Kate Sanborn

My favorite lectures of long ago, for friends who remember

Kate Sanborn

My favorite lectures of long ago, for friends who remember

ISBN/EAN: 9783337056926

Printed in Europe, USA, Canada, Australia, Japan

Cover: Foto ©Thomas Meinert / pixelio.de

More available books at **www.hansebooks.com**

My

Favorite Lectures

Of Long Ago

For Friends who Remember

———

KATE SANBORN

— — —

BOSTON

1898

ACROSS THE YEARS

Sitting on my southern piazza, this perfect after-noon in the perfect month of June, looking out over "Breezy Meadows," with their rich growth of grass, fields of waving grain, and ripening crops, while my cows graze in the distant pasture; listening to the raucous yet not unpleasant voices of the conceited turkey-gobbler and his meek, drab-hued mates, the geese, always perfectly at home on my farm, the mournful "koquet, koquet" of the imprisoned guineas, and the cheerful cackle of the business hen, I realize that my happiest hours are now those devoted to outdoor sports and agricultural enter-prises — no longer a blue-stocking, but a full-fledged farmer!

Emerson says that "a farm is a mute gospel." To me it has rather proved to be a revelation, noisy, expensive, and at times depressing or exasperating. Still, I love this life and shall never give it up.

Looking back to the time when, intensely ambi-tious, and audacious because so ambitious, so ignor-ant of the world, and so empty as to purse, I dared to announce a course of ten lectures on literary themes in New York city, a young woman, almost unknown,

I am amazed at the venture, and bless, as I have
always done, the patrons who, believing in me, gave
such effective aid. Do you recall my painful timidity, my face, which turned all colors from excitement, and how every bit of that nervous fear
vanished under the radiant inspiration of the en-
couraging faces before me? Dear happy hours!
Dear faces! Dear faithful friends!

How far away it all seems! Since then I have
talked to thousands, have enjoyed the honors of
somewhat successful authorship, have been professor
of literature in a woman's college, president of a
woman's club, have learned to make butter, and
manage hens. But nothing stays so agreeably in
my memory as that first audience of New York
women. How public opinion changes as time rolls
on! Twenty-five years ago there were plenty of
persons who considered me an oddity on account
of my profession; some would not care to know
a woman who unsexed herself by speaking on a
platform. I was an unconscious pioneer: now the
number of women doing the same work is legion.
I started a class in Dr. Holland's parlor on Park
Avenue for his wife and a score of friends, condensing new books and speaking of current events; now
every village has such a class, or else a thriving club
able to do its work without a guide.

Egotism (on paper) is sometimes allowable. I
confess without any apology that, like Montaigne, I
have always "hungered to make myself known."

have desired earnestly to be known especially, as a thorough, well-equipped student of literature.

And now I am not willing to let these pet lectures grow yellow in a desk, or, after my death, be stored in an attic as food for mice, or, later, given to the flames. I am not so exacting as to expect you to read them: just give the book an honorable place in your libraries — perhaps some grandchildren of yours may look them over. They represent a deal of "digging," careful condensing and elimination, and are still worth preserving.

The kindest of publishers fight shy of lectures; all want something light and amusing from me — farm bulletins and comic adventures. That is only a small part of my life, so I offer some serious work made easy reading by hard labor, to those who still retain a kindly interest in

Kate Sanborn.

Farmer, Henwoman, and ex-Litterateur.

CONTENTS

MY FAVORITE LECTURES

SPINSTER AUTHORS OF ENGLAND

OLD Maids have been classified, by one who has written a book about them, as Voluntary, Involuntary, Inexplicable, and — Literary. These various modifications are honored with a chapter of comment; each type is clearly defined — except the Literary Spinster; she is left severely alone. Possibly, the terms were thought synonymous, for in the hearts of many there is still an innate shrinking from a Blue Stocking, a name first applied to a man, the agreeable Dr. Stillingfleet, whose blue stockings were often noticed at Mrs. Montagu's Receptions.

Jeffrey hit the happy medium when speaking of a literary woman: "I don't care how blue her stockings are, if her petticoats are long enough to hide her hose."

An engraving in an English Annual, entitled " The Husband of a Blue," illustrates the once popular theory that a woman who writes must of necessity be a failure in home-life. The luckless man, in extremely simple toilette, is walking the floor; a screaming baby in his arms, a pendulum between patience and despair; while Madam, all unconscious of the situation, unless, perhaps, annoyed by the cries of one and the heartfelt groans of the other, is perched up in bed with tangled locks flowing and eyes wildly rolling, as she rounds some fine sentence, or, with gaze uplifted, is waiting for further inspiration.

Both in England and our own country there are many distinguished authors who are also good wives and mothers, women, in happy homes, with husbands proud and fond, sure of three good meals each day, and every button on.

But Literary Spinsters are to be enumerated in this paper; scarcely more, for there are so many to be mentioned that I can merely evoke, and dismiss, like the showman of a panorama.

I must go back to the Fourteenth Century for my first Spinster Author, to the pretty Prioress and practical sportswoman — Juliana Berners, a Minerva in her studies, a Diana in her diversions, the highborn beauty, once famous, now forgotten, cotemporary with Chaucer. Her works, printed in black letter, and adorned with extraordinary wood-cuts, have lately been reproduced in luxurious binding. Her treatise on the Art of Fishing is the best known. She is the author of the " Book of St. Albans," which contains essays on Hawking, Hunting, Coat-Armor, Fishing, and Bearing of Arms — printed at Westminster by Wynkyn de Worde, a rival of Caxton, in 1486.* She was practical as well as learned and

---

* BERNERS (Dame Juliana). A Treatyse of Fysshinge wyth an Angle. A facsimile reproduction of the first book on the subject of fishing, printed in England by Wynkyn de Worde at Westminster in 1496. With an introduction by Rev. M. G. Watkins, M.A.   4to, printed on hand made paper, rough edges, blind tooled, vellum boards.   London, E. Stock, n. d. (1880). $4.50.

enjoyed the chase as does the empress of Austria to-day. It is paradoxical to imagine a holy Prioress, accustomed to severe restriction and serene meditations, chasing over the woodlands with hound and horn, or collecting recipes for the extinction of vermin on her pet hawks, which she cared for with untiring devotion. We owe to her the earliest English treatise on fishing.

Her picture, as seen in Zouch's Life of Walton, shows a striking face, full of decision, spirit, and sweetness, a handsome figure, attractive in spite of her ugly gear. On her right is seen the landing net, with fish and creel, on the left, emblems of the chase, and a hooded falcon at top.

Good-bye, pretty and pious Juliana of so long ago. I would like to linger with you — but a brilliant crowd is beckoning, led by Queen Elizabeth herself. "Queen Bess" (1553–1603) was an accomplished linguist, translated from Greek and Latin and occasionally "dropped into poetry."

A sonnet on Mary, Queen of Scots, is preserved, also some verses on her own feelings, at the departure of a rejected lover.

You recall her couplet, added to Raleigh's, on a window of her palace. He scratched :

> " I fain would climb,
> But that I fear to fall."

She rejoined :

> " If thy heart fails thee
> Do not climb at all."

A bit of impromptu doggerel is ascribed to her
on entering a certain town, where the mayor, a pom-
pous, rotund little personage, mounted on a stool, to
make his address of welcome more impressive.

Her reply was brief and curt :

" You great fool,
Get off that stool !"

Disraeli speaks of a manuscript volume of her
poems still to be seen in the Hatfield collection.

She was ambitious to shine as a poet, although
affecting to be angry when one of the ladies of her
bedchamber copied some rhymes from her tablet,
" fearing her people should imagine she was busied
in such toys."

Her courtiers lavished extravagant praise on her
royal ditties, which any editor of to-day would con-
sign to the waste basket, and the Latin poem of her
cousin will live, while the verses of Elizabeth Re-
gina are forgotten.

We are more interested in another Elizabeth, the
celebrated classical scholar, Miss Carter (1717–1806),
in the words of Allibone, " an ornament to her sex and
an honor to her race." Of her translation of Epictetus, which brought her £1,000, Dr. Warton said " It
excels the original."

Dr. Johnson, her friend and admirer for nearly
half a century, composed a Greek epigram in her
honor. He remarked of a fine Greek scholar : " Sir,
he is the best Greek scholar in England,— except
Elizabeth Carter."

Upon hearing a lady commended for her learning, he said, "A man is in general better pleased when he has a good dinner upon his table than when his wife talks Greek. My old friend, Miss Carter, could make a pudding as well as translate Epictetus, and work a handkerchief as well as compose a poem."

William Hayley, Cowper's biographer, wrote several volumes on "Old Maids, Ancient and Modern," and dedicated the work to Mrs. Carter,* saying:

"Permit me to pay my devotions to you, as the ancients did to their three-fold Diana, and to reverence you in three distinct characters as a poet, as a philosopher, and as an old maid."

Miss Carter was a first-rate housekeeper and needle-woman, took lessons in drawing and music, was an excellent dancer, could play cards, or share in any social diversion when young, even somewhat of a romp. She jots in her diary, "I walked three miles yesterday in a wind that I thought would have blown me out of this planet, and afterwards danced nine hours, and then walked back again. No girl pedant was she, and they said she had many opportunities of marriage.

Miss Elizabeth Carter once went to a puppet show at Deal with some five friends. Punch was uncommonly dull and serious, though usually more jocose than delicate. "Why, Punch," says the showman, "what makes you so stupid?" "I can't talk my

* English spinsters, after arriving at the mature age of fifty, were addressed as Mrs., not Miss.

own talk," answers Punch, " because the famous Miss Carter is here ! "

Next in order Miss Catherine Talbot (1720 1777), a most worthy spinster, who can only be mentioned. for several pages must be given to Hannah More (1745-1832), whose talent for writing showed itself early. When but a little child, if she could get hold of a sheet of paper, she would scribble some essay or poem, never omitting a moral, and then hide it in a dark closet with the brooms and duster. When she composed verses at night, her admiring sister would often steal down stairs for a light and then jot them down.

One of her favorite games was a prophecy, for her mother proudly relates how she used to make a carriage of a chair and invite her sisters to ride with her to London to see bishops and booksellers Her highest ambition was a whole quire of paper, all her own, and when the prize was obtained she covered sheet after sheet with letters to depraved characters to reclaim and reform them, and the replies, expressive of contrition and resolutions of amendment. She was as brilliant as good. When Sheridan, the elder, delivered his lectures on eloquence in Bristol, she sent some verses to the orator, which led to a pleasant acquaintance. As a talker she was remarkable, When about sixteen, a dangerous illness brought an eminent physician to her bedside. Like every one else who met her he was completely charmed by her conversation. On one occasion he entirely forgot

the purpose of his visit in the fascination of her talk,
till suddenly, recollecting himself, when he was half
way down stairs, he cried out : " Bless me ?   I forgot
to ask the girl how she was," and hurried back to the
room exclaiming, " How are you to-day, my poor
child ? "

In her 17th year she wrote a pastoral drama,
" The Search after Happiness," a success.   She had
already a wide correspondence with distinguished
men.   One sent her this verse on her promise to
visit his garden :

> " Blow, blow my sweetest rose,
>   For Hannah More will soon be here,
>   And all that crowns the ripening year
> Should triumph where she goes."

Her father disliked pedantic women, and having
taught her a little Latin and mathematics was
alarmed at her progress; at twenty she was an
uncommon linguist.   But, if learned, never poky in
her brilliant youth ;   popular in London society;   full of spirit and humor;   a special favorite
of Dr. Johnson, Garrick.   Horace Walpole called
her his " holy Hannah."   Garrick gave her the pet
name of " Nine," referring to the Muses.   He wrote
prologue and epilogue for her play of " Percy," a
success, which gave her 750 pounds.   She earned
more than $150,000 by her pen, one-third of which
she gave away, and did not begin her career until
after thirty.   Millions of her tracts and ballads were
sold.   It is said that her books were more numerous,

passed through more editions, printed in more languages, read by more people, than those of any woman on record. Her popular story, " Coelebs in Search of a Wife," unendurably tame now, went through ten editions in one year. Of course, she was severely criticised by rivals. She said she " was battered, hacked, scalped, tomahawked." After Garrick's death she never went to a theatre, even to see her own tragedies performed, and lived more quietly, but always eagerly sought for by the best society. Only one love affair is spoken of in connection with this beautiful woman, so witty and attractive, and that most unfortunate and mortifying. A rich widower, kept postponing their marriage until her friends interfered. He declared that he had the deepest regard and respect for Miss More, and at his death he bequeathed her a thousand pounds. She had other offers, but avoided a second entanglement. Most people think of Hannah More as an aged spinster with black mits, corkscrew curls, and a mob cap, always writing or presenting a solemn tract, ignoring her youthful fascinations.

Her kindness to Macaulay, when a precocious little lad he often visited her, is pleasant to remember.

She stimulated him to read, giving the money to buy his first valuable books, laying, as she said, " the tiny cornerstone of his library," and encouraged without flattery.

If, after listening to this high estimate, you go to your library and taking down Hannah's prosy disquisitions, rather dusty on the edges, and, turning over the various volumes, look for something interesting or lively, you will be disappointed. Her tracts and homely poems, written for practical effect among the poor (for instance, the dialogue between the two weavers over the half-made carpet), are still excellent. But who reads Hannah More now? Her day has gone by. Her "Percy," like Addison's "Cato," would be wretchedly dull on any stage. Towards the close of her life she fell into a common error, and grew narrow in her views, and unnecessarily solemn. Never found time to read Scott's novels, and accused him of being not immoral but non-moral, which was unjust; and said she would rather present herself at Heaven's gate with her tract, "The Shepherd of Salisbury Plain," in her hand, than encumbered with all the novels of the mighty "Wizard of the North."

A good novel is as useful in its way as a good tract, and Jeannie Dean's character and her speech to the Queen in behalf of her sister, seems to me more Christlike, than the stilted submission of the saintly shepherd.

"And when we come to die, my Leddy, its not what we hae dune for ourselves, but what we hae dune for others that we think on maist pleasantly."

"I wonder if you ever heard a story told to me by your countryman, Mr. Northmore, a great Devonshire reformer, one of the bad epic poets and very pleasant men in which that country abounds. He said that Jeremy Bentham being on a visit at a show-house in those parts, at a time when he was little known except as a jurist, certainly before the publication of the Church of Englandism, or any such enormities — Mrs. Hannah More, being at a watering-place in the neighborhood, was minded to see him, and availed herself of the house, being one which was shown on stated days, to pay a visit to the philosopher. He was in the library when the news arrived, and the lady being already in the ante-chamber and no possible mode of escape presenting itself, he sent one servant to detain her a few minutes and employed another to build him up with books in a corner of the room. When the folios and quartos rose above his head, the curious lady was admitted. Must it not have been a droll scene? The philosopher playing at bo-peep in his intrenchment and the good lady, who had previously ascertained that he was in the room, peering after him in all the agony of baffled curiosity!"

I have sketched Hannah More's picture as faithfully as possible, with no idea of blaming her for being too good, but it would be partial not to allude to her narrowness lest a shadow might fall on the picture.

She said many good things, as: "I used to wonder why people should be so fond of the company of their physician, till I recollected he is the only person with whom one dares to talk continually of one's self without interruption, contradiction, or censure."

"There are only two bad things in this world, *sin* and *bile*." Speaking of Woman's Rights, how many ways there are of being ridiculous? I am sure I have as much liberty as I can make good use of, now I am an old maid, and when I was a young one I had, I dare say, more than was good for me."

Anna Seward (1747–1809) was a most sentimental, lackadaisical, affected creature, with a particularly florid and stilted style, called by her admirers of the " Della Cruscan " school the " The Swan of Litch-field," but who impresses more impartial observers as a Goose. Still, at nine years old she could repeat the first three books of Paradise Lost, which proves her appreciation of good poetry whatever we may think of her own. She wrote a succession of Elegies, Monodies, and Odes; Sonnets, Poetical Epistles, and Adieus; all about Capt. Cook and Major André, and a variety of other notables; also a metrical novel, " Louisa," and laid claim to the first fifty lines of Dr. Darwin's " Botanic Garden "; was afterwards his biographer, a real misfortune for the doctor's fame, though a ludicrous one. Walter Scott, who was her literary executor, pronounced her two volumes of poems " absolutely execrable," and her six volumes of published correspondence proved an utter failure. I grieve to say that this voluminous publication was regarded as a display of " vanity, egotism, and malignity ! "

Leigh Hunt says, " Miss Seward is affected and superfluous, but now and then she writes a goop line, for example :

'And sultry silence brooded o'er the hills,'

and she can paint a natural picture." Horace Walpole wrote to the Countess of Ossory, " Misses Seward and Williams, and half a dozen more of those harmonious virgins, have no imagination, no novelty. Their thoughts and phrases are like their gowns, old remnants cut and turned." Her style is the acme of high-flownativeness and stewed prunism. She says that Dr. Darwin purchased about the year 1777, "a little wild umbrageous valley, a mile from Litchfield, irriguous from various springs and swampy from their plentitude."

When this bog was transformed into a Paradise, she took her tablets and pencil and. seated on a flowery bank in the midst of that luxurious retreat, composed some lines, " while the sun was gilding the glen, and while birds of every plume poured their songs from the boughs."

Four lines from the " Botanic Garden " will suffice for a specimen :

" My plumy pairs in gay embroidery dressed,
    Form with ingenious bill the pensile nest,
    To Love's sweet notes attune the listening dell,
    And Echo sounds her soft symphonious shell."

Richard Lovell Edgeworth, the eccentric father of Maria, who liked to pose as a bachelor, met Miss Seward at Litchfield, when " she was in the height of youth and beauty, of an enthusiastic temper, a votary of the Muses, and of the most eloquent and brilliant conversation." He adds that Mrs. Darwin had a little pique against Miss Seward, who had in fact been her rival with the doctor. "At Mrs. Darwin's tea-table I was placed next Miss Seward, and a number of lively sallies escaped her that set the table in good humor. I remember she repeated some of Prior's "Henry and Emma," and dwelling upon Emma's tenderness she cited the care that she proposed to take of her lover if he were wounded,

" 'To bind his wounds my finest lawns I'd tear,
Wash them with tears, and wipe them with my hair."

I represented that the lady who must have had by her own account a *choice* of lawns might have employed some of the coarse sort for this operation instead of having recourse to her hair. I then paid Miss Seward some compliments on her own beautiful tresses, and at that moment the watchful Mrs. Darwin took this opportunity of drinking *Mrs. Edgeworth's health.*"

As Americans, we ought to think kindly of Miss Seward, as she was on our side during the War for Independence. Boswell has recorded Johnson's remark, "I am willing to love all mankind except an American," adding that "his inflammable corruptions bursting with horrid fire, he breathed out threatenings and slaughter, calling them rascals, robbers, and pirates, and exclaiming he'd burn 'em and destroy 'em." Miss Seward, looking to him with mild but steady astonishment, said: "Sir, this is an instance that we are always most violent against those whom we have injured." Johnson said to Miss Seward, "Madam, there is not anything equal to your description of the sea round the North Pole, in your ode on the death of Captain Cook."

In one of her letters she exclaims: "How prone are our hearts perversely to quarrel with the friendly coercion of employment at the very instant in which it is clearing the torpid and injurious mists of unavailing melancholy."*

We come next to Jane Austen (1755–1817). who, like Mrs. Browning, has been called "a feminine Shakespeare." Her life was most simple and secluded, domestic, and she really wrote for her own amusement — idolized by her nephews and nieces, who were always pleading to go to "Auntie's Room" for a frolic, a petting, or a story. It was not then thought desirable for young ladies to study or write, so Miss Austen compromised matters by a large piece of fancy work kept on parlor table to hide her manuscripts when callers appeared. Much money was not necessary for the moderate expenses of her quiet home, and so modestly did she estimate her work, that when she received one hundred and fifty pounds from the sale of " Sense and Sensibility," she considered it a prodigious recompense. She called her exquisite word painting " little bits of ivory, two inches

---

*This sort of writing emigrated to America, but died with Mrs. Sigourney.

wide." She never posed as a literary light, had a dislike of being lionized, was a little embarrassed when introductions were sought, saying, "If I am a wild beast I cannot help it ; it is not my fault." She wrote early two of her masterpieces, published before she was twenty-one.

We always like to know how such a famous person looked. She was tall, slender, with clear brunette complexion, fine rich color, hazel eyes, brown curling hair.

She was lively, graceful, witty, a good dancer, fond of a good play, a little satirical, full of quiet humor, and very lovable. She had many admirers, flirted a little, loved seriously once, another unfortunate romance which Miss Thackeray speaks of, and then settled down with her beloved sister Cassandra, to a quiet old maid life, in a happy home. Miss Mitford, one of her warmest admirers, declared she would almost be willing to cut off one of her hands if it would enable her to write like Miss Austen with the other.

Walter Scott, after reading " Pride and Prejudice " for the third time, said: " That young lady had a talent for describing the involvements, feelings, and characters of ordinary life, which is to me the most wonderful I ever met with. The big *bow-wow* I can do myself, like any one going ; but her exquisite touch is denied to me. What a pity that so gifted a creature died so early !"

Coleridge would sometimes burst out into high

encomiums of her novels as being in their way perfectly genuine and individual productions, and Archbishop Whately was an enthusiast in her praise.

Macaulay, with all his love for new novels, seemed never to tire of hers, and called her a prose Shakespeare. He intended to write her memoir, and erect a monument to her memory with the proceeds. This biography, which would have been her best monument, he never accomplished, but in his letters we find constant allusions to his delight in reading her stories. In our day such a woman would have had her memoirs written by enthusiastic admirers before the breath had left her body. But her talent, her rare gift of depicting every-day types in daily life with pre-Raphaelite distinctness and truth, was fully appreciated by many of England's most famous men. Seven distinguished men, among them Hallam and Macaulay, being asked at a dinner party to mention the novel which had given them the most pleasure, gave the name as Mansfield Park, by Jane Austen.

Miss Thackeray says : " The simple family annals are not without their romance, but there is a cruel one for poor Cassandra, whose lover dies abroad and his death saddens the whole family party."

Jane, too, " receives the addresses " (do such things as addresses exist nowadays?) of a gentleman possessed of good character and fortune and of everything in short except the subtle power of touching her heart."

And another sorrowful story.   The sisters' fate (there is a sad coincidence and similarity in it) was to be undivided, their life, their experience, was the same.   Some one without a name takes leave of Jane one day, promising to come back.   He never comes back ; long afterwards they hear of his death. The story seems even sadder than Cassandra's, in its silence and uncertainty, for silence and uncertainty are death in life to some people."

We have a picture of Lord Holland lying on his bed, agonizing with an attack of gout, while his sister sat beside him diverting his mind with one of Miss Austen's novels, of which he never wearied.

And Sydney Smith, more than once, dwelt with eloquence on her merits, and said he should have enjoyed giving her the pleasure of reading her praises in the " Edinburgh." George Eliot considered her the greatest artist that has ever written ; the most perfect master over the means to her end, " surpassing all male novelists." Tennyson and Howells are her devoted admirers.

Her novels have been translated into French, and in the *Atlantic Monthly* of February, 1863, you will find an excellent article on this charming woman. To say that the Prince Regent read and liked her stories and invited her to examine his library seems a small honor in comparison with the appreciation of the others mentioned. With all her fondness for literary work she was a true woman, fond of children, amusing them with stories, playful doggerel, and merry games, skillful with her needle, embroidering exquisitely, "great in satin-stitch," sang sweetly, and played well on piano.

She inherited her love of fun from her witty and agreeable grandfather, of whom Mrs. Thrall wrote to Dr. Johnson: "Are you acquainted with Dr. Leigh, master of Balliol College, and are you not delighted with his gaiety of manner and youthful vivacity now that he is eighty-six years of age?" When some one told him how, in a dispute among the Priory Counsellors, the Lord Chancellor struck the table with such violence that he split it. " No, no," replied the master, "I can't persuade myself that he split the table, though I believe he divided the board."

He was once calling on a gentleman notorious for never opening a book, who ushered him into a room overlooking the Bath Road, then a great thoroughfare for travelers of every class, remarking, rather pompously, " This, Doctor, I call my study." Dr. Leigh, glancing around the room in which not a book was to be seen, replied, " And very well named too, sir, for you know Pope tells us, " The proper study of mankind is man." Only three days before he died, being told of a man whom his friends regarded as *egged* on to matrimony, as he married after a long illness cured by eating eggs, he trumped the joke saying, " Then may the YOKE sit easy on him."

Two of Miss Austen's epigrams have been preserved. The first was suggested by reading in a

newspaper the marriage of Mr. Gell to Miss Gill of
Eastborne.

> " At Eastburn, Mr. Gell, from being perfectly well,
> Became dreadfully ill for love of Miss Gill ;
> So he said with some sighs, ' I'm the slave of your ii's,
> Restore if you please, by accepting my ee's.' "

The second on the marriage of a middle-aged
flirt with a Mr. Wake, whom gossips averred she
would have scorned in her prime.

> " Maira, good-humored, and handsome and tall,
> For a husband was at her last stake,
> And having in vain danced at many a ball,
> Is now happy to *jump at a Wake!* "

Her novels were at first published anonymously,
which prevented her enjoying the praise they received.   She received seven hundred pounds for her
novels.   The old verger in Winchester Cathedral
had been so often asked to point out her grave, that
he inquired of some traveler if " she ever did anything in particular."   She had a happy, peaceful life
and left behind an enduring fame.

Jane Porter, another novelist, now comes upon
the scene (1776–1850).   She began the system of historical novel-writing which attained the climax of
renown in the hands of Scott.   Like Jane Austen,
she lived in a very quiet way with her mother and
her sister Anna, who also wrote novels.   All that we
need to know of her is that she wrote " Thaddeus
of Warsaw " and the " Scottish Chiefs," both of which
were famous in their day.

Thaddeus was translated into several of the Continental languages. A relation of the Polish Patriot, Kosciusko, sent her a gold ring containing a miniature of the hero, and Gen. Gardiner, who was then British Ambassador at the Court of Stanislaus, could hardly believe that some of the scenes could have been described by one who was not an eye witness. In 1809, appeared the Scottish Chiefs, and Scott admitted to George IV that this was the veritable begetter of the Waverly novels.

There was a touch of Old World and sentimental eloquence in her manners which we shall hardly see reproduced. She conversed like an accomplished woman who had kept much worshipful company in her time, without, however, the slightest parade or pretension. Maginn in " The Fraserians " (a delightful book to own) rambles on in his own way about her, saying, as he looked at her picture, "handsome the face is still." " We hope Miss Porter has sufficient philosophy to pardon us for that fatal adverb. Time and tide wait for no man, nor woman either, and there is the fact extant that she published the ' Spirit of the Elbe ' in 1800, some five-and-thirty years ago. Allowing that she was then but twenty, it brings her now-a-days to the Falstaffian age of some seven-and-fifty, or inclining to threescore. Many a lady of Miss Porter's standing, if she had kept Miss Porter's good looks, could well smuggle off ten or a dozen years from the account if she had not dabbled in printer's work. Joe Miller informs us that a coal porter having inquired what the crime was for which he saw a man hanging at Tyburn tree, and being told it was forgery, exclaimed: 'Ah! that's what comes of knowing how to read and write, my good fellow!'

"We are tempted to make a similar exclamation when we find a lady rendering the footsteps of time traceable by manifesting her powers of penmanship."

"In private she is a quiet and good-humored lady, rather pious and fond of going to evening parties, where she generally contrives to be seen patronizing some sucking lion or lioness. In which occupation may she long continue, devoting her mornings to the prayer-book and the evenings to the conversazione.

> "And may no ill event cut shorter
> The easy course of Miss Jane Porter."

Joanna Baillie, 1762-1798, being a veritable Scotch woman, can hardly be classed among the English spinsters, although she spent most of her long life near London, the center of a literary circle, literally the friend of two generations of authors. Her ambition was to be a dramatist, and her plan to devote a play to each passion, but they were very poor imitations of Shakespeare and Beaumont and Fletcher, just as her Scottish songs have the rhyme and the pronunciation of Burns without his spice and spirit and soul. There was a want of business in her scenes. Her stock of words was deplorably scanty, her pages were marred by affectations of antiquated phraseology, and she unduly magnified little things, as when alluding to goose flesh she says:

> " When every hair-pit in my shrunken skin
> A knotted knoll becomes."

Not a pleasing idea of the state of that young woman's person.

The *Edinburgh Review* decided that she must not write comedies and could not possibly write a tragedy.

Still, her name commands attention. No woman before had attempted so high a vein of poetry.

When she first appeared, the drama throughout England seemed expiring, and she roused it to new life.

Mrs. Siddons and Kemble, both acted in De Montfort, and that would make anything a success.

She made the mistake of attempting too much. Her voice was pitched for a more select audience, not for the public.

Her fireside lyrics are quite charming. Very appropriately (as an old maid) she wrote poetical addresses to her Kitten and a Teapot, both of them worth reading, and a touching tribute to her sister, Agnes, a spinster, too, with whom she had lived for years, and to whom she was thoroughly devoted.

Scott, who always said such kind things of women, declared " that her merit as a dramatist was so great to prevent all attempts at competition on his part," and Lord Byron said: " Women (saving Joanna Baillie) cannot write tragedy ; they have not seen enough nor felt enough of life for it." Yet Byron, when invited to attend this good woman to the opera, sat and made faces at her all the evening.

As Maria Edgeworth (1767-1849) was proud to be called an Irish woman and Irish Story Teller, she will not be dwelt upon in this rapid survey. She has lately had a great deal of attention, Mrs. Grace Oliver having written her life and also edited some of her stories, and she figures in the "Eminent Women" series. This will gratify Donald Mitchell, who, in a book for children, devotes a chapter to her. "Those stories which were the delight of all young people forty years ago, and those novels which were the delight of all the grown people of her time," and pleads that it is quite too soon to forget good Miss Edgeworth and her books. Like Miss Baillie, she aimed to make each work an elucidation of one passion or one vice. Scott averred that it was her tender, humorous, admirable delineations of Irish character which led him to do the same thing for his country, and Tourgenieff, the late Russian novelist, said he should never have written about the woes of the peasanty of his land if not inspired by what Miss Edgeworth had done.

The Life and Letters of Maria Edgeworth have been edited by Augustus J. C. Hare. She said:

"As a woman, my life, wholly domestic, can offer nothing of interest to the public."

Macaulay considered her "the second woman of her age."

Scott said of Simple Susan that when the boy brings back the lamb to the little girl, there is nothing for it but to put down the book and cry. She remarked of Madame Roland, "She was a great woman and died heroically, but I don't think she became more amiable and certainly not more happy by meddling with politics; for — her head is cut off and her husband has shot himself." Here is a capital epigram:

"Theory was born in Brobdignag and Practice in Lilliput."

Next in order, Jane Taylor, 1783–1824. The "Original Poems for Infant Minds, by the Taylor Family," did a great and good work in their day. They sound oddly enough now, and the little folks accustomed to the delicious nonsense verses of Edward Lear, the grotesque playfulness of the rhymes in Lewis Carrol's stories, and the really beautiful poetry now written expressly for their delectation, would hardly relish these crude efforts to instruct children by means of poetry suited to their capacity.

The preface alludes to them as " that interesting little race," as if they were a quite distinct species from their parents — like the Aztecs!

The book opens rather dismally. First poem, " The Churchyard."

> " And see, from those darkly green trees
>   Of cypress and holly and yew,
>   That wave their black arms in the breeze,
>   The old village church is in view.

> The owl from her ivied retreat
> Screams hoarse to the winds of the night,
> And the clock with its solemn repeat
> Has tolled the departure of night."

This is followed by a cheerful, alluring invitation:

> "My child, let us wander alone,
> When half the wide world is in bed,
> And read o'er the mouldering stone
> That tells of the mouldering dead.
> And let us remember it well,
> That we must as certainly die;
> For us, too, may toll the sad bell,
> And in the cold earth we must lie.
>
> "You are not so healthy and gay,
> So young, so active, and bright,
> That death cannot snatch you away,
> Or some dreadful accident smite.
> Here lie both the young and the old,
> Confined in the coffin so small,
> And the earth closes over them cold,
> And the grave-worm devours them all."

In a poem on "Beasts, Birds, and Fishes," Adelaide Taylor managed to bring in a metrical catalogue an entire menagerie, without the slightest connection:

> "The Dog will come when he is called,
> The Cat will walk away,
> The Monkey's cheek is very bald,
> The Goat is fond of play,
> The Parrot is a prate-a-pace, ·
> Yet knows not what she says,
> The noble Horse will win the race,
> Or draw you in a chaise.
> The Sparrow steals the cherry ripe,

> The Elephant is wise,
> The Blackbird charms you with his pipe,
> The false Hyena cries,
> The Hen guards well her little chicks,
> The useful Cow is meek,
> The Beaver builds with mud and sticks,
> The Lapwing loves to squeak.
> The spotted Tiger's fond of blood,
> The Pigeon feeds on peas,
> The Duck will gobble in the mud,
> The Mice will eat your cheese,
> A Lobster's black, when boiled he's red,
> The harmless Lamb must bleed,
> The Codfish has a clumsy head,
> The Goose on grass will feed."

The moral, from which there is no escape, comes at the close of the ninth verse :

> " The child that does not these things know,
>   May yet be thought a dunce ;
> But I will up in knowledge grow,
>   As youth can come but once."

Jane, under the *nom de plume* " Q. Q. " (a doubly Qrious signature), published two small volumes of tiresome, sermonizing essays, relieved occasionally by something really bright and entertaining, like the " Discontented Pendulum," an allegory so popular with our grandmothers, found in most of the reading books of the last generation, and now used by elocutionists as an example of the circumflex, as employed to express irony and gentle sarcasm :

"It is vastly easy for you, Mistress Dial, who have always, as everybody knows, set yourself up above me — it is vastly easy for you, I say, to accuse other people of laziness."

And "the Weights, who had never been accused of light conduct."

But there is little of that sort. The reading for children was either in the form of a short sermon or a prolonged conundrum, in stilted, formal language. Due credit must be given to Jane Taylor and her sisters, for their work was far better than any that preceded it. Some of the best have lately been revived and published.

And now we come to dear, rosy, sunny-faced, brave-hearted Miss Mitford (1786–1855), whose life was one long struggle, hidden by a patient, cheery smile; the highest type of a dutiful, loving daughter. Her mother was an heiress, her father a handsome, lazy, selfish spendthrift and gambler, who utterly ruined their future by wasting all the money of the mother. She won, at the age of ten, twenty thousand pounds in a lottery ticket, and Dr. Mitford promised to settle this sum on her, but this was soon squandered, like the wife's fortune. As Mr. Stoddard puts it: "To sum Dr. Mitford up in a word, he was a beast."

So the brave little woman had to support both, and did it without a murmur, for he had not even the grace to die, but lived on most unconscionably until his child nearly broke down under the terrible weight.

She says: "If he could tell how *debt* presses upon the mind — upon the heart, as if it were a sin, and

sometimes, I do believe, makes me ill, when otherwise I should be well, he *would* be more careful.
But men do not change at eighty."

"I am doubly thankful to have my dear father
spared to me. If I could but give my whole life to
him, reading to him, driving out with him, playing
cribbage with him, never five minutes away from
him, except when he is asleep — for this is what
makes him happy — it would be the breath of life
to me!"

After he was utterly ruined financially, she
writes: "Whatever your embarrassments may be,
of one thing I am certain, that the world does not
contain so proud, so happy, or so fond a daughter.
I would not exchange my father, even though we
toiled together for our daily bread, for any man on
earth, though he could pour all the gold of Peru
into my lap."

He died at eighty-two, deep in debt. "Everybody shall be paid," wrote Mary, "if I sell the gown
off my back, or pledge my little pension."

Poetry was not her forte, but she wrote many
poetic dramas, some of which were quite successful
when put on the stage. Her most popular work was
a series of sketches called "Our Village." The
first volume passed through fourteen editions, and
Stoddard declares that "never before or since has
the country been painted with such a loving and
accurate pencil as hers." She also published two
poor novels and several volumes of poetry, but she

was neither poet nor novelist. Her " Recollections of a Literary Life," and her letters will always be enjoyed.

In the letters of Mrs. Browning to Richard Horne frequent allusions are made to her friend, Miss Mitford, and visits to Three Mile Cross, the original of " Our Village."

She says, " It would be impossible for any engraving or photograph, however excellent as to features, to convey a true likeness of Mary Russell Mitford. During one of these visits Charlotte Cushman was also staying at the cottage, and exclaimed the first time Miss Mitford left the room, " What a bright face it is!" This effect of summer brightness all over the countenance was quite remarkable. A floral flush overspread the whole face, which seemed to carry its own light with it, for it was the same indoors as out. The silver hair shone, the forehead shone, the cheeks shone, and above all the eyes shone; it was very like a rosy apple in the sun. The forehead and chin were strong.

She was, to speak the truth, decidedly *fat*, and always craved elegance of style and figure, disliking what she called her " rotundity and rubicundity."

Her " Recollections " are full of agreeable anecdotes; her criticisms one-sided and worthless.

From the " Noctes Ambrosianæ ":

Shepherd.—" I'm just verra fond o' that lassie Mitford. She has an ee like a hawk's that misses naething however far aff, and yet like a dove's, that sees only what is nearest and dearest and round about the hame circle o' its central nest. I'm just excessive fond o' Miss Mitford. I'm fond o' a gude female writers. They're a bonnie and every passage they write carries, as it ought to do, their femininity alang wi it. The young gentlemen of England should be ashamed o' theirsells for letting her name be Mitford. They should marry her whether she will or no, for she wad mak baith a useful and agreeable wife. That's the best creetishism on her warks."

I find but one allusion anywhere to matrimony, and this in a note to some one who congratulated her on a supposed approach of that condition :

" Alas! my dear friend, you are quite mistaken, I assure you, I am not going to be married. ' No such good luck,' as papa says. I have not been courted, and I am not in love. So much for this question. If I ever should happen to be going to be married (elegant construction this) I will then not fail to let you into the secret, but alas! alas! alas!! In such a *then* I write a never."

It is related of the dear old lady that she once went to an evening party wearing a peculiarly showy cap from which she had forgotten to remove the price mark, and walked about in her gracious way with " Cheap at one pound six," on a fluttering ribbon, in benign unconsciousness of her ludicrous oversight.

Miss Sedgwick's visit to Miss Mitford.

"She led us directly through the house into her garden, a perfect bouquet of flowers. 'I must show you my geraniums while it is light, for I love them next to my father.' The garden is filled, matted with flowering shrubs and vines. The trees are wreathed with honeysuckles and roses, and the girls have brought away the most splendid specimens of heartsease to press in their journals. Oh, that I could give my countrywomen a vision of this little paradise of flowers that they might learn how taste and industry and an earnest love and study of the art of garden culture might triumph over small space and humble means."

You remember Mrs. Browning's sonnet:

TO MARY RUSSELL MITFORD.
IN HER GARDEN.

"What time I lay these rhymes anear thy feet,
  Benignant friend, I will not proudly say,
  As better poets use, 'These *flowers* I lay,'
Because I would not wrong thy roses sweet,
Blaspheming so their name. And yet repeat,
Thou, overleaning them this springtime day,
With heart as open to love as theirs to May.
Low rooted verse may reach some heavenly heart,
Even like my blossoms, if as nature true,
Though not as precious. Thou art unperplext,
Dear friend, in whose dear writings drops the dew,
And blow the natural airs — thou who art next
To nature's self in cheering the world's view —
To preach a sermon on so known a text."

She was devotedly fond of her pets, says Mr. Fields.

"Her voice had a peculiar ringing sweetness in it, rippling out sometimes like a beautiful chime of silver bells. When she told a comic story, hitting off some one of her acquaintances, she joined in with the laugh at the end with great heartiness and *naïveté*."

"Her dogs and her geraniums were her great glories. She used to write me long letters about ' Fanchon,' a dog whose personal acquaintance I had made."

She would have agreed with Hamerton : "I humbly thank Divine Providence for having invented dogs."

Walter Savage Landor wrote some lines to her a few months before she died :

> " None hath told
> More pleasing tales to young and old.
> Fondest she was of Father Thames,
> But rambled to Hellenic streams,
> Nor even then could any tell
> The country's purer charms so well
> As Mary Mitford."

Harriet Martineau said : " Miss Mitford's descriptions of scenery, brutes, and human beings have such singular merit that she may be regarded as the founder of a new style." They were devoted friends. She was grateful for the kind reception given to her books in America. " It takes ten years to make a literary reputation in England, but America is wiser and bolder and dares to say at once, ' This is fine.' " She also dared to say : " I have seen

things of Longfellow's as fine as anything in Camp-
bell or Coleridge or Tennyson or Hood." As an old
lady she was as lovely as a winter rose, retaining her
vivacity and enthusiasm.

"I love poetry and people as well at sixty as I
did at sixteen."

In summer time when she gave strawberry parties at her cottage, the road leading to it was
crowded with carriages of all the rank and fashion
in the country.

Her conversation was simply charming; considered better than her finished compositions.

She was a successful dramatist, edited several
Annuals, was a frequent contributor to periodicals,
wrote delightful letters, but she will live through
the simple annals of village life, which are so natural
and vivid that they seem to have written themselves.

I do not believe it is generally known that in
1832 she made a collection of American Stories for
Young People.

She said: "In turning over a large mass of the
lighter literature of America, the little books intended for children appeared to me to possess
peculiar excellence, distinguished by the acute
observation and cheerful common sense to be expected from the country of Franklin."

She retained the "Americanisms" and gave her
reason: "It seems to me no mean part of an enlarged and liberal education to show our English
children that the standard of gentility differs in dif-

4

ferent countries, and that intelligent and cultivated people may, without the slightest tincture of vulgarity, use words and idioms of which these little exclusives never heard before. Thus, in America a shop is called a store and autumn the fall, and children frequently address their parents with the affectionate and homely appellations of father and mother, instead of the colder and more infantile elegancies of papa and mamma."

Miss Martineau (1802-1876), seems a sharp contrast to Miss Mitford, but those who knew her best, testified of sweetness as well as strength. No one has an indifferent opinion about her if he studies her character at all.

Miss Mitford said: "The woman I like best is Harriet Martineau, who is cheerful, frank, cordial, and right-minded in a very high degree."

To some she is a heroine of free thought, an uncrowned queen. "A product of the higher culture of the nineteenth century," or, as Mrs. Browning sketched her,

> "The noblest female intelligence between the seas,
> As sweet as spring; as ocean, deep."

Others differ so positively with her decisions, that they look upon her as repulsive and her influence as dangerous. All must agree as to her ability. No woman of modern or past time has left such a number of solid, interesting, instructive books. She wrote with unusual power and facility on Political

Economy, History, Psychology, Education, the Forest and Game Laws, Health, Husbandry, and Handicraft, The Effect of Machinery on Wages, The Relation of Wages and Population, Free Trade, Protection, was a successful journalist, a regular writer of leaders for a London daily (1642 Articles for *Daily News*), shaping the current politics of her day, influencing men and nations. Also published several volumes of travels, books for children, was a frequent contributor to the best reviews.

She wrote a series of tales illustrating important doctrines of Political Economy, saying: " I knew the work wanted doing, and that I could do it." These tales had a tremendous and unlooked-for success.

Lord Brougham declared " the whole Society for the Diffusion of Knowledge had been driven out of the field by a little deaf woman at Norwich."

When she visited the United States she became an abolitionist.

W. E. Forster said: " It seemed as if Harriet Martineau, alone, kept England straight in regard to America." She was a practical philanthropist, started a Mechanics' Institute, a building society, evening lectures for the people, and thought of starting a correspondence class.

Even when kept in bed by illness, she went on writing, and produced that pleasant work, " Life in a Sick Room." She managed her little farm at Ambleside with the skill of a practical agriculturist, and was regarded as an affectionate friend and peculiarly thoughtful and generous neighbor.

Here I pause to take a long breath, and to admire anew such versatility of achievement under such depressing conditions. She said: "My life has had no spring. When three senses out of five are deficient, the difficulty of cheerful living is great."

Her childish days were pitiably sad: first, as a half-starved body, with an undemonstrative mother, sternly just, and lacking in common tenderness, then afflicted with the wild vagaries of a diseased imagination, suffering from trifling causes, deprived of the sense of smell and of taste, and at twenty hopelessly deaf. Try to realize her position, and always judge her leniently. She determined never to inquire what was said, as she dreaded becoming a burden to her friends. She felt that no one cared for her, and when her brother James was obliged to leave her, he advised her to try to forget her loneliness by an attempt at authorship. She wrote laboriously at first, "coldly correct," and without marked signs of genius, choosing the Latin *nom de plume* "Discipulus," a masculine name, like George Sand, George Eliot, and the Brontë sisters. She became engaged, and for a short time was truly happy. She poured out her soul in letters and in disguised characters in print. She wrote: "Do you really think there are any people that have passed through life without knowing what that moment was, that stir in one's heart, as being first sure that one is beloved? It is more like the soul getting free of the body and rushing into Paradise, I should think." But it was, after all, a sad and stormy experience. They were both abnormally sensitive and over anxious. At last her lover became insane, and her mother, as cruel in her way as Dr. Mitford in his, refused to allow her daughter to visit him. It was inexcusable prudishness. After his death came the sudden loss of all their property. One of this young clergyman's causes of mental distress was the fact that Miss Martineau had wealth, therefore a poor man ought not to try to win her. Not a prevailing source of anxiety among young men in general! And as all the money was soon to be swallowed up in a financial crash, this special form of worry was quite futile, as is all worry. Miss Martineau said afterwards, " If I had a husband dependent on me for his happiness, the responsibility would have made me wretched. If he had not depended on me for his happiness, I should have been jealous." It was, perhaps, best that her lover went when he did!

Her fortitude, energy, and persistence should not be called masculine, but womanly, true womanly endurance and heroic patience and courage.

She was left with absolutely only one shilling and her dreadful mother to discourage all her efforts, with a silly aunt who gave her some pieces of silk, lilac, blue, and pink, to make into little bags to earn a few pennies! Imagine Harriet Martineau giving herself up to making patchwork and crazy quilts!

She was never impractical. She said: "I could make shirts and puddings, and iron and mend, and get my bread by my needle, if necessary. And at first she did sew all day, and sit up most of the night to write. Her articles were often refused, and the pay for a long time was ridiculously small.

"It was truly life I lived in those days."

In March, 1830, she received at the age of twenty-nine, the three prizes (£45) offered by a Unitarian Association for promoting their faith among the Roman Catholics, Mohammedans, and Jews, a convincing proof of her ability. She was deeply religious in her younger days and prepared a small volume of devotional exercises, prayer, and meditations for the use of young people. Later on she lost her faith in prayer, and finally gave up all belief in a future existence. "I have no wish for future experience, nor have I any fear of it. I am frankly satisfied to have done with life. I neither wish to live longer here nor to find life elsewhere. It seems to me simply absurd to expect it."

Her last year was spent in her pretty country home at Ambleside. She studied practical farming and made it pay, her farm of two acres supporting the laborer and his wife, and the home had a constant supply of vegetables, milk, eggs, etc.

Mrs. Wordsworth pronounced her a model in household economy; always careful to make her servants happy. Miss Bronté spoke, after a week's visit, of the combination of the highest mental culture with the nicest discharge of feminine duties.

I like to read how she set up a cross-pole fence around her estate, and, like a true woman, planted roses all along the line to wreathe and decorate it in summer. She had a keen sense of humor, dearly loved a good story, was truly affectionate in private life, with a warm and sensitive heart; never refused herself to children callers. By the way, she had an immense acquaintance and found her social duties rather irksome. Sidney Smith advised her to hire a carriage and engage an inferior authoress to go round in it to drop her cards.

Her complete cure by magnetism, after years of suffering, excited great comment, and, as a result, her beloved brother James was hopelessly alienated from her. She simply dared to tell the truth and express gratitude for her wonderful recovery.

Her last fancy work was a blanket for some little baby. Does not her character seem less hard and unlovely to you as you study it impartially? Deprived of all that is best and most precious in a woman's life, never knowing a mother's love, shut out by her deafness from the society where she would have shone so brilliantly, how much she accomplished, how nobly she struggled.

As a spinster author, I will quote one of her sensible remarks about marriage : " Women who are furnished with but one object—marriage, must be as unfit for anything when that aim is accomplished, as if they never had any object at all." " She served the

Right, that is God, all her life," said Florence Night-
ingale.

James Payn, in his " Literary Recollections," does
complete justice to a great woman who has been long
misunderstood — Harriet Martineau. " To call Miss
Martineau a deaf and disagreeable atheist is, in the
opinion of many persons, to treat her according to
her deserts. A great philosopher, who was, evidently, not amiable, used to pretend that Miss Martineau could always hear when she liked, and only
used her trumpet when she wanted to hear ; whereas,
at other times, she laid it down as a protection
against argument. Nothing could be more untrue."
Mr. Payn lays stress upon the domesticity and
tenderness of Miss Martineau's nature. She was
always anxious to do good to one of her friends.
Mr. Payn says, for instance, " A year after my first
introduction to her I came to Ambleside a married
man, and my first child was born there in the winter.
Her kindness to myself aud my wife I shall never
forget ; I went in and out of the knoll as I pleased,
like a cat which had a hole cut in the door for it,
and her library was not only placed entirely at my
service while on the premises, but I was permitted
to take home with me whatever books I wanted."
When the child was born — she was named after
Miss Martineau — the latter wrote to Mr. Payn in
this lovable spirit: "I send to the back door (for
quiet's sake) for a bulletin, and shall continue to do
so instead of coming, so long as quiet is necessary.

Oh! your news makes me so happy. Your little Christmas rose! I am glad it was a clear bright morning when it began to blow. How happy your dear wife must be, only not too happy to sleep, I hope. Come here, you know, as much as you like, and make any use of me and mine." Miss Martineau appears, indeed, as a sympathetic and noble personality in Mr. Payn's bright pages.

"There never was such an industrious lady," said the maid, who was with her the last eleven years of her life. "When I caught sight of her, just once, leaning back in her chair, with her arms hanging down, and looking as though she wasn't even thinking, it gave me quite a turn. I felt she must be ill to sit like that."

Her wise brother said to her, "Now, dear, leave it to other women to make shirts and darn stockings, and do you devote yourself to writing." She said:

"I am, in truth, very thankful for not having married at all. I am, probably, the happiest single woman in England, and am glad my fortune went.

"Many and many a time since have I said that, but for that loss of money, I might have lived on in the ordinary provincial method, of ladies with small means, sewing and economizing and growing narrower every year. Whereas, by being thrown on my own resources, I have worked hard and usefully, have friends, reputation, and independence ; seen the world abundantly abroad and at home, and, in short, have truly lived instead of vegetated."

We must not forget Matilda Betham, the beloved friend of Coleridge, Southey, Charles and Mary Lamb, Mrs. Barbauld, and many other persons of that time, who, at the age of fourteen, read Thomas Paine's works, and set herself to refute his arguments. She, like so many of our spinster authors, had no advantages of education beyond those afforded by her father's library and his teaching. In those days, women lived in terror of being thought learned, but her friends encouraged her aspirations, both literary and artistic. "I tell you," said one, " for the thousandth time, that you are full of genius; several paths to fame lie open to you, and if you don't continue to march through one of them, you deserve to have your mental feet cut off."

Her portraits were charming, but there were no art schools for women, no thorough teaching. Still her pictures were exhibited at Somerset House. She wrote poetry for the magazines and prepared a Biographical Dictionary of Celebrated Women.

Her declining years were spent in London. At certain literary receptions, the oddly-dressed old lady, who entered the room leaning on a cane, her face beaming with animation and intelligence, was usually surrounded by a little court. " I would rather talk to Matilda Betham than to the most beautiful young woman in the world," said one of her many admirers. She inherited her ready wit from her father, who lived to be ninety-six. Almost his last words were a witticism. He was walking up and down the room leaning on his daughter's arm the day before he died, and said smiling, " I'm walking slowly but I'm going fast."

There are many other literary spinsters who deserve much more than honorable mention, but you know we're going " 'cross lots," and must not tarry.

As the beautiful Mary Berry (1762–1852), who shone in society for nearly seventy years, whose memoirs are more interesting than the average novel, the special friend of Horace Walpole and his literary executor, besides publishing a History of England and France and a life of Lady Rachel Russell.

After all her social triumphs and universal popularity, Miss Berry gave her verdict in favor of " the dusty highway of married life " and owned her loneliness.

Caroline Herschel, the distinguished astronomer (1750–1848), who discovered eight comets, and gave to the world a general index of reference to every observation of every star inserted in the British Catalogue. She is so associated with her brother William that we cannot think of one without the other. She was his constant helper for fifty years. Night after night she shared his vigils, wrote down his observations as he made them, and when he was sleeping in the morning reduced the rough jottings to clearness and planned the labor of the next evening. Reversing the usual time of woman's sweeping we often read, " Swept the heavens from nine to six."

Here are some of the points she wrote down to ask her brother about at breakfast :

" Given the true time of the transit — take a transit."

" Time of a star's motion to be turned into space."

" A logarithm given to find the angle."

With all this care she kept the house with marvelous economy, and in every spare moment, when she should have been napping, her tireless fingers were knitting, knitting for the nephews and nieces in Germany.

And such lovely modesty ! She only " minded the heavens " for her brother, and said sincerely : " I am nothing ; I have done nothing. All I am I know I owe to my brother. I am only a tool which he shaped to his use ; a well-trained puppy dog would have done as much."

Yet she was an original thinker. Scientific men gladly gave her that praise. How often it happens that great men and great causes have some helper of which the outside world knows but little.

She is the devoted sister, as Miss Mitford was the model daughter. She might have been successful as a public singer; all that ambition was put aside. She lived most economically, rarely spending more than forty dollars a year on herself.

William worked night and day; she fed him that he might lose no time.

Her ink often froze as she was working; if it were not for cloudy nights she must have died of overwork.

" In her latest moments her only thought for herself was embodied in a request that a lock of her beloved brother's hair might be laid with her in her coffin."

The Astronomical Society of London rewarded her work with a gold medal in 1828. She lived to be almost " a centurion," as Mrs. Partington would say, nearly ninety-eight years old. Side by side stand the brother and sister. Without her unwavering love and steadfast service he could never have. achieved what he did. Give to her then, at least, a third of Alison's eloquent tribute :

" Herschel, by multiplying with incredible labor and skill the powers of the telescope, was enabled to look further into space than man had ever done before, discover a world hitherto unseen in the firmament, and in the Georgium Sidas add 'a new string to the lyre of heaven.' "

This story suggests another devoted brother and sister, Charles and Mary Lamb. Every one knows all about that pathetic oft-told tale. Mary (1764–1847), owes her literary fame to her " Tales from Shakespeare," and original " Poetry for Children."

" You must die first, Mary," he said, yet she survived him thirteen years. When she was ill and absent Charles wrote : " I am like a fool, bereft of her co-operation." Again : " I expect Mary will get better before many weeks are gone; but at present I feel my daily and hourly prop has fallen from me.' I totter and stagger with weakness, for nobody can supply her place to me."

Read this sonnet written in an asylum in "a lucid interval."

TO MY SISTER.

" If from my lips some angry accents fell,
    Peevish complaint, or harsh reproof unkind,
    'Twas but the error of a sickly mind
And troubled thoughts clouding the purer well
    And waters clear of reason ; and for me
    Let this my verse the poor atonement be.
My verse which thou to praise wert e'er inclined
    Too highly, and with a partial eye to see
    No blemish.   Thou to me didst ever show
Kindest affection ; and wouldst oft-times lend
    An ear to the desponding love-sick lay,
    Weeping my sorrows with me, who repay
But ill the mighty debt of love I owe,
Mary, to thee, my sister, and my friend."

She is the Bridget of his Elia Essays.

Next comes Miss Elizabeth Smith, the feminine Mezzofanti (1716-1806), who taught herself the Latin, Greek, Hebrew, Syriac, Arabic, Persian, Spanish, and German languages, wrote well in prose and verse, and published memoirs of Frederick and Margaret Klopstock.

Helen Maria Williams (1762-1827), a voluminous author, at first a warm supporter of the French Revolution, imprisoned at Paris on that account, later, a friend of the Bourbon. She wrote legendary tales, novels, odes, and miscellaneous poems, several volumes of letters of travel, various translations, but will be remembered by that well-known hymn :

"Whilst Thee I seek, Protecting Power."

At the last she was a hypochondriac, often summoning her intimate friends to her death-bed from from which she rose with rapidity and frequency. One wit, after being present on several such trying occasions, remarked "he could not afford to waste so much time on a mortuary uncertainty."

The learned Mary Astell (1668–1731), one of the first to advocate the higher education of women, and proposed a college for co-education. She was a writer of considerable note in her day, and published an "Essay in Defense of the Female Sex," with reflections on marriage, caused it is said by a disappointment of her own. Also six familiar essays on Marriage, Crosses in Love, and Friendship. In these she dwells on the rights and privileges of women with some asperity. As she grew older and more resigned to her solitary fate, she wrote on religious themes. She was so devoted to her studies that when she saw visitors coming whom she knew to be incapable of any improving conversation, she would look out of her window and jestingly tell them, as Cato did Nasica, "Miss Astell is not at home," and so kept gossips from making inroads on her precious time! Miss Philipps is remembered by a book, entitled " My Life, and what shall I do with It. By an old maid."

A magazine by this name was commenced in London many years ago, but it did not succeed.

Agnes Strickland and Lucy Aiken were both excellent historians. That trio of sweet singers, Adelaide Procter, Jean Ingelow, and Christina Rosetti can only be named. And that other remarkable trio, the Brontë sisters, for Charlotte won her fame as a spinster, who on the lonely Yorkshire heath, in their gloomy home, wrote so wonderfully of the outside world and of human nature.

Eliza Cook (1817–1889), the editor of the popular journal bearing her name, has seated herself comfortably on the hill of fame in her "Old Arm Chair."

Miss Mulock and Miss Thackeray slipped quietly out of the ranks, both married happily to men much younger than themselves. Miss Mulock wrote before she became Mrs. Craik:

> " My worldly name the world speaks loud,
> Thank God for well-earned fame;
> But silence sits at my cold hearth,
> I have no household name."

Frances Power Cobbe, a woman whose influence is felt through England and in this country, an independent, warm-hearted, clear-headed author of a score of valuable books, full of liberal, earnest, original thought. She deserves a special chapter as does Jean Ingelow and Frances Ridley Havergal. There are so many more that I stop, and will group these latter-day spinsters in a separate essay.

The longevity of unmarried literary women is remarkable. Average age, eighty-one.

Reviewing this throng renowned for their attractiveness in various ways, who can help wondering at their unmated condition. ′

> " Alas, nor chariot nor barouche,
>   Nor bandit cavalcade,
>   Tore from the trembling father's arms
>   Their all-accomplished maids."

For them how happy had it been !

Literary woman are accused of being eccentric and ugly, but the majority of these woman were beautiful. Some hag once said that every woman who wrote had one eye on her paper, the other on some man ; — except the Baroness Hahn Hahn, and she had lost one eye !

Dorothy Pattison, " Sister Dora," the heroic hospital nurse, said she believed the true sphere for woman was home, after all, and toward the end of her life, remarked: "If I had to begin life over again, I would marry, because a woman ought to live with a man, and be in subjection."

Dorothea Dix always advised young girls to marry rather than seek a career. The irony of fate or " Sarcasm of Destiny" or the Hand of Providence sometimes directs a woman's life very differently

5

from her own ideal. She may be lovable, affectionate, fond of home, devoted to children, yet be denied
all.

> " The needs God gave us disallowed ;
> Our unkissed faces in a shroud —
> Tis this to be a woman."

Derision and neglect used to be added to this
discipline. But the world is more tolerant, enlightened, and kindly, and the old maid is now allowed to do what she can to make others happy, and
no position of usefulness or distinction is closed to her
if she has the power to fill it. Gail Hamilton says
frankly and truly that every woman would marry if
she got a chance, meaning thereby the right chance.

Some of these spinsters who have been so brave
and cheerful, and accomplished so much, have
doubtless felt what Mrs. Browning has expressed so
perfectly in Aurora Leigh :

> " My father ! thou hast knowledge, only Thou,
> How dreary 'tis for woman to sit still
> On winter nights by solitary fires,
> And hear the nations praising them far off,
> Too far ! Ay, praising our quick sense of love,
> Our very heart of passionate womanhood,
> Which could not beat so in the verse without
> Being present also in the unkissed lips
> And eyes, undried, because there's none to ask
>   The reason they grew moist.

> To have our books
> Appraised by love, associated with love,
> While *we* sit loveless. Is it hard, you think ?
> At least 'tis mournful.
>   The love of all

Is but a small thing to the love of one.
You bid a hungry child be satisfied
With a heritage of many corn-fields ; nay,
He says he's hungry ; he would rather have
That little barley cake you keep from him
While reckoning up his harvests. So with us
We're hungry.
But since we needs must hunger,
                    Better for man's love
Than God's truth ! Better for companions sweet
Than great convictions. Let us bear our weights,
Preferring dreary hearths to desert souls."

This quotation has roused severe criticism. One spinster, whose own career has been both brilliant and useful, exclaims : "It is too bad ! You depict these woman as talented, attractive, admired, lovely characters, and making lots of money. Then all is spoiled by this doleful picture of pining and sighing by a dreary hearth."

I add, in deference to such appeals, that if some old maids are lonely, there are plenty of wives who would like to be !

Josiah Allen's wife has similar opinions of matrimony:

"Good land !" says I. "Is marryin' the only theme anybody can lay holt of ? It seems to me that the best way would be to lay holt of duty now, and then, if a bo comes, lay holt of him. But not get married !

"Oh dear me, suz !" screamed Delila Ann, for truly the thoughts seemed to scare her to death. "O how awful ! How lonely, lonely, they must be !"

"Who said they wasn't?" says I in pretty middlin' short tones, for she was a beginnin' to wear me out some, but I continued on in more mild accents. " I have seen married folks before now that I knew was in their souls as lonesome as dogs, and lonesomer" says I. "A disagreeabler feeling I never had than to have company that haint company stay right by you for two or three days. And then what must it be to have 'em stand by you from forty to fifty years! Good land! it would tucker anybody out!"

I am weary of this old bachelor life. It is a dog's life — no,
not a dog's ; that is a reflection on canine sagacity ; it is a log's
life, if life that may be called, which life is none.— *Pres. Raymona
of Vassar College.*

What do you know by any possibility about women ? You,
who are bachelor, bachelorum? I tell you, sir, that until you marry,
you are in utter darkness and desolation.— *Black.*

BACHELOR AUTHORS IN TYPES

THIS is a hard subject to manage, as bachelors
usually are.

The Spinsters of literature placidly took the
places assigned them, their pure, unselfish lives arranged themselves easily in accordance with my
plan, shedding a perfume of self-abnegation and
charitable deeds over the page.

But bachelors in literature, as in life, are fascinating, evasive, and inscrutable.

Then, there is such a numerous throng, that, like
the Fisher in the " Arabian Nights," gazing at the
Genii he had released from the bottle, it seems almost impossible to capture and confine so much in
so small compass.

Any one of these distinguished men would furnish abundant material for a volume, their combined
works the reading of a lifetime, and I can almost see

their smiles and their sneers, at the idea of being massed together in this daring, irreverent way by a woman !

To play the critic to these mental monarchs in a brief review would be an impertinence.

As the old broker remarked: " What we want is *pints*," bits of heart history, pen photographs, and now and then a quotation or anecdote that reveals character.

Still: if these sketches seem odd, unconnected, and a trifle bald, they will be truer to the theme. Without going back to the days of Homer, Virgil, Horace, and Juvenal, or dilating on the literary achievements of the Roman Catholic Clergy (though sorry to omit Father Prout), the mind recalls an illustrious company.

Tasso, Ariosto, Petrarch, Boccaccio, Congreve, Erasmus, Scaliger, Herrick, Goldsmith, Gray, Thomson, Collins, Cowley, Marlowe, Pope (the interrogation point of English literature, so called by an author he had quizzed too closely, "a little crooked thing that asks questions"), Pollock, his friend hoped he would marry in " the course of time." Cowper, Akenside (his were pleasures of the imagination), Hume, Gibbon, Macaulay, Gay, remembered by the Beggars' Opera and " Black-Eyed Susan." Rich was his manager, and 'twas said that " this opera made Rich gay, and Gay rich." Prior, Shenstone, and Collins, Rogers, Crabbe Robinson, that great talker of whom Rogers once said at breakfast : "If you have anything to say, say it quickly, for Crabbe Robinson is coming." Sir Isaac Newton and another Isaac, the good Dr. Watts, who made the longest visit on record, a forty-years visit, and was so delightful a guest that Lady Abney said it was the shortest visit she ever had : yet no lady ever seemed to be struck with "Watts and Select Hymn." Yet he had his romance. Few who have read Dr. Watts' hymn beginning

"How vain are all things here below,"

are aware that it was composed just after his suit had been rejected by Miss Singer, afterwards the celebrated Mrs. Rowe. The lady would have preferred the Doctor, but he was so slow in declaring his passion, that, tired of waiting, she had accepted Mr. Rowe, when the worthy divine at last made known his wishes.

Cruden, of Concordance fame, charmed with Miss Abney's wealth and virtues, determined to marry her. For months he annoyed her with calls, letters, petitions, memorials, and remonstrances; when she left home, he caused "praying-bills" to be distributed in various places of worship requesting the prayers of ministers and congregations for her preservation and safe return, and afterwards further bills for said congregations to return thanks. Finding that these peculiar attentions did not produce the desired effect, he drew up a long paper which he called a "Declaration of War," in which he announced

that he should yet compass her surrender by " shooting off great numbers of bullets from his camp,
namely, by earnest prayer to Heaven day and night,
that her mind might be enlightened and her heart
softened." But the young lady never relented, and
this grotesque courtship ended in defeat.

Herder, Hobbes (I jot down the names as they
come to me), Grimm, the German Philologist, to
whom the children are indebted for those wondrous
stories, known as "Grimm's Tales." Frederick
Grimm, the critic and diplomat; Voltaire, Alexander
Humboldt, Hans Andersen, Neander, the German
theologian, Jaffé, the Jewish historian of Popery,
Bishops Butler, Hammond, and Leighton, Locke,
Jeremy Bentham, Spinoza, Kant, Swedenborg, the
mystic; Dr. Barrow, who gave the best definition of
wit yet known.

Beranger, the lovable French lyrist. Rabelais,
who, like Swift, concealed deep meaning and grave
rebuke under coarse satire. Boileau, the satirist,
whom Mad. Sevingé affirms was only cruel in his
writings. He may be called the French Horace.

St. Beuve, whom Matthew Arnold considered the
finest critical spirit of our time. Burton, the author
of the " Anatomy of Melancholy," and Matthew
Green, who wrote "The Spleen."

George Buchanan, tutor to James the VI, and
James Buchanan, our bachelor president and something of an author, publishing love verses in the
New York *Herald*. His romance developed into a
tragedy.

Captain John Smith, a sworn champion of the ladies, all of whom he admired too ardently to be guilty of the invidious offense of marrying any one of them. Perhaps the last professional knight errant that the world ever saw. He was a prolific author and his " True Relation of Virginia " was the first book in American literature.

By the way, what an interesting book could be written about the Smiths who have distinguished themselves! To another John Smith we owe the key to Pepy's Diary.

If my subject included musicians, sculptors, artists, what a famous list could be added, as Raphael, Michael Angelo,* and Leonardo da Vinci, dear deaf old Sir Joshua Reynolds, Landseer, who, as some one well said " discovered the dog," Handel, Beethoven, Schubert, Berloiz.

Handel was a hopeless bachelor. He was never in love and had an aversion to marriage. In 1707 he went to Lübeck to compete for the place of successor to the famous organist Buxtehude ; but when he found that one of the conditions of obtaining the place was the compulsory privilege of marrying the daughter of his predecessor, not noted for her beauty, he fled precipitately.

Of Beethoven it is said that he found more pleasure in the society of women than of men. He made up his mind repeatedly to get married, and

* When Michael Angelo was asked why he did not marry, he replied, " Painting is my wife and my works are my children."

proposed more than once, but was refused in each case.   One of these women confessed that she rejected him because he was "so ugly, and half-cracked."

Beethoven was enamored of the Countess Guicciardi, but she married another.   He was often very lonely and once exclaimed, "O Providence, vouchsafe me one day of pure felicity!"

A touching romance was that of young Schubert. He was the teacher of Count Esterhazy's beautiful daughter and soon adored her, but the passion was not returned.   "You have dedicated none of your works to me," she said.   "What's the use," he sadly replied, "you already have all."   Later he wrote: "Imagine a man whose health will never come again, whose brilliant hopes have come to naught — to whom the happiness of love and friendship offers nothing but sorrow.   Every night when I go to sleep, I hope I may never wake again."   His grave is near Beethoven.

A learned physician, whose heart is as large as his practice, and knowledge of human nature as keen as his own scalpel, tells me it would not be possible to classify women.*   You could not find two alike, nor predicate with certainty what any one of that capricious sex would do under given circumstances; but men, as regards mental peculiarities, could be more easily arranged in bundles or types.

* As Heine puts it: "Do you say that woman has no character? She has a new character every day."

I shall therefore try to simplify matters, by classifying this interesting crowd of bachelor authors, naming a few representative men.

And first, the Lady-killer, with Congreve, the dramatist, as a specimen.

It is said that Congreve had too much wit in his comedies, not a prevailing fault now-a-days, and Dryden pronounced his play, " The Old Bachelor," the best first play he had ever seen. Macaulay speaks of its dialogue as resplendent with wit and eloquence in such abundance that the fools come in for an ample share. He was attacked and nearly demolished by Jeremy Collier in his " Short View of the Stage." The poet spoke of " The Old Bachelor " as a trifle to which he attached no value, and which had become public by a sort of accident. " I wrote it," he said, "to amuse myself in a slow recovery from a fit of sickness."

" What his disease was," says Collier, "I am not able to inquire, but it must be a very ill one to be worse than the remedy."

Congreve was handsome, witty, and a universal favorite. Ladies found him irresistible. His last admirer was the Duchess of Marlborough, daughter of the Dowager Duchess Sarah.

Gouty and blind, he was charming to the last, and after his death her grace " had a statue of him in ivory, which moved by clockwork, and was placed daily at her table." She also had a large wax doll made in his likeness, and its feet were regularly blistered and anointed by the doctors as poor Congreve's had been.

The inscription on his monument in Westminster Abbey was written by this appreciative friend, to whom he bequeathed his small fortune, which she wore round her neck in superb diamonds. Thackeray dwells on Congreve in his Lectures on the Humorists.

Swift might be ranked as a lady-killer in a serious way, but bachelors will not allow him in their ranks.

As the greatest contrast, think of Cowper as a sensitive plant closing its delicate, shrinking petals, affected by every passing cloud, unable to endure contact with the rough-handed world.

"O poets, from a maniac's tongue was poured the deathless
          singing !
O Christians ! at your cross of hope a hopeless hand was clinging !
O men ! this man in brotherhood your weary paths beguiling,
Groaned inly while he taught you peace, and died while you were
          smiling.
And now, what time ye all may read, through dimming tears his
          story ;
How discord on the music fell and darkness on the glory,
And how, when one by one sweet sounds and wandering lights
          departed,
He wore no less a loving face because so broken-hearted."

Cowper, at twenty-eight, became deeply attached to his cousin, Theodora, and she fully returned his affection ; was perhaps controlled by it through life, as she never married. But her father refused his

consent on the grounds of relationship and hered-
itary insanity. Cowper writes to Lady Hesketh of

"Her through tedious years of doubt and pain
Fixed in her choice, and faithful, but in vain."

Keats belongs to this class, shy, pure. sensitive,
too delicately organized for health or lasting happiness. In one of his letters he hoped that after his
death he "would be among the English poets." With
one or two exceptions, no poet of the last generation
stands higher in the estimation of those fitted to
judge.

His letters to that disagreeable young woman,
Fanny Brawne, must be mentioned. Another instance of "brawn and brain." where, as usual,
Brawn gets the better of brain. His quivering,
bleeding heart is laid open for inspection, a painful
sight.

There are the Embittered Bachelors, like Pope,
who avenge their deformity and unhappiness or in-
validism in satire, that, when applied to women, has
neither delicacy nor genuine wit. Lady Montague's
mocking laughter after his professions of passion
must have hurt him. I can hear it now.

Those governed by an Early Love like Irving.
He was social, charming, enjoyed the society of
ladies, was ever complimentary and courteous, sometimes indulging in sentiment, yet we like to believe
that his deepest love was buried in the grave of Matilda Hoffman, of whom he said : " She died in the

beauty of youth, and to me she will always be young and beautiful."

In a letter to Paulding, Irving writes: "Your picture of domestic enjoyment indeed raises my envy. With all my wandering habits, which are the results of circumstances rather than of disposition, I think I was formed for an honest, domestic, uxorious man, and I cannot hear of my old cronies snugly nestled down with good wives and fine children round them, but I feel for the moment desolate and forlorn. Heavens! what a haphazard, schemeless life mine has been that here I should be at this time of life, youth slipping away, and scribbling month after month and year after year, far from home, without any means or prospect of entering into matrimony, which I absolutely believe indispensable to the happiness and even comfort of the after part of existence."

It was by the death-bed of his love that the well-beloved Dr. Muhlenberg wrote: "I would not live alway," and his devotion to her memory was unwavering to the end.

Gilbert White, the lovable, retiring old bachelor who gave us that delightful book, "The Natural History of Selbourne," making his name famous by an intelligent, enthusiastic, exact study of the birds and animals around his own home, belongs to this class. I think Miss Hetty Mulso made a mistake in refusing such a lover.

In Mary Howitt's translation of the autobiography of Hans Andersen, we find that he had his trials, but nothing could spoil the sunshiny, child-like nature of this best of story-tellers — a man of crystal innocence and amusing conceit. He gives the romance in his own ingenuous way.

"Sentiment, which I had so often derided, would now be avenged. I arrived in the course of my journey at the house of a rich family, in a small city, and here, suddenly a new world opened before me, an immense world, which yet could be contained in four lines, which I wrote at that time:

> ' A pair of dark eyes fixed my sight,
> They were my world, my home, and my delight.
> The soul beamed in them, and childlike peace,
> And never on earth will their memory cease.'

New plans of life occupied me. I would give up writing poetry, to what would it lead? I would study theology and become a preacher. I had only one thought and that was she. But it was self-delusion. She loved another; she married him. It was not till several years later that I felt and acknowledged that it was best both for her and myself that things had fallen out as they were. She had no idea, perhaps, how deep my feeling for her had been, or what an influence it produced in me. She had become the excellent wife of a good man, and a happy mother. God's blessing rest on her."

It was in the company of Thorwaldsen, the sculptor (a bachelor, also) that Andersen wrote several of his stories. He says, that often in the twilight, when the family circle sat in the open garden parlor,

Thorwaldsen would come softly behind me, and, clapping me on the shoulder, would ask, " Shall we little ones have any tales to-night?"   Often during his most glorious works would he stand with laughing countenance and listen to the story of " The Top and Ball," " The Ugly Duckling."   It is sad to think that one who had made Christmas merry for so many little folks should ever be solitary on that day. He tells the story in his artless, touching way: " And yet, amid these social festivities, with all the amiable zeal and interest that there was felt for me, I had one disengaged evening, one evening on which I felt solitude in its most oppressive form — Christmas eve, that very evening of all others, in which I would most willingly witness something festal, willingly stand beside a Christmas tree, gladdening myself with the joy of children, and seeing the parents joyfully become children again.   Every one of the many families in which I, in truth, felt that I was received as a relation, had fancied, as I afterwards discovered, that I must be invited out, but I sat quite alone in my room at the inn, and thought on home. I seated myself at the open window and gazed up to the starry heavens which was the Christmas tree lighted up for me.   ' Father in Heaven,' I prayed as the children do, ' what dost Thou give to me?'"   It was he who said, " Every man's life is a fairy tale, written by God's finger."   His own fairy tales have been read with delight in every modern language, Do you recall his epitaph?

"Thou art not dead though thine eyes are closed ;
In children's hearts thou shalt live forever."

Hans Andersen is the only literary bachelor I remember who received and refused an offer of marriage. You can imagine his surprise on being told by a young and handsome girl, who had traveled far to meet him, that she wished to marry him. "I should be so very good to you," said the admiring, simple-hearted maiden, "and always take good care of you." "But, my dear girl, I don't wish to be married," answered the charming old man, and she departed as suddenly as she came.

Turner, the artist, had his life shaped and shadowed by an early diappointment. "A boyish fancy ripened into love, but his idol was influenced to marry in his absence, and the treachery wrought incalculable harm on his sensitive nature. He gradually changed into a self-concentrated, reserved money-maker." The very peculiar appearance of his "Slave Ship" may be due to this misfortune. Emotional insanity on canvas. I have always liked the story of the farmer's wife whose city cousin took her to see a collection of paintings in London. She looked at Turner's "The Day after the Deluge" and read the title. "Well, I should think it was!" she said, and passed on. Something serious also seems to affect his literary work.

Turner is not generally known as an author, yet he has written a good deal, so faulty in spelling, grammar, and construction, that it would serve as an exercise for little boys at school to correct.

Hamerton says he never did anything worse than his poetry, except his prose. You shall judge of their respective merits from brief extracts.

> " Where the soft river, flowing, gives renown,
>   'Mid steep worn hills, and to the low sunk town ;
>   Whose trade has flourished from early time
>   Remarkable for thread called Bridport twine."

Now for the prose :

" They wrong virtue, enduring difficulties or worth. in the bare imitation of nature, all offers received in the same brain, but where these attempts arise above mediocrity, it would surely not be a little sacrifice to those who perceive the value of the success, to foster it by terms so cordial that cannot look so easy a way as those spoken of convey doubts to the expecting individual. For as the line that unites the beautiful to grace and these offering forming a new style not that soul can guess as ethics. Teach them of both, but many serve as the body the soul, but presume more as the beacon to the headland which would be a warning to the danger of mannerism and the disgustful."

(I trust this is clear to you !)

Adam Smith, the distinguished writer on Political Economy, was never married. Dugald Stewart gives this interesting bit of history :

" In the early part of Mr. Smith's life, it is well known to his friends that he was for several years attached to a young lady of great beauty and accomplishment. What prevented their union I am not able to learn, but I believe it is pretty certain that after this disappointment, he laid aside all thoughts of marriage. The lady also died unmarried. At eighty she still retained evident traces of her former beauty. The powers of her understanding and the gaiety of her temper seemed to have suffered nothing from the hands of Time."

The Hermit, as Thoreau — "The Bachelor of Thought and Nature." Thoreau was a recluse, a genuine apostle of solitude, standing aloof from other men and scorning them.

"They do a little business each day to pay their board; then they congregate in sitting rooms and feebly fabulate and paddle in the social slush.

"The whole enterprise of this nation is totally devoid of interest to me. Would I not rather be a cedar post than the farmer that sets it, or he that preaches to that farmer?

"I could do easily without the post-office; never read any memorable news in a newspaper. Nothing at the North Pole that I could not find at Concord.

"What a foul subject is this of doing good instead of minding one's own life, which should be his 'business.'

"The youth gets together the materials to build a bridge to the moon, or a temple on the earth, and the middle-aged man concludes to build a wood-shed with them." . .

On picking up a button from the coat of the drowned Marquis of Ossoli on the seashore, Thoreau reached the acme of self-aggrandizement. "Held up, it intercepts the light, an actual button, and yet all the life it is connected with is less substantial to me and interests me less than my faintest dream."

He also said : " The stars and I belong to a mutual admiration society. I would put forth sublime thoughts daily.

" I love my friends very much, but I find that it is of no use to go to see them.

"I hate them commonly when I am near them ; they belie themselves and deny me continually. Silence alone is worthy to be heard."

" 'I love Henry,' said a friend, 'but I cannot like him, and as for taking his arm, I should as soon think of taking the arm of an elm tree." Still Thoreau had a love affair, and the heroine is now a grandmother. He and his brother John made love to the same nymph, and she went and married a parson.

To the average observer, a hut by a pond, and intimacies with mice and woodchucks, are even less desirable than " social slush." After all his outdoor excursions and a life in fresh air, Thoreau died of consumption like any common mortal who had been of more use to mankind.

Do not say that I fail to appreciate the peculiar charm of this student of nature. " No one ever came nearer to the great heart of nature." What are guesses with others are a revelation to him. But he affected to despise humanity, always a mistake. Men and women as a rule are more interesting than chipmunks. All this was caused by his intense sympathy with nature.

" It appears to me," said this fascinating dreamer, " that to one standing on the heights of philosophy mankind and the works of man will have sunk out of sight altogether; that man is altogether too much insisted on. Man is too much with us. It is our weakness that so exaggerates the virtue of philanthropy and charity, and makes it the highest human attribute. The world will sooner or later tire of philanthropy and all religion based on it mainly. In order to avoid delusions, I would fain let man go by, and behold a universe in which man is but a grain of sand."

He may have inherited his self-consciousness from his mother, who when heard it she remarked that Thoreau's style resembled Emerson's, replied placidly: " Yes, Mr. Emerson *does* write like my son." Lowell, who does not believe in Thoreau's originality, nor his arrogant omniscience about nature, says: " He turns commonplaces end for end, and fancies it makes something new of them. He discovered nothing, but thought everything a discovery of his own, from moonlight to the planting of acorns and nuts by squirrels."

The Self-denying bachelor, like Lamb, who gave up marriage for the sake of his sister. I am proud to say there are many equally noble in our day.

Lamb said of celibacy: "There is a quiet dignity in old bachelorhood, a leisure from cares, noise, and so on ; an enthronization upon the armed chair of a man's feeling, that he may sit, walk, read unmolested ; to none accountable." Writing to Procter on his marriage, Lamb said : " I am married myself to a severe step-wife, who keeps me, not at bed and board, but at desk and board, and is jealous of my morning aberrations. I cannot slip out to congratulate kinder unions. It is well she leaves me alone o' nights ; the d——d Day-hag Business."

The Old-Maidish bachelor, like Gray, who always had his room in the most exact order, and a fire-escape at the window, who labored eight years on a single poem, and made it perfect. " No man ever went down to immortality with a smaller book under his arm."

Erasmus was fanciful, and often old-maidish in his tastes. He must have a certain kind of fire-place, and a particular brand of wine. He almost fainted at the sight of fish, declaring that while his " heart was Catholic, his stomach was Lutheran."

The late Francois Mignet, the French historian, was a confirmed old bachelor. A private passage was opened for him from his fourth-story lodgings into the house of Mr. Thiers, with whom he was on very intimate terms. He retired at ten, rose at five, did his own cooking, allowed no one to touch his papers, and in winter sat and wrote with a rug around his legs and feet, rather than have the trouble of tending the fire.

Walt Whitman stands by himself, "the good, gray poet" he is called by his admirers. I am not one of them. I do not find fault with his extraordinary ideas of "true art," refusing to expurgate his Leaves of Grass, although I cannot understand why we should excuse, tolerate, or admire in a book what would be tabooed as blasphemous or obscene in pictures or conversation. Why do women write of the rollicking vulgarity of Chaucer's tales as "delicious *naïveté*," and lady teachers advise the young girls under their guidance to read his description of intrigue, and hot, lawless, unbridled passion. It is not only unwise, but positively dangerous and wicked. Why not tell the truth about old Dan Chaucer? He spoils his own feast with needless filth. So does Rabelais. Gross indelicacy is not wit. Swift enjoyed revolting subjects that give a decent person a mental nausea. Many who have erred in this direction have realized the harm, and repented before death. But Walt Whitman sees nothing that is in the least objectionable in any of his poems. Let him represent the Egotist.

"Divine am I inside and out and I make holy whatever I touch or am touched from.
The scent of these arm-pits aroma finer than prayer."
or
"I do not snivel that snivel the world over."
"I find no sweeter fat than sticks to my own bones."
"I dote on myself."
"I am an acme of things accomplished."
"My feet strike an apex of the apices of the stairs."

> " My lovers suffocate me,
> Bussing my body with soft balsamic busses."
> " Let me have my own way;
> After me vista ! "
> " I bestow upon any man or woman the entrance to all the gifts of the universe."
> " Who thinks the amplest thoughts? for I would surround those thoughts."
> " Who has gone farthest? for I would go further."
> " To be conscious of my body, so satisfied, so large !"
> " To be this incredible God I am."

His stringing together of nouns has been parodied so often and so well, that I will only give three of his own lines to prove that nothing can be more ridiculous :

> " Flail, plough, pick, crowbar, spade,
> Shingle, rail, prop, wainscot, jamb, lath, panel, gable,
> Citadel, ceiling, saloon, academy, organ, exhibition,
> house, library."

Yet, once in a while you stumble on a striking and good sentence, as, " How beggarly appear arguments before a defiant deed! " " I think heroic deeds were all conceived in the open air." His warble for Lilac-time I cheerfully acknowledge is exquisite, full of the very soul of spring. His love of nature is the redeeming quality. His Army Lyrics also have the true martial ring, and a deal of tenderness and pathos.

And the *Happy-go-lucky* type, the blundering darling, whom every woman likes, but no woman wants to marry; as poor "Goldy." He loved the beautiful Miss Horneck, the beautiful "Jessamy Bride," who was beautiful at seventy. After his coffin had been closed, a lock of hair was requested for a lady who wished to preserve it as a memento. She laughed at her awkward admirer while he lived, but his regard for her " has hung a poetical wreath above her grave."

Says Irving: " Had it been his fate to meet a woman who could have loved him despite his faults and respected him despite his foibles, we cannot but think that his life and genius would have been made more harmonious, his desultory affections would have been concentrated, his craving self-love appeased, his pursuits more settled, his character more solid. A nature like Goldsmith's, so affectionate, so confiding, so susceptible to simple, innocent enjoyments, so dependent on others for the sunshine of existence, does not flower if deprived of the atmosphere of home."

Next, for contrast, a large family of CLAMS, cold, encased in a hard shell. Hume takes the lead as a bivalve; apathetic and frigid. In his essays, he frequently discusses the passion of love, dividing it into its elements as systematically as if he had subjected it to a chemical analysis, and laying down rules regarding it as distinctly and specifically as if it were a system of logic. Hume's elder brother John was married in 1751, and the following letter full of light and elegant raillery refers to that event:

DEAR MADAM

Our friend has at last plucked up a resolution and has ventured on that dangerous encounter. He went off on Monday morning, and this is the first action of his life wherein he has engaged himself without being able to compute exactly the consequences. But what arithmetic will serve to fix the proportion between good and bad wives, and rate the different classes of each. Sir Isaac Newton himself, who could measure the course of the planets, and weigh the earth as in a pair of scales, even he had not algebra enough to reduce that amiable part of our species to a just equation, and they are the only heavenly bodies whose orbits are as yet uncertain.

It is recorded of Hume that he once made an offer of marriage to a lady who refused him, but whose friends afterwards told him that she had changed her mind. " So have I." replied the historian. At times he seems to be depressed by his self-imposed solitude, and spoke of himself as left utterly abandoned and desolate. " Fain would I run into the crowd for shelter and warmth, but cannot prevail with myself to mix with such deformity. I call upon others to join me in order to make a company apart, but no one will hearken to me. Everyone keeps at a distance, and dreads that storm which beats upon me from every side."

The Corpulent Bachelor Authors make a long list. Hume was one of the fattest of fat bachelors, and often alludes to it. In a letter he says, " Pray tell his solicitorship (Alexander Home) that I have been reading in an old author called Strabo, that in some cities of ancient Gaul there was a fixed legal standard established for corpulency. that the senate kept a measure, beyond which if any form presumed to increase, the proprietor was obliged to pay a fine proportionable to its rotundity. Ill would it fare with us if such a law should pass our parliament." Unappreciated in his own country, he was the rage in Paris. The incense of praise was enough to intoxicate even his cool head. But he could not shine in the society of ladies. In their salons he was an exquisitely comical failure. Mad. D. Épinay gives a vivid scene. He is seated between the two prettiest women in Paris, but could only look admiringly, then blankly, from one to the other, absolutely unable to think of a word to say. His French, indeed, was some excuse. " The French," said Walpole with his customary cynicism, " believe in Mr. Hume, the only thing in the world that they believe implicitly, for I defy them to understand any language which he speaks."* But Gibbon's corpulency placed him in an even more embarrassing position.

It is generally imagined that Gibbon was faithful to his early and romantic love for Susan Curchod, afterwards Madam Necker, and the mother of Mad. de Stael. To be sure he never married, but one critic's enthusiasm over his fidelity to this disappointed passion is a trifle excessive. He comments in this way on some extracts from his journal during the time of his courtship: " What raptures these simple memoranda hint, and how dreary a void in his life is suggested by the historian's future recurrences

* He made a similar criticism on Dante, saying, " His reputation will go on increasing, because scarcely anybody reads him."

to the sole passion of his life. He never loved nor thought of loving any other woman : his hurt was not bravely received, but, apparently, it was incurable." When attributing to the man who grew, year by year, more famous and more enormously fat, in the society of Madam Necker, such constancy, this writer should have mentioned, if only to refute it, a malicious story told concerning an occasion, when Gibbon, lured by the charms of a beautiful woman, not only forgot his loyalty to what is described as the sole love of his life, but, what was a matter of more importance to him, forgot that his fat had kept pace with his fame. It is averred that Gibbon, charmed with the beautiful Lady Elizabeth Foster, invited the fair one to breakfast in a bower fragrant with circling acacias, and read to her several passages from his " History of the Decline and Fall of the Roman Empire," just completed. Enchanted with the masterly narrative, her ladyship, wholly unsuspicious of all amorous pretensions from a man of his mature years, ungainly figure, and love-repelling countenance, complimented him with a charm of language and warmth of address which he instantly converted in effusions of tender inspiration. Falling on his knees, he gave utterance to an impassioned profession of love, greatly to the surprise of its object, who, recoiling, entreated him to rise at once from this humiliating posture. Thus recalled to cooler feeling, but prostrate and helpless from his unwieldly form, he vainly sought to regain his feet, and the lady, whose first astonishment soon yielded to irrepressible laughter, was equally powerless in affording relief, until, at length, with the aid of two strong women, he was reseated in his arm-chair, from which it was supposed he had accidentally slipped. But this reversal of his " Decline and Fall " (I refer to his fall and her decline) did not interrupt their friendship, which shows him in a much more amiable light than Pope with Lady Montague.

This absurd tableau has also been laughed over in France with Mad. de Cronza as the heroine.

Thomson, the poet of the Natural School, after the brilliant finish of Pope's studied couplets was also noticeably corpulent. " More fat than bard he seems." Famous for his lays and his laziness, biting mouthfuls from the luscious peaches hanging on the garden wall, too lazy to take his hands out of his pockets to pick them. He loved to lie in bed. He refused entirely to get up one morning in 1748, and after a proper period had elapsed they buried him. He had at least one romance, an unfortunate affair, being deeply interested in a Miss Amanda Somebody, whose mother did not want a poor poet for a son-in-law.

He exclaimed :

> " For once, O Fortune, hear my prayer,
> And I absolve thy future care ;
> All other blessings I resign,
> Make but the dear Amanda mine."

Poor Jemmy ! He sung of the seasons but had no summer of his own.

> " 'Tis mine, alas ! to mourn my wretched fate,
>   I love a maid who all my bosom charms,
>   Yet lose my days, without this lovely mate,
>   Inhuman fortune* keeps her from my arms."

And next " The Cadaverous Skeleton," as Rogers, extremely sensitive about his appearance, but his friends were unmerciful. Byron wrote a scathing lampoon, ending :

> " Is't a corpse stuck up for show?
>   Galvanized at times to go !
>   Vampire, ghost, or ghoul, what is it?
>   I would walk ten miles to miss it ! "

Sydney Smith named him " The Death Dandy," and wicked Theodore Hook advised him to call his hearse instead of his carriage. Even the cabby, whom he hailed at midnight from St. Paul's church-yard, knew too much to desire a ghost as passenger, and cried out, as he drove rapidly on, " Go back ! go back to your grave, old man ! "

He was handsome in youth, but at ninety-four one might be pardoned for looking slightly shriv-eled.

Jack Bannister maintained that more good things had been said and written on Rogers' face than on that of the greatest beauty.

When Rogers repeated the couplet —

> " The robin with his furtive glance,
>   Comes and looks at me askance."

* In the shape of Amanda's mother.

Ward struck in with

"If it had been a carrion crow he would have looked you full in the face!"

One wag insisted that he had been once shut up in the Catacombs, mistaken for a mummy! And they said of his picture, a faithful likeness, that it was "painted to the death!"

Byron placed Rogers next to Scott as a poet. He had a decided talent for epigrams, and his table talk is delightful. A friend remarked, "If you enter his house, his drawing-room, his library, you of yourself say, 'This is not the dwelling of a common mind.' There is not a gem, a coin, a book thrown aside on his chimney-piece, his sofa, his table that does not bespeak an almost fastidious elegance. But this very delicacy must be the misery of his existence. He was reputed a wit, as well as poet, and did say some good things and many severe ones. Going to Holland House by the Hammersmith stage-coach, a lumbering old tortoise of a vehicle, he asked the driver what he called it. Being answered "The Regulator," he observed "it was a very proper name, as all the others *go by it*."

"When Croker wrote his review in the Quarterly of Macaulay's 'History,' he intended murder, but committed suicide."

On somebody remarking that Payne Knight had become very deaf — "'Tis from want of practice," replied Rogers ; "he is the worst listener I know."

Rogers' breakfasts were even better than his poems.

He might also be classed as "an opulent catch, who wouldn't be caught."

His epigram on Ward, Lord Dudley, is excellent:

> " Ward has no heart, they say, but I deny it,
>   He has a heart and gets his speeches by it."

Byron pronounced this to be one of the best epigrams in the English language, with the true Greek talent of expressing by implication what is wished to be conveyed.

Miss Sedgwick, who breakfasted with Rogers and called him the " king of old bachelors," said that he pronounced matrimony a folly at any period of life, and quoted the saying of some one that, " No matter whom you married, you would find afterwards you had married another person ! "

Yet Hayward, in a recent essay in the *Edinburgh*, tells us that during the last four or five years of Rogers' life he was constantly expatiating on the advantages of marriage, and regretting he had not married, because then he should have had a nice woman to care for him.

His own version of his nearest approximation to the nuptial tie was, that when a young man, he admired and sedulously sought the society of the most beautiful girl he then, and still thought, he had ever seen. At the end of the London season, at a ball, she said : " I am going to-morrow to Worthing. Are you coming there?" He did not go. Some months afterwards, being at Ranelagh, he saw the attention of everyone drawn towards a large party, in the center of which was a lady on the arm of her husband. Stepping forward to see this wonderful beauty, he found it was his love.

She merely said:

" You never came to Worthing."

Voltaire was remarkable for his attenuated figure and thin face. " Wicked Mummy " was one of his nicknames. He makes merry in his letters over the meagerness of his countenance, speaking of himself as " a dried herring," and once when he had said " I hope soon to see you face to face," he added, " that is if I may apply the word *face* to such a phiz as mine ? "

He was once completely discomfitted by Young, author of the " Night Thoughts." Voltaire was depreciating Paradise Lost, particularly disposed to ridicule Milton's celebrated personifications of death, sin, and the devil. Young, who had a happy talent for impromptu wit, retorted :

> " Thou art so witty, profligate, and thin,
> Thou art at once, the devil, death, and sin."

Many famous metaphysicians, philosophers, and scientists have been bachelors. Jeremy Bentham, Kant, Locke, Butler, Spinoza, Hobbes, Newton, Robert Boyle, Humboldt, Buckle, Spencer, etc. In looking over the life of Isaac Newton to find some romance, I only encountered such headings as " History of Fluxions," " Lunar Theory," " Achromatic Telescopes," and lose courage to seek further. It is

7

reported that his friends, fearing he would be insane
from such constant mental exertion, induced a beautiful lady to enter his study and sit beside him, hoping her presence might divert him from his labors.
He had his pipe in his mouth as usual, and the only
notice taken of the fair invader was to borrow her
dainty finger to punch his pipe bowl. She declared
she would not be used as a tobacco stopper, and so
the affair ended, in smoke !

Bunsen, the celebrated German chemist, became
so engrossed in an experiment on his wedding day
as to entirely forget his waiting bride, who was carried off by another.

Humboldt was described by a woman who knew
him well, as an amiable, good-looking man ; a graceful dancer, devoted to the ladies ; a wit, a diplomat,
and a philosopher, a great favorite in society. As he
entered a drawing-room, a joyous exclamation was
heard from all present, and as soon as the company
were again seated, the hostess would exercise her
privilege of starting conversation, by suggesting some
topic to her distinguished guest. The theme need
not be scientific ; it served the purpose equally well,
if it were a bit of general news or town gossip. This
intellectual giant could play with it as he pleased,
and could turn and twist it in such a manner as to
make it an opportunity for the display of wit, irony,
wordly wisdom, memory, and versatile genius. He
was a little feared for his witticisms. One young
matron lingered at a reception until he departed,

saying, " I will never leave so long as that gentleman remains. I should not like to be the subject of his remarks!" (not so courageous as a friend of mine who was obliged to hurry away from a dinner for the opera, who said with a smiling bow to a witty French woman among the guests, who would always sacrifice a friend for an epigram : " Madam, I leave my reputation in your hands!") But there was no malevolence in Humboldt's character-sketches. Bismarck, who disliked him, is reported as saying that he was a conceited, insupportable chatterer, and a disgusting glutton! To offset this harsh estimate is Ingersoll's eloquent tribute : " We associate the name of Humboldt with oceans, continents, mountains, and volcanoes; with the great palms, the wide deserts, the snow-tipped craters of the Andes ; with primeval forests, and European capitals; with wildernesses and universities ; with savages and savans ; with the lovely views of unpeopled wastes ; with peaks and pampas, and steppes, and cliffs, and crags. With the progress of the world ; with every science known to man; with every star glittering in the immensity of space — the world is his monument!"

Here are a few unique statements from this inveterate bachelor: " I regard marriage as a sin. It is my conviction also that he is a fool, and still more a sinner, who takes upon himself the yoke of marriage : a fool, because he thereby throws away his freedom, without gaining a corresponding recompense; a sinner, because he gives life to children without being able to give them the certainty of happiness. The whole of life is the greatest insanity."

Buckle, who was always an invalid, declared that he owed everything to his mother, with whom he lived. After her death he said: " For the opinion of the world I care nothing, because, now at least, there is no one whose censure I fear, or whose praise I covet." In her society he found all the aid and sympathy he needed, and through her influence he was led to value the mental sympathy and companionship of women, with whom he was a great favorite. One of his finest discourses was on " The influence of woman on the progress of knowledge."

A bachelor is apt to have his hobbies, his were books, chess, cigars, and " averages". He also declared he would not marry until he had $5,000 a year, and never attained that comfortable income.

The Pessimist, as " Schopenhauer, who did not wish to be loved by his fellow-men, for, in order to be loved by them, one must be like them, which, God forbid! When the cat is a kitten, she plays with little paper balls; she imagines that they are alive and like herself. When she is old, she knows better, and lets them lie."

Such had been his experience with the bipeds. He was a woman-hater, and gloried in his celibacy. " The so-called career of most young men," he said, "ends in their becoming beasts of burden to women. The married man bears the full burden of life ; the unmarried but half. All genuine philosophers have been celibates — Descartes, Leibnitz, Malebranche, Spinoza, Kant. The ancients are not to be taken into account, because woman with them occupied a subordinate position. Moreover, Socrates' matrimonial experience did not recommend the nuptial state to scholars."

Josiah Royce tells us of insanity in his family, and says, " the man, unquestionably, was incapable of a permanently cheerful view of life — a born outcast, doomed to hide and be lonely." His mother did not enjoy his "rhetorically gloomy" letters. " Everything," he writes to her, "is washed away in time's stream. The minutes, the numberless atoms of pettiness into which every deed is dissolved, are the worms that gnaw at everything great and noble to destroy it." His mother found this sort of thing rather tedious. A most brilliant company often gathered at her house in Weimar, with Goethe at the head, and her son, a youth of twenty, could not add grace to such a scene so long as he could talk of nothing but time and worms.

She wrote him plainly, being a woman as clearheaded as she was charming : " When you get older, dear Arthur, and see things more clearly, perhaps we shall agree better. Till then let us see that our thousand little quarrels do not hunt love out of our hearts. To that end we must keep well apart. You have your lodgings. As for my house, whenever you come you are a guest, and are welcome, of course, only you mustn't interfere. I can't bear objections.

Days when I receive, you may take supper with me if you'll only be so good as to refrain from your painful disputations which make me angry, too, and from all your lamentations over the stupid world and the sorrows of mankind, for all that always gives me a bad night and horrid dreams, and I do so like sound sleep."

How short-sighted are the students who insist that it is not necessary to know an author's history to understand his work. Schopenhauer, the morbid mystic, was simply a result of an unfortunate combination of inherited mental qualities. He could not help it; he lived alone, he died alone. " His name is everywhere a symbol for all that is most dark and deep and sad and dangerous about the philosophy of our time." We pity him, and if we are wise, avoid his unhealthy influence.

Cowley was spoken of in youth as the most amiable of mankind, but, being ill-treated in a love affair in his latter days, could not afterwards endure the sight of a woman, and would leave the room if one came into it.

James Smith of the famous " Rejected Addresses," was a bachelor. "I have had a horrid dream," he wrote in his diary, " namely, that I was engaged to be married; introduced to my bride, a simpering, young woman, with flaxen hair, in white gloves, just going to declare off — *coûte que coûte* — when, to my inexpressible relief, I awoke.

It is noticeable that the best Letter-writers have

been bachelors — Erasmus, Walpole, Gray, Pope, Cowper, and Macaulay. They were not subjected to the domestic interruptions so comically described by Hood in his " Parental Ode," ending —

> " I'll tell you what, my love,
> I cannot write unless HE's sent above."

Erasmus was the most facetious man and the greatest critic of his age — a moderate reformer who satisfied neither side. He exposed with great freedom the vices and corruptions of his own church, yet never would be persuaded to leave the communion. In his most remarkable work, " The Praise of Folly," he laughs at the faults and foibles of all classes and professions in a good-humored way. Open the book at random, you will find something to entertain you.

In a gossipy letter to Faustus Andrelinus, poet-laureate of France, another bachelor author, Erasmus dwells with delight on a custom never to be sufficiently commended (saluting ladies with a kiss on meeting or leaving), saying: " Faustus, if you well knew the advantages of Britain, you would hasten hither with wings to your feet, and if your gout would not permit, you would wish you possessed the art of Dardalus."

Erasmus left the bulk of his fortune as dowries for young maidens.

Horace Walpole, who satirized for sixty years the men and women, manners and morals of his times in letters to friends, " loved letter writing and studied it as an art." Macaulay thinks " his letters his best performances." Macaulay's " Essay on Walpole " is so brilliant, critical, and complete that all who are not familiar with it should enjoy it at once.

Such racy, natural, spiteful pictures of life as Walpole loves to give are invaluable, and when mixed with brains they embody history.

The letters were carefully prepared for publication. Nothing else that he has written will live.

In his old age he was devoted to the beautiful and talented Mary Berry, but, from fear of being laughed at by the world he had so mercilessly ridiculed, assumed an equal interest in her sister, Agnes, who was comparatively commonplace, and did not dare to own himself a more than septuagenarian lover. His letters prove his deep and ardent attachment, and his fascinating friend deserved the title of Lady Orford. How much happier the rheumatic, lonely old fellow might have been!

Miss Martineau, who knew the Berrys, asserts in her positive way that he did offer himself to both. Impartial, certainly, but as there is no other reference to this, it is safe to presume that her trumpet reported inaccurately, as was frequently the case. Irving compares such an elderly bachelor to an old moth, attempting to fly through a pane of glass towards a light, without ever approaching near enough to warm itself or scorch its wings!

Pope took great pains with his letters, and was so proud of them as to send duplicate copies to different ladies.

When women feel inclined to dislike "the Wasp of Twickenham" they should remember his fond reverential devotion to his mother. Dean Swift declared that he had not only never witnessed, but had never heard of anything like it. She lived to be ninety-three, and had been for some time in her dotage, but to him her death was a deadly wound.

Pope was often atrociously abused before he stung his enemies, and is represented as warm-hearted and self-sacrificing by those who knew him best.

The epigrammatic, quotable couplet was Pope's best mode of expression. Regarding marriage he wrote :

> " Who would bear the dull unsocial hours,
> Spent by unmarried men, cheered by no smile.
> To sit like hermit at a lonely board,
> In silence."

We think of Macaulay as a learned historian, a brilliant essayist, an extraordinary talker. " Poor Macaulay," said the roguish Sydney Smith, when both had been talking at the same time, " will be very sorry some day to have missed all this." He also alluded most wittily to Macaulay's " flashes of silence," and some one accounts for his never marrying, on account of his passionate love for clever talk of his own. Brougham wrote of Macaulay as the greatest of bores in society. He said: " I have seen people come in from Holland house breathless and able to say nothing but 'Oh dear, Oh mercy!'

'What's the matter?' 'Oh Macaulay!' Then everyone said, 'That accounts for it. You're lucky to be alive.'" But read his life, more interesting than any novel, and see how his loving nature shines out in home life and in his letters to his idolized sisters.

Macaulay, as a bachelor, is a mystery. When he loved, he loved more entirely and more exclusively than was well for himself.

" It was improvident in him to concentrate such intensity of feeling upon relations, who, however deeply they were attached to him, could not always be in a position to requite him with the whole of their time and the whole of their heart. He suffered much for that improvidence. After the marriage of his sister Margaret, he never again recovered his tone of thorough boyishness," and he wrote :

"I have still one more stake to lose. There remains one event for which, when it arrives, I shall, I hope, be prepared. From that moment, with a heart formed, if ever any man's heart was formed for domestic happiness, I shall have nothing left in this world but ambition.

"After all, what am I more than my fathers? Than the millions and tens of millions who have been weak enough to. pay double price for some favorite number in the lottery of life, and who have suffered double disappointment when their ticket came up a blank.

"I am sitting in the midst of two hundred friends, all mad with exultation and party spirit, all glorying over the Tories, and thinking me the happiest man in the world. And it is all I can do to hide my tears and to command my voice when it is necessary for me to reply to their congratulations. Dearest, dearest sister, you alone are now left to me. Whom have I on earth but thee? But for you, in the midst of all these successes, I should wish that I were lying by poor Hyde Villiers. But I cannot go on."

At the close of his life, the prospect of a separation from his sister Hannah, with whom he had lived in close and uninterrupted companionship since her childhood and his own early manhood, darkened his last hours. He endured it manfully, but his spirits never recovered the blow.

"This prolonged parting — this slow sipping of the vinegar and the gall — is terrible. A month more of such days as I have been passing of late would make me impatient to get to my little narrow crib, like a weary factory child."

You see that now and then a literary bachelor's own confession proves his solitude and forlornity.

Thomas Hollis, a devotee to literature and republicanism, who would not marry lest marriage should interrupt his labors, writes in his autobiography of his deep dejection, and cries out wearily that he has no one to advise, assist, or cherish him, that he goes nowhere for the pleasure of it, but as a used man, always laboring for others, with no sunshine or comfort for himself.

Mark Akenside, who, "when he walked the

streets, looked for all the world like one of his own Alexandrines set upright," was an irritable, cross-grained bachelor, but this infirmity was excused as caused by two disappointments in love.   He sighed for domestic comfort in this fashion :

> " Though the day have smoothly gone,
>   Or to lettered leisure known,
>   Or in social duty spent,
>   Yet at eve, my lonely breast
>   Seeks in vain for perfect rest,
>   Languishes for true content."

It is said that he neglected the sick women in his visits to the hospital, so great was his antipathy to the sex !

One of our modern literary bachelors (James Whitcomb Riley) writes thus:

BEREAVED.

> " Let me come in where you sit weeping — Aye,
>   Let me, who have not any child to die,
>   Weep with you for the little one whose love
>   I have known nothing of.
>
> The little arms that slowly, slowly loosed
>   Their pressure round your neck ; — the hands you used
>   To kiss. — Such arms — such hands I never knew.
>   May I not weep with you?
>
> Fain would I be of service — say some thing,
>   Between the tears, that would be comforting, —
>   But ah ! so sadder than yourselves am I,
>   Who have no child to die."

The Bachelor Wit and Diner-out is another type,

like Theodore Hook, whom Coleridge pronounced to have had a genius equal to Dante, but sadly misused, and his life a miserable failure. Theodore, with his improvisations and practical jokes, deserves more space.

Many bachelors might be mentioned of this type, their morals in an inverse ratio to their ability. Herrick, Hook, Shenstone, and others, preferred the companionship of their servants to orthodox home life.

Halleck, " the first poet-laureate of New York city," who modestly alluded to himself as but an amateur in the literary orchestra, posed as a bachelor, but was privately married and had two lovely daughters said to have inherited much of their father's ability. He must have been extremely attractive, for a lady of position and culture said of him : " If I were on my way to church to be married — yes, even if I was walking up the aisle, and Halleck were to offer himself, I'd leave the man I had promised to marry and take him."

His " Marco Bozarris " ran like wild-fire through the country. Rogers, who was fond of reading it to his guests, said : " It is better than anything we can do on this side of the Atlantic." " Fanny," his longest poem, a pleasant satire on follies in fashions and politics, was immensely liked in its day.

Bryant said of his poem on Burns, " I am not sure that these verses are not the finest in which one poet ever celebrated another. The lines

> " None knew thee but to love thee,
> None named thee but to praise,"

which he wrote on the death of his literary partner, Drake, could well be used for himself. Here is an amusing letter he wrote to a friend on hearing of the approaching marriage of an old man :

" My Dear Sir:

" I am very glad, indeed, to learn from your kind letter of remembrance, that there are sensible young women besides Mrs. Enoch (see Genesis v, 21) and the late Lady Leicester, who believe it takes sixty-five years to make a good husband. Mrs. Enoch became the mother of Methusalem, a millionaire in years, and Lady Leicester, the mother of five sons, each a multi-millionaire in money. May your marriage destiny be the long life of the one and the long purses of the other. For my own part, I still continue to fancy that Methusalem's resolution, not to marry until he was one hundred and eighty-one, was wise and prudent as a general rule. I am fast approaching that interesting period ; and, unless Mrs. Hackett, when I have the pleasure of conversing with her, shall by reference to her own pleasant example persuade me into an early marriage, I shall wait patiently another century for the happy day."

The Jilted literary bachelors are numerous, from Jeremy Bentham to Chorley, but I regard them too highly to recall their lack of reciprocated affection.

The Timid bachelor. I make this division, because a bachelor assures me there are many unhappy men, who actually have not the courage to undertake the solemn responsibilities of matrimony, but that, if a lady would only take such a specimen kindly but firmly by the ear and lead him to the altar, he would go and be grateful.

The Ideal bachelor. No need to give the name. Every heart prompts, every mouth utters the same—

simple-hearted, kindly, shy; a " friend " in the truest
sense, not only to the slave and the suffering, but to
children, to the homely country life, and the simple
wayside flowers of New England, to humanity; whose
breadth is seen in his creed rather than his hat-brim
— the revered, beloved Whittier.   Yet he often
speaks regretfully of what he has lost in his single
life.   Here is a bit from a letter addressed to an old-
time friend.

> " The years, that since we met have flown,
>   Leave, as they found me, still alone.
>   Nor wife, nor child, nor grandchild dear,
>   Are mine, the heart to cheer.
>   More favored thou; with hair less gray
>   Than mine, can let thy fancy stray
>   To where thy little Constance sees
>   The prairie ripple in the breeze.
>   For one like her to lisp thy name,
>   Is better than the voice of fame. "

Reference is made to his friend's grandchild,
Constance.

Lastly, the Irresistibles.   I hear a wild commotion
round me at this announcement, and find that almost
every man I had otherwise placed is pushing into
this division as his proper sphere.   You see how 'tis.
I can do nothing with them, after all.   But there is
woman's last refuge — I can still talk about them.

To the conundrum, " Why are men of genius
so often bachelors?" it may be answered that
such instances are not owing to anything like a
want of appreciation of woman's worth or charms,

but to unfavorable circumstances. Most of these celebrated celibates have been deep in love. "I have seldom met with an old bachelor," said Irving, "who had not, at some time or other, some trait of romance in his life to which he looks back with fondness, and about which he is apt to grow garrulous occasionally."

It is self-evident that all bachelors remain unmarried from preference. They may not be able to win the one woman of their choice — but there are always plenty more from which to make a selection.

Dr. Holmes observes that even Lazarus could have married if he could have picked up crumbs enough to support a wife!

You remember that when a lady suggested a tax on bachelors, one of them promptly acquiesced, saying: "They ought to be taxed for freedom, as it was certainly a luxury. In the Annual Register of London, a serious proposition from the House of Commons is recorded, that all unmarried men over thirty-five should pay a special tax, and it has been proposed by Robert Dale Owen for our country. This law was carried into execution in Sparta, and in Athens there were persons whose business was matchmaking. In Prof. Felton's Greece, Ancient and Modern, a detailed account is given of this.

I fear it would be difficult to collect a tax of this sort from bachelors of the present day, even a small yearly stipendum for the oakless vines, hanging in limp profusion all about them. The

Roman Censor, Metellus, appeals to bachelors in this way: "Fellow citizens, if we could live without wives, we should be free of this burden, but since nature has willed that it is as impossible to live without them as it is unpleasant to live with them, let us lay these disagreeablenesses of this short life as offerings on the altar of the state."

I wonder that Cato's sentiments have not been blazoned on the banners of the agitators for Women's Rights. "Recall," he says, "all the ordinances of our forefathers, designed to keep women in subjection, and yet, ye could hardly keep them bridled. What shall be the result if ye give them freedom and the same rights which ye have yourselves. At the moment when they became your equals, they will become your superiors!"

Lord Bacon's dicta are familiar to all:

"Certainly the best works and of greatest merit for the public have proceeded from the unmarried or childless men, who, both in affection and means, have married and endowed the public."

The conjugal troubles of Shakespeare and Dryden, Milton, Addison, Shelley, Bulwer, Byron, Dickens, with a score of lesser lights, may have alarmed some bachelor authors. As women are supposed to have personal reasons for disapproving of bachelors, please notice that I only quote the severe criticisms of other men.

Dickens says of them: "Old bachelors are like those strange, wandering fires that seem to have no fixed spheres, serve no known law in the moral universe, the purpose of whose existence being a mystery to themselves and all about them. These singular specimens of humanity are in an anomalous condition, for they are not only isolated in their selfishness, but they have also outlawed themselves from the rights and privileges of domestic life."

In Thackeray's Pendennis you will find a touching description of a bachelor's forlorn apartments, ending —" To be well in chambers is melancholy and lonely and selfish enough, but to be ill in chambers, to pass nights of pain and watchfulness, and long for the morning and the laundress, to have no other companion for long hours but your own sickening fancies and fevered thoughts, no kind hand to give you drink if you are thirsty, or to smooth the hot pillow that crumples under you, this indeed is a fate so desolate and tragic that we shall not enlarge upon its horror."

Franklin compares a bachelor to a half-pair of scissors, and Beecher says: " A bachelor is like an old hemlock tree, dead at top, and ragged all the way down."

For a farewell picture let me give from Praed, an old bachelor's violent protest against matrimony:

> " When the dim eyes shall gaze and fear
>   To close the glance that lingers here,
>   Watching the faint, departing light,
>   That seems to flicker in its flight ;
>   When the lone heart in that long strife
>   Shall cling unconsciously to life;

I'll have no shrieking female by
To shed her drops of sympathy,
To listen to each smothered throe,
To feel or feign officious woe,
To bring me every useless cup,
And beg, dear Tom, to drink it up !
To turn my oldest servants off,
E'en as she hears my gurgling cough,
And then expectingly to stand,
And chafe my temples with her hand ;
And pull a cleaner nightcap o'er 'em,
That I may die with due decorum;
And watch the while my ebbing breath,
And count the tardy steps of death ;
Grudging the Leech his growing skill,
And wrapped in dreams about the *will;*
I'll have no furies round my bed,
They shall not plague me till I'm dead.

Believe me, ill my dust would rest,
If the plain marble on my breast,
That tells in letters large and clear,
The bones of Thomas Quince lies here,
Should add — a talisman of strife —
Also, the bones of Jane, his wife !"

LADY MORGAN.

IF the veritable Lady Morgan, with her wit and vanity, poor French and fine clothes, good common sense and warm Irish heart, could be with you this moment, she would be a most entertaining companion. A spirited, versatile, spunky little woman, her whole life a grand social success, one of the most popular and voluminous writers of her day; but, with all her sparkle and dash, ambition and industry, destined in a few generations more to be almost unknown, vanishing down that doleful "back entry" where Time sends so many bright men and women. As the founder of Irish fiction — for the national, tales of Ireland begin with her — and the patron of Irish song (she stimulated Lover to write " Rory O'More," and " Kate Kearney " is her own), always laboring for liberty and the interests of her oppressed countrymen, and preserving her name absolutely untouched by scandal through a long and brilliant career, she deserves a place among distinguished women. She evidently had no idea of being forgotten, and completed twenty chapters of autobiography — its florid egotism at once its fault and its charm — besides keeping a diary in later years, and preserving nearly all the letters written to her, from tributes of poets and exiles to the petitions of weavers and chimney sweeps, and even cards left at her door. But on those cards were the names of Humboldt, Cuvier, Talma, and the most celebrated men of that epoch, down to Macaulay, Douglas Jerrold, and Edward Everett, while she could count among her correspondents the noted men and women of three countries. La Fayette declared he was proud to be her friend; Byron praised her writings, and always expressed regret that he had not made her acqaintance in Italy; Sydney Smith coupled her name with his own as "the two Sydneys"; Leigh Hunt celebrated her in verse; Sir Thomas Lawrence, Ary Scheffer, and other famous artists begged for the honor of painting her portrait. Was it strange after all this, and being told for half a century that she was an extraordinarily gifted and fascinating woman, that (being a woman) she should believe it?

She was extremely sensitive in regard to her age, and if forced to state it on the witness-stand would doubtless have whispered it to the judge in a bewitching way, as did a pretty but slightly *passé* French actress under similar embarrassing circumstances. She pleads: "What has a woman to do with dates — cold, false, erroneous, chronological dates — new style, old style, precession of the equinox, ill-timed calculation of comets long since due at their station and never come? Her poetical idiosyncrasy, calculated by epochs, would make the most natural points of reference in woman's autobiography. Plutarch sets the example of dropping dates in favor of incidents; and an authority more appropriate, Madame de Genlis, who began her own memoirs at eighty, swept through nearly an age of incident and revolution without any reference to vulgar eras signifying nothing (the times themselves out of joint), testifying to the pleasant incidents she recounts and the changes she witnessed. *I* mean to have none of them!"

Sydney Owenson was born in " ancient ould Dublin " at Christmas: the year is a little uncertain. The encyclopædias say about 1780; 1776 has been suggested as more correct, but we will not pry into so delicate a matter. A charming woman never loses her youth. Doctor Holmes tells us that in traveling over the isthmus of life we do not ride in a private carriage, but in an omnibus — meaning that our ancestors or their traits take the trip with us; and in studying a character it is interesting to note the combinations that from generations back make up the individual. Sydney's father was the child of an ill-assorted marriage. " At a hurling-match long ago, the Queen of Beauty, Sydney, granddaughter of Sir Maltby Crofton, lost her heart, like Rosalind, to the victor of the day, Walter McOwen (anglicised Owenson), a young farmer, tall and handsome, graceful and daring, and allowed him to discover that he had ' wrestled well and overthrown more than his enemies.' Result, an elopement and mésalliance never to be forgiven — the husband a jolly, racketing Irish lad, unable to appreciate his refined, accomplished wife, a skillful performer on the Irish harp, a poet, and a genius, called by the admiring neighbors 'the Harp of the Valley.'" Their only child, the father of Lady Morgan, was a tolerable actor, of loose morals and tight purse, who could sing a good song or tell a good story, and who was always in debt.

Sydney was a winsome little rogue, quite too much for her precise and stately mother, who was ever holding up as a model a child, in her grave fifty years agone, who had read the Bible through twice before she was five years old, and knitted all the stockings worn by the coachmen! All in vain; Sydney was not fated to die early or figure as a young saint in a Sunday-school memoir. She took a deep interest in chimney-sweeps from observing a den of little imps who swarmed in a cellar near her home, and on one occasion actually scrambled up a burning chimney, followed by this sooty troop. Her pets were numerous, the prime favorite being a cat named Ginger, from her yellow coat. Her mother, who was shocked by Sydney adding to her nightly petition, "God bless Ginger the cat!"* did not share this partiality, as is seen in the young lady's first attempt at authorship:

* Puzzling Theological Questions :
" Why may I not say, bless Ginger ? "
" Because Ginger is not a Christian."
" Why isn't Ginger a Christian ? "
" Because Ginger is only an animal."
" Am I a Christian, mamma, or an animal? "

" My dear pussy cat,
Were I a mouse or a rat,
  Sure I never would run off from you,
You're *so* funny and gay
With your tail when you play,
  And no song is so sweet as your mew.
But pray keep in your press,
And don't make a mess,
  When you share with your kittens our posset,
For mamma can't abide you,
And I cannot hide you
  Unless you keep close in your closet."

Her voice was remarkable, but her father, knowing too well the temptations that beset a public singer, refused to cultivate her talent for music, saying, " If I were to do this, it might induce her some day to go on the stage, and I would prefer to buy her a sieve of black cockles from Ring's End, to cry about the streets of Dublin, to seeing her the first prima donna of Europe." A genuine talent for music will assert itself in spite of neglect, and one evening at the house of Moore, where, with her sister Olivia, she listened in tearful enthusiasm to some of his melodies, sung as only the poet could sing them, was an important event in her life. She tells us that after this treat they went home in almost delirious ecstacy, actually forgetting to undress themselves before going to bed. This experience developed a longing to know more of the early Irish ballads, and roused a literary ambition. If the grocer's son could so distinguish himself, she could surely relieve her dear father from his embarrassments ; and she began at once to write with this noble object. Her unselfish and unwavering devotion to her rather worthless father is the most attractive and touching point in her character. His watchful care was certainly creditable. Living in a town where soldiers were stationed, he allowed them no acquaintance with his daughters. One of them said : "Owenson looks at us as if he'd like to pitch our entire mess-room of Ensigns out of the window in an armfull." After her mother's death she was sent to boarding-school, where she studied well, scribbled verses, accomplished herself in dancing, and furnished bright home-letters for her less brilliant mates.

She next figures as a governess in the family of a Mrs. Featherstone of Bracklin Castle. There was a merry dance for adieu the night she was to leave, but, like Cinderella, she danced too long; the hour sounded, and Sydney was hurried into the coach in a white muslin dress, pink silk stockings, and slippers of the same hue, while Molly, the faithful old servant, insisted on wrapping her darling in her own warm cloak and ungainly headgear. Being ushered in this plight into a handsome drawing-room, there was a general titter at her grotesque appearance, but she told her story in her own captivating way until they screamed with laughter — not at her now, but with her — and she was carried off to an exquisite suite of rooms — a study, bedroom and bathroom, with a roaring turf fire, open piano, and lots of books, and after dinner, when she was toasted, she sang sev-

eral songs, which she said had an immense effect.
and the evening ended with a jig, the host regretting
they had no spectators besides the servants. This.
her first jig out of the schoolroom, she contrasts
with her last one in public, when invited by the
Duchess of Northumberland to dance with Lord
George Hill. She accepted the challenge from the
two best jig dancers in the country, Lord George
and Sir Philip Crampton, and had the pleasure of
flooring them both. Apropos of her fondness for
jigs, in Fanny Kemble's Old Woman's Gossip, you
will find an amusing reminiscence.

She was a successful teacher, although she could
not restrain her love of fun. Once, indeed, they
threatened to write to her father, but were conquered
by an evening of song.

Her father's pride rose in revolt against her position. He wished to place her under the protection
of some purse-proud cousins, but Sydney rebelled.
She writes to dear papa: "A humble companion I
will *not* be to any one. I could never walk out with
little dogs or run little messages. What objections
can you have to my occupying the position of a
teacher, a calling which enrolls the names of Madame
de Maintenon and Madame de Genlis." And she kept
her place and her self-respect.

"St. Clair" was the name of her first novel. She
had kept her work a profoun dsecret, and one morning, full of ambitious dreams, she borrowed the cook's
market bonnet and cloak and sallied out to seek her

fortune. Before going far she saw over a shop door "T. Smith, Printer and Bookseller," and ventured in. It was some minutes before T. Smith made his appearance, and when he did come he had a razor in one hand, a towel in the other, and only one side of his face shaved. After hearing her errand, he told he did not publish novels, and sent her to Brown. Brown wanted his breakfast and was not anxious for a girl's manuscript, but his wife persuaded him to look it over, and, elated with success, Sydney ran home, forgetting to leave any address, and never heard of her first venture until, taking up a book in a friend's parlor, it proved to be her own! It had a good sale and was translated into German, with a biographical notice, which stated that the young author had strangled herself with an embroidered handkerchief in an agony of despair and unrequited love. The "Sorrows of Werther" was her model, but with a deal of stuff and sentimentality there was the promise of better things. In all her early works her characters indulge in wonderful digressions; historical, astronomical, and metaphysical, in the midst of terrible emergencies where danger, despair, and unspeakable catastrophes are imminent and impending. No matter what laceration of their finest feelings they may be suffering, they always have their learning at command and never fail to make quotations from favorite authors appropriate to the occasion. ("St. Elmo" resembles this.)

The "Novice of St. Dominick" was Miss Owenson's

second novel, she going alone to London to arrange
for its publication. It was no small undertaking,
and when the coach drove into the yard of the Swan
with Two Necks, the young lady was utterly ex-
hausted, and, seating herself on her little trunk in the
inn yard, fell fast asleep. But, as usual, she found
friends and luck was on her side. The novel was
cut from six volumes to four, and with her first literary earnings, after assisting her father, she bought
an Irish harp and a black mode cloak, always devoted
to music and dress.

Next came " The Wild Irish Girl," her first national story, which gave her more than a national
fame and £300 from her fascinated publisher. It
contains much curious information about the antiquities and social condition of Ireland, and a passionate
pleading against the wrongs of its people. It made
the piquant little governess all the rage in fashionable society, and until her marriage she was
known by the name of her heroine — Glorvina. As
a story it is not worth reading to-day. In the " Book
of the Boudoir," a sort of literary rag-bag, she gives
under the heading " My First Rout in London," a
graphic picture of an evening at Lady Cork's. She
says: " A few days after my arrival in London and
while my little book was running rapidly through
successive editions, I was presented to the Countess-
dowager of Cork, and invited to a reception at her
fantastic and pretty mansion in New Burlington
street. Oh, how her Irish historical name tingled in

my ears and seized on my imagination, reminding
me of her great ancestor, 'the father of chemistry
and uncle to the earl of Cork'! I stepped into my
job carriage at the hour of ten, and, all alone by myself, as the song says, 'to Eden took my solitary
way.' What added to my fears and doubts and hopes
and embarrassments was a note from my noble
hostess received at the moment of departure:
'Everybody has been invited expressly to meet the
Wild Irish Girl; so she must bring her Irish harp.
M. C. O.' I arrived at New Burlington street without my harp and with a beating heart, and I heard
the high-sôunding titles of princes and ambassadors
and dukes and duchesses announced, long before my
poor plebeian name puzzled the porter and was ban-
died from footman to footman. As I ascended the
marble stairs with their gilt balustrade, I was agitated
by emotions similar to those which drew from a
frightened countryman his frank exclamation in the
heat of the battle of Vittoria: 'Oh, jabbers! I wish
some of my greatest enemies was kicking me down
Dame street.' Lady Cork met me at the door:
'What! no harp, Glorvina?'—'Oh, Lady Cork!'—
'Oh, Lady Fiddlestick! You are a fool, child: you
don't know your own interests.— Here, James, William, Thomas! send one of the chairmen to Stan-
hope street for Miss Owenson's harp.'"

After a stand and a stare of some seconds at a
strikingly sullen-looking, handsome creature who
stood alone, and whom she heard addressed by a

pretty sprite of fashion with a " How-do, Lord Byron ?" she says : " I was pushed on, and on reaching the centre of the conservatory, I found myself suddenly bounced upon a sort of rustic seat, a very uneasy pre-eminence, and there I sat, the lioness of the night, shown off like the hyena of Exeter 'Change, looking almost as wild and feeling quite as savage.   Presenting me to each and all of the splendid crowd which an idle curiosity, easily excited and as soon satisfied, had gathered round us, she prefaced every introduction with a little exordium which seemed to amuse every one but its object : ' Lord Erskine, this is the Wild Irish Girl whom you are so anxious to know.   I assure you she talks quite as well as she writes.— Now, my dear, do tell my Lord Erskine some of those Irish stories you told us the other evening.   Fancy yourself among your own set, and take off the brogue.   Mrs. Abingdon says you would make a famous actress ; she does indeed.   You must play the short-armed orator with her ; she will be here by and by.   This is the duchess of St. Albans : she has your novel by heart.   Where is Sheridan ? — Do, my dear Mr. T——(This is Mr. T——, my dear : geniuses should know each other) — do, my *dear* Mr. T——, find me Mr. Sheridan.   Oh ! here he is ! — What ! you know each other already ? So much the better.— This is Lord Carysford.— Mr. Lewis, do come forward.— That is Monk Lewis, my dear, of whom you have heard so much, but you must not read his works ; they are very naughty.'

Lewis, who stood staring at me through his eye-
glasses, backed out after this remark, and disappeared. 'You know Mr. Gell,' her ladyship continued, 'so I need not introduce you; he calls you the
Irish Corinne. Your friend Mr. Moore will be here
by and by; I have collected all the talent for you.—
Do see, somebody, if Mr. Kemble and Mrs. Siddons
are come yet, and find me Lady Hamilton.— *Now*,
pray tell us the scene at the Irish baronet's in the
rebellion,' and then give us your blue-stocking dinner
at Sir Richard Phillips. Here is Lord L.— he will
be your bottle holder.'

"Lord L—— volunteered his services. The circle
now began to widen — wits, warriors, peers, and ministers of state. The harp was brought forward, and
I tried to sing, but my howl was funereal. I was
ready to cry, but endeavored to laugh, and to cover
my real timidity by an affected ease which was both
awkward and impolitic. At last Mr. Kemble was
announced. Lady Cork reproached him as the *late*
Mr. Kemble, and then, looking significantly at me,
told him who I was. Kemble acknowledged me by
a kindly nod, but the stare which succeeded was not
one of mere recognition; it was the glazed, fixed
look so common to those who have been making liba-
tions to altars which rarely qualify them for ladies'
society. Mr. Kemble was evidently much preoccu-
pied and a little exalted. He was seated my *vis-a-vis*
at supper, and repeatedly raised his arm and stretched
it across the table for the purpose, as I supposed, of

helping himself to some boar's head in jelly. Alas! no! The *bore* was that *my* head happened to be the object which fixed his tenacious attention, which, dark, cropped and curly, struck him as a particularly well-organized '*Brutus*,' and better than any in his repertoire of theatrical perukes. Succeeding at last in his feline and fixed purpose, he actually stuck his claws in my locks, and, addressing me in the deepest sepulchral tones, asked, 'Little girl, where did you get your wig?' Lord Erskine came to the rescue and liberated my head, and all tried to retrieve the awkwardness of the scene. Meanwhile, Kemble, peevish, as half-tipsy people generally are, drew back muttering and fumbling in his pocket, evidently with some dire intent lowering in his eyes. To the amusement of all, and to my increased consternation, he drew forth a volume of the *Wild Irish Girl*, and reading with his deep, emphatic voice one of the most high-flown of its passages, he paused, and patting the page with his forefinger, with the look of Hamlet addressing Polonius, he said, 'Little girl, why did you write such nonsense? and where did you get all those damned hard words?' Thus taken by surprise, and smarting with my wounds of mortified authorship, I answered, unwittingly and witlessly, the truth: 'Sir, I wrote as well as I could, and I got the hard words from — Johnson's Dictionary.' He was soon carried off to prevent any more attacks on my head, inside or out."

Lady Cork was a unique character, and her name

suggests several anecdotes. She entertained frequently, giving parties of various colors: pink for the exclusives, blue for the literary, gray for the religious, and her pet and protegé suggested dundukettry mud color as a good name for a mixed crowd.

On a pink evening, she wore such an enormous plume, that one of the wits present compared her to a shuttle-cock — all Cork and feathers.

At a dinner where this eccentric dowager was the only lady present, she said to Colman, " You are so agreeable that you shall drink a glass of champagne with me."

" Your ladyship's wishes are law to me," said Colman, " but really, champagne does not agree with me ;" upon which, Jekyll called out, " Faith, Colman, you seem more attached to the cork than the bottle."

She was a person of extraordinary power for making herself comfortable, and did anything that it pleased her to do — would invite a number of guests to dinner at a friend's house before telling said friend of the pleasure in store for him, and would make use of a friend's carriage without asking permission. Once, on leaving a breakfast party, she claimed a carriage in this way ; told the footman that she took it by his mistress's orders ; kept it out the whole afternoon, and on meeting the owner exclaimed, " I wish you would have the steps of your carriage lowered before I use it again."

Sydney Smith said that she was once so much

affected by one of his charity sermons, that she borrowed a guinea from a friend to put in the plate.

Darwin tells us how once, when dining at Dean Milman's, Sydney said, " It is generally believed that my dear old friend, Lady Cork, has been overlooked," and he said this in such a manner that no one could, for a moment, doubt that his dear old friend had been overlooked by the Devil.

Glorvina was now very much the fashion, visiting in the best Dublin society and making many friends, whom she had the tact to retain through life. When articles of dress or ornament are named for one, it is an unfailing sign that they have attained notoriety, if not fame, and the bodkin used for fastening the " back hair " was called " Glorvina " in her honor. Like many attractive women of decided character, she had her full share of faults and foibles. Superficial, conceited, sadly lacking in spirituality and refinement, a cruel enemy, a toady to titles, a blind partisan of the Liberal party,— that is her picture in shadow. Her style was open to severe criticism, and Richard Lovell Edgeworth suggests mildly that Maria, in reading her novel aloud in the family circle, was obliged to omit some superfluous epithets.

In this first flush of celebrity she never gave up work, holding fast to industry as her sheet-anchor. Soon appeared two volumes of patriotic tales. " Ida of Athens" was Novel No. 3, but written in confident haste, and not well received. The names of her books would make a list rivaling that of the loves of

Don Giovanni (nearly seventy volumes), and any extended analysis or criticism would be impossible in this rapid sketch. "Every day in my life is a leaf in my book," was a motto literally carried out, and she tried almost every department of literature, succeeding best in describing the broad characteristics of her own nation. "Her lovers, like her books, were too numerous to mention," yet her own heart seemed untouched. She coquetted gayly, but her adorers were always the sufferers.

Sir Jonah Barrington wrote her at this time a complimentary and witty letter, in which he says of her heroine Glorvina, "I believe you stole a spark from heaven to give animation to your idol." He thought the inferiority of "Ida" was owing to its author's luxurious surroundings. "I cannot conceive why the brain should not get fat and unwieldy, as well as any other part of the human frame. Some of our best poets have written in paroxysms of hunger, and I really believe that Addison would have had more point if he had had less victuals; and if you do not restrict yourself to a sheep's trotter and spruce beer, your style will betray your luxury." But soon came an increase of the very thing feared for her fame, in the form of an invitation from Lady Abercorn and the marquis to pass the chief part of every year with them. This was accepted, and thus she met her fate. Lord Abercorn kept a physician in his house, Doctor Morgan, a handsome, accomplished widower, whom the marchioness was anxious to provide with a second wife. She had fixed upon Sydney as a suitable person, but the retiring and reticent doctor had heard so much of her wit, talents, and general fascination, that he disliked the idea of meeting her. He was sitting one morning with the marchioness when a servant threw open the door, announcing "Miss Owenson," who had just arrived. Dr. Morgan sprang to his feet, and, there being no other way of escape, leaped through the open window into the garden below. This was too fair a challenge for a girl of spirit to refuse, and she set to work to captivate him, succeeding more effectually than she desired, for she had dreamed of making a brilliant match. Soon a letter was written to her father asking his leave to marry the conquered doctor, yet she does not seem to have been one bit in love. He was too grave and good, though as devoted a lover as could be asked for. It was a queer match and a dangerous experiment, but after a while, their mutual qualities adjusted themselves. He kept her steady, and she roused him from indolent repose. As a critic of that time says: "She was as bustling, restless, energetic, and pushing as he was modest, retiring, and unaffected." Lover gives this picture of them : "There was Lady Morgan, with her irrepressible vivacity, her humor that indulged in the most audacious illustrations, and her candor which had small respect for time or place in its expression, and who, by the side of her tranquil, steady, contemplative husband, suggested the notion of a

Barbary colt harnessed to a patient English draught-horse."

She had a certain light, jaunty air peculiarly Irish, celebrated by Leigh Hunt in verses which embody a faithful portrait:

"And dear Lady Morgan, see, see where she comes,
  With her pulses all beating for freedom like drums,
  So Irish, so modish, so mixtish, so wild,
  So committing herself, as she talks, like a child ;
  So trim, yet so easy, polite, yet high-hearted,
  That Truth and she, try all she can, won't be parted.
  She'll put on your fashions, your latest new air,
  Aud then talk so frankly, she'll make you all stare.
  Mrs. Hall may say " Oh !" and Miss Edgeworth say " Fie !"
  But my lady will know the what and the why.
  Her books, a like mixture, are so very clever
  That Jove himself swore he could read them forever.
  Plot, character, freakishness, all are so good,
  And the heroine herself playing tricks in a hood."

After a happy year with her patrons, Glorvina married and moved to a home of her own in Kildare street, Dublin, whence she writes to Lady Stanley: "With respect to authorship, I fear it is over. I have been making chair-covers instead of periods, hanging curtains instead of raising systems, and cheapening pots and pans instead of selling sentiment and philosophy." But even during this first busy year of housekeeping she was working upon "O'Donnel," another national tale, for which she was paid five hundred and fifty pounds. It was highly praised by Sir Walter Scott, and sold with rapidity, but her liberal politics made her unpopular with the

leading Tory journalism of England. In point of
pitiless invective the criticism of the *Quarterly* and
Blackwood has, perhaps, never been exceeded. Her
books were denounced as pestilent, and the public
advised against maintaining her acquaintance. Miss
Martineau, an impartial critic, if impartiality consists in punching almost every one she passed, did
not fail to give our heroine a black eye, speaking of
her as "in that set to which Mrs. Jameson belonged,
who make women blush and men grow insolent."

Sir Charles and his wife next visited Paris with
the intention of writing a book. Their letters carried them into every circle of Parisian society, "in
the course of one evening, assisting at a Royalist
dinner, drinking ultra tea, and supping *en republi-
caine.*" And in each the popularity of Lady Morgan
was unbounded. Madame Jerome Bonaparte wrote
to her: "The French admire you more than anyone
who has appeared here since the battle of Waterloo
in the form of an Englishwoman." When "France"
appeared the clamor of abuse in England was
enough to appall a very stout heart. John Wilson
Croker was one of her most bitter assailants, and
attempted to annihilate her in the *Quarterly*. She
balanced matters by caricaturing him as "Counsellor
Crawley" in her next novel, in a way that hit and
hurt, and by a witticism which lives, while his en-
venomed sentences are forgotten. Some one was
telling her that Croker was among the crowd who
thought they could have managed the battle of

Waterloo much better than Wellington, whose success, in their estimation, was only a fortunate mistake. She exclaimed, " Oh, I can believe it. He had his secret for winning the battle ; he had only to put his " Notes on Boswell's Johnson " in front of the British lines, and all the Bonapartes that ever existed *could never have got through them !* " Maginn in *Blackwood* gave unmerciful cuts at her superficial opinions, ultra sentiments, and chambermaid French. *Fraser's Magazine* complimented her sardonically on her simple style, being happy to observe that she had reduced the number of languages used, as the Sibyl did her books, to three, wisely discarding German, Spanish, the dead and Oriental languages. But she received the cannonade, which would have crushed some women, with perfect equanimity. As a compensation, she was the toast of the day, and at some grand reception had a raised dais only a little lower than that provided for the duchess de Berri. At a dinner at Baron Rothschild's, Carême, the Delmonico of those times, surprised her with a column of ingenious confectionery architecture on which was inscribed her name spun in sugar. It was a more equivocal compliment when Walter Scott christened two pet donkeys, Hannah More and Lady Morgan.

The chapters on society are extremely readable. She tells us how Robespierre, during the most sanguinary period of his career, wore a muslin waistcoat lined with rose-colored silk, and a coat of the most tender blue. Josephine she represents as absurdly whimsical about her toilettes. "I am very ill to-day," she said one morning. "Give me a cap which suggests delicate health." This style was presented. "But this is too sick, they will believe now I am about to die." A more healthy head-dress was presented for inspection. "And now," said the Empress, with a languid yawn, "And *now*, you make me too robust."

"Florence Macarthy" another novel, attacking the social and political abuses in Irish government, was her next work. Colburn, her publisher, who had just presented her with a beautiful parure of amethysts, now proposed that she and her husband should go to Italy. "Do it, and get up another book —the lively lady to sketch men and manners, the metaphysical balance wheel contributing the solid chapters on laws, politics, science, and education." They accepted the offer, and received the same extraordinary attention as in their former tour, and her picture was displayed in shop windows. This may be accounted for by the fact that it was well known that they were to prepare a book on Italy. It was equally well known that Lady Morgan had a sharp tongue and still sharper pen; so that people who lived in glass houses, as did many of the magnates, were remarkably civil to "Miladi," even those who regarded her tour among them as an unjustifiable invasion. "Byron pronounced this book an excellent and fearless work. During her sojourn in Italy, Lady Morgan became enthusiastic about Salvator

Rosa, and began to collect material for writing the history of his life and times, which was her own favorite of all her writings."

In 1825 the "Dairy" is started, chatty, full of gossip and incident. She writes, October 30th: "A ballad-singer was this morning singing beneath my window, in a strain most unmusical and melancholy. My own name caught my ear, and I sent Thomas out to buy the song. Here is a stanza:

> " ' Och, Dublin City, there's no doubting,
> Bates every city upon the say ;
> 'Tis there you'll hear O'Connell spouting,
> And Lady Morgan making tay ;
> For 'tis the capital of the foinest nation,
> Wid charming pisantry on a fruitful sod,
> Fighting like divils for conciliation,
> An' hating one another for the love o' God.' "

"The O'Briens and O'Flahertys" was published in 1827, and proved more popular than any of her previous novels. There is an allusion to it in the interesting account which Lord Albemarle gives us of his acquaintance with Lady Morgan : "A number of pleasant people used to assemble of an evening in Lady Morgan's ' nut-shell ' in Kildare street. When I first met her she was in the height of her popularity. In her new novel she tells me I am to figure as a certain count, a great traveler who made a trip to Jerusalem for the sole object of eating artichokes in their native country. The chief attraction in the Kildare street ' at homes ' was her sister Olivia (Lady Clark), who used to compose and sing charming

Irish songs, for the most part squibs on the Dublin
society of the day. One of the verses ran thus :

> " We're swarming alive,
> Like bees in a hive,
>> With talent and janius and beautiful ladies ;
> We've a duke in Kildare,
> And a Donnybrook Fair ;
>> And if that wouldn't plaze, why nothing would plaze yez.
> We've poets in plenty,
> But not one in twenty
>> Will stay in ould Ireland to keep her from sinking.
> They say they can't live
> Where there's nothing to give.
>> Och, what business have poets with ating or dhrinking !"

Justly proud of her sister, Lady Morgan was in
the habit of addressing every new comer with, " I
must make you acquainted with my Livy." She
once used this form of words to a gentleman who
had just been worsted in a fierce encounter of wit
with the fascinating lady. " Yes, madam," he replied,
" I happen to know your Livy, and I only wish 'your
Livy' was *Tacitus*."

Few of Lady Morgan's bon-mots have been preserved, but one is given which shows that she occasionally indulged in a pun. Some one, speaking of
a certain bishop who was rather lax in his observance
of Lent, said he believed he would eat a horse on
Ash Wednesday. " Very suitable diet," remarked
her ladyship, " if it were a *fast* horse."

The " Diary" progresses slowly by fitful jerks.
Here is a characteristic entry : " *April 3, 1834.* My
journal has gone to the dogs. I am so fussed and

fidgeted with my dear charming world, that I cannot write ; I forget days and dates. Ouf ! last night,
at Lady Stepney's, met the Milmans, Mrs. Norton,
Rogers, Sydney Smith, and others ; among them,
poor, dear Jane Porter. She told me she was taken
for me the other night, and talked to as such by a
party of Americans. *She* is tall, lank, and lean, and
lackadaisical, dressed in the deepest black, with
rather a battered black gauze hat and the air of a
regular Melpomene. *I* am the reverse of all this,
and, without vanity, the best-dressed woman wherever I go. Last night, I wore a blue satin trimmed
fully with magnificent point lace — light blue velvet
hat and feather, with an aigrette of sapphires and
diamonds. Voilà! Lord Jeffrey came up to me, and
we had *such* a flirtation! When he comes to Ireland
we are to go to Donnybrook Fair together ; in short,
having cut me down with his tomahawk as a reviewer,
he smothers me with roses as a man. I always say
of my enemies before we meet, ' Let me at them ! ' "
Of the same soirée she writes again : " There was
Miss Jane Porter, looking like a shabby canoness.
There was Mrs. Somerville in an astronomical cap.
I dashed in in my blue satin and point lace, and
showed them how an authoress should dress."

Her conceit was fairly colossal. The reforms in
legislation for Ireland were, in her estimation, owing
to her novel of " Florence Macarthy." She professed
to have taught Taglioni the Irish jig. Of her toilette,
made largely by her own hands, she was comically

vain. In "The Fraserians," a charming off-hand description of the contributors to that magazine, Lady Morgan is depicted trying on a big, showy bonnet before a mirror with a funny mixture of satisfaction and anxiety as to the effect.

Chorley, the feared and fearless critic of the *Athenæum*, speaks of Lady Morgan as one of the most peculiar and original literary characters he ever met. After a long and searching analysis he adds: "However free in speech, she never shocked decorum — never had to be appealed or apologized for as a forlorn woman of genius under difficulties." "A compound of the most startling contradictions, impossible to be overlooked or forgotten, though possible to be described in two ways, both true, yet the one diametrically opposed to the other. Her life, were it truly told, would be one of the most singular contributions to the history of gifted woman that the world has ever seen."

An American paper, the *Boston Literary Gazette*, gave a personal description which was not sufficiently flattering, and roused the lady's indignant comments. It dared to state that she was "short, with a broad face, blue, inexpressive eyes, and seemed, if such a thing may be named, about forty years of age." Imagine the sensations this paragraph produced! She at once retorted, exclaiming in mock earnest, "I appeal! I appeal to the Titian of his age and country — I appeal to you, Sir Thomas Lawrence. Would you have painted a short, squat, broad-faced, inexpressive, affected, Frenchified, Greenland-seal-like lady of any age? Would any money have tempted you to profane your immortal pencil, consecrated by nature to the Graces, by devoting its magic to such a model as this described by the Yankee artist of the *Boston Literary?* And yet, you did paint the picture of this Lapland Venus — this impersonation of a Dublin Bay Codfish! . . . Alas! no one could have said that I was forty then ; and this is the cruelest cut of all! Had it been thirty-nine or fifty! Thirty-nine is still under the mark, and fifty so far beyond it, so hopeless ; but forty — the critical age, the Rubicon — I cannot, will not, dwell on it. But, O America! land of my devotion and my idolatry! is it from *you* the blow has come? Let *Quarterly* and *Blackwoods* libel, but the *Boston Literary!* Et tu Brute!"

In 1837 she received a pension of three hundred pounds a year, a handsome recognition of her literary merits, and entirely unsolicited.

And in '39 she published a book entitled, "Woman and Her Master," solid and dull. She endeavored to prove that woman is composed of finer clay than man, or is rather a bit of precious porcelain. And a masculine critic says: "The lady, having all the talk to herself, rides to the end upon a gently undulating wave of triumph."

One more peep into her diary :

"Moore looked very old and bald, but still retains his cock-sparrow air. He was very pleasant but

rather egotistical and shallow. He exclaimed bitterly against writing-women, even against the beautiful Mrs. Norton.

"'In short,' said he, 'a writing-woman is one
unsexed,' but suddenly recollecting himself. and
pointing at me, said to my sister, 'except *her*.'"

August 19th.

"My soireé very fine. Learned, scientific. and
tiresome. Fifty philosophers passed through my
little salon last night. My sister, Lady Clark, made
a song about them, which she sang to the amusement of all."

In December, 1846, she writes: "I dare not trust
myself to chronicle my feelings as to passing years.
To forget is my philosophy; to hope would be my
insanity; to endure, and that I can, is my system.
I am grateful for the good I yet enjoy; to be so. is
my religion."

In 1850, she thoroughly enjoyed a sharp pen-to-
pen encounter with Cardinal Wiseman on a statement made in her Italy. She writes: "Lots of
notices and notes of my letter to Cardinal Wiseman.
It has had the run of all the newspapers. The little
old woman lives still."

Lady Morgan had vanity, but it was a vanity so
quaint and sparkling, so unlike in its frank honesty
to all other vanities that it became absolutely a
charm.

"I am vain," she once said to Mrs. Hall, "but I
have a right to be so. Look at the number of books

I have written (over 70). Have I not been ordered to leave a kingdom and refused to obey? Did ever woman move in a brighter sphere than I do? My dear, I have three invitations to dinner to-day. One from a duchess, another from a countess, a third from a diplomatist. What am I? A pensioned scribbler! Yet I am given gifts that queens might covet."

Horace Smith, the wit and poet, was a frequent and delighted as well as delightful guest of Lady Morgan's.

Once when invited to visit her he was suffering from an acute attack of bronchitis, and sent with his regrets the following doggerel:

> "O dear Lady Morgan, this pain in the organ
>   Of sound, that the doctors call larynx,
>   Is a terrible baulk to my walk and my talk,
>   While my pen its extremity ne'er inks.
>   Tho' I know its not sage, I'm transported with rage,
>   Cause I can't be transported to Sydney.

> "When my daughters come back from your dwelling, alack!
>   What lots of facetiæ they *can* tell us !
>   While *I* within clutch of a feast I can't touch,
>   Am condemned to the tortures of Tantalus !
>   When last you came here, *you* had illness severe,
>   Now *I* must call in the physician.
>   We would meet, but the more we're disposed (what a bore)
>   The greater our indisposition !

> "O Morgans and Fate, do not bother my pate,
>   With this Fata Morgana probations ;
>   If ye can't make me well, rob Sir Charles of his spell,
>   And his wife of her rare fascinations."

In Ireland, at the vice-regal drawing-rooms of the Marchioness Wellesley, Lady Morgan frequently figured. "Here," writes one, "here it was that I saw Lady Morgan for the first time, and as I had long pictured her to my imagination as a sylph-like person, nothing could equal my astonishment when the celebrated authoress stood before me. She certainly formed a strange figure in the midst of that dazzling scene of beauty and splendor. Every lady present wore feathers and trains, but Lady Morgan scorned both appendages. Hardly more than four feet high, with a slightly curved spine, uneven shoulders and eyes, she glided about in a close-cropped wig bound by fillet or solid band of gold, her face all animation and with a witty word for everybody."

Mrs. Kemble thought her a clever, vain, lively, good-natured woman. She says, " My relations with the lively, amusing authoress consisted merely in an exchange of morning visits, during one of which she plied me with a breathless series of pressing invitations to breakfasts, luncheons, dinners, evening parties, to meet everybody that I did not know, and upon my declining all these offers of hospitable entertainment, for I had at that time withdrawn myself entirely from society, and went nowhere, she exclaimed, " But what in the world do you *do* with yourself in the evening ? "

" Sit with my father, or remain alone."

" Ah ! " said the society-loving little lady, with an

exasperated Irish accent, " Come out of that sphare of solitary self-sufficiency ye live in, *do !* " which ob-jurgation certainly presented in a most ludicrous light my life of very sad seclusion, and sent us both into fits of laughter.

In 1828, O'Connell paid a graceful tribute to the achievements of Lady Morgan. " To Irish female talent and patriotism we owe much. There is one name consecrated by a generous devotion to the best interests of Ireland — a name sacred to the cause of liberty and of everything — great, virtuous, or patriotic ; the name of an illustrious woman, who has suffered unmanly persecution for her talented and chivalrous adherence to her native land."

" It is to me delightful," writes Sir Jonah Bar-rington, " to see a woman solely by the force of her own natural talent, succeed triumphantly in the line of letters she has adopted, and in despite of the most virulent, illiberal, and unjust attacks ever yet made on any author by mercenary reviewers."

Chorley, the feared and fearless critic of the *Athenaeum,* speaks of Lady Morgan as one of the most peculiar and original literary characters he ever met.

" A composition of natural genius, acquired accomplishments, audacity, that flew at the highest game, shrewd thought ; and research at once intel-ligent and superficial ; personal coquetries and affectations balanced by sincere and strenuous fam-ily affection ; extreme liberality of opinions, religious and political; extremely narrow literary sympathies, united with a delight in all the most tinsel pleasures, and indulgent of the most inane aristocratic society; a genial love for art, limited by the most inconceivable prejudices of ignorance; in brief, a compound of the most startling contradictions impossible to be overlooked or forgotten, though possible to be described in two ways, both true, yet the one diametrically opposed to the other."

Her life, were it truly told, would be one of the most singular contributions to the history of gifted woman that the world has ever seen.

However free in speech she never shocked decorum — never had to be appealed or apologized for as a forlorn woman of genius under difficulties.

The closing chapters of any biography must of necessity be sad; friends falling to the grave like autumn leaves.

First her beloved husband, then her darling sister Olivia, and her journal she now calls her "Doomsday Book."

December 25, 1858, was Lady Morgan's last birthday. "She assembled a few old friends at dinner and did the honor, with all the brilliancy of her best days. She told stories with infinite *finesse* and drollery, and after dinner sang a broadly comic song, which she said must be good, as it was written by a church dignitary, so she gave from Father Prout 'The Night before Larry was Stretched.' It was a custom of those days to wake a man, who was to be |hung, the night before his execution, so the poor lad might enjoy the whisky drank in his honor."

There was one book more, positively the last, " The Odd Volume," but she never gave up her pen, that "worn-out stump of a goose-quill" until her physician literally took it from her fingers.

She grew old gracefully, showing great kindness to young authors, enduring partial blindness and comparative neglect with dignity and cheerfulness. Her heart was always young.

Some one writes: " The last time we saw the ' Wild Irish Girl ' she was seated on a couch in her bedroom as pretty and picturesque a ruin of old-lady womankind as ever we looked upon; her black silk dressing-gown fell round her petite form, which seemed so fragile that we feared to see her move. We recalled to memory Maria Edgeworth, having believed her to be the smallest great woman in the world, but Lady Morgan seemed not half her size."

Another says: " Everything in her room was artistic, and you might have imagined yourself in the presence of Mad. de Genlis, feeling that after the passing away of that small form, which enshrined so much vitality and so large and expansive a mind, the last link between us and the Atkins, the Barbaulds, the D'Arblays would be gone."

She met death patiently and with unfailing courage rather than religious resignation on the evening of the 16th of April, 1859.

Deference to her sensitiveness prevents any allusion to her age.

"She lived through the love, admiration, and malignity of three generations of men and was, in short, a literary Ninon, as brisk and captivating in 1859 as when George was Prince and the author of ' Kate Kearney' divided the laureateship of society and song with Tom Moore," one of the most popular and best abused writers of her time. No one reads her now. Why do I resurrect her? Because she was such a charming personality, industrious, cheerful, lovable, womanly; making the most and the best of her life according to her convictions. And because, as I read her life, and moralized over the hosts of ambitious men and women who wrote so much and so well, and are almost unknown, she seemed to stand at my elbow, merry, but eager, and shaking her fan, she whispered, " Tell your friends all about me, that's a darling. Give me one more chance to be heard of in your beautiful broad America." So I offer this pen photograph of Sydney, Lady Morgan.

CHRISTOPHER NORTH AND HIS FRIENDS.

I devote this hour with special pleasure to John Wilson — grand old lion of the North ; with the body of an athlete, the brain of a genius, the heart of a woman ; as remarkable as a pugilist, pedestrian, sportsman as for his literary criticisms, sketches of Scottish life, and logical eloquent lectures on moral philosophy.

Oh for the power to bring the man before you as he *was*, of commanding stature, with the brow and features of a god, clear blue eyes, a wonderfully mobile face, locks of the true keltic yellow floating over his broad shoulders, the embodiment and ideal of vigorous manhood.

"*You* are a *man!*" said Napoleon, when he first saw Goethe. So exclaimed strangers as they passed Wilson on the street. Walter Scott is supposed to have depicted him in his sketch of Richard the Lion-hearted. He certainly fulfilled Emerson's idea that it is the first duty of every man to be a splendid animal, anticipating Gail Hamilton's flattering statement: "There is nothing so splendid as a splendid man." He has always been one of my heroes, and although the rose-color and glamor which surrounded him in childish days is dimmed, so that I can see his faults, there is still a wondrous charm connected with his name.

Such enthusiasm, such strong personal magnetism, is incapable of oblivion. I know that at the
last, his mind and body failed — that like other men.
he died and was buried; but, to me, he is still in the
prime of life, never old, never changed.

I think about him, read about him, picture him,
till he glows a living being beside me. Up to his
neck in water, fishing; or running, leaping, wrest-
ling, rowing, and excelling in all; delighting the
students in Edinburgh University; an odd successor
to Dugald Stewart and Dr. Brown, a victorious rival
of Sir William Hamilton; walking with his wife over
the hills of Scotland, chatting and chaffing with the
Ettrick Shepherd at Ambrose Tavern; boating on
the Windemere; "laboring in his study when the
fever of composition was upon him, upon poem,
essay, or story, his eyes gleaming like a panther's, his
unkempt beard adding a grim wild force to his expression, the whole effect that of 'an inspired
buffalo'; spending several weeks with a camp of
Gypsies; riding in mad chase after a neighbor's *bull*,
at half-past two on a summer's morning, with a
couple of jolly friends, all armed with immense
spears fourteen feet long; leaping in rivalry with
some tinkers who had pitched their tents by the
roadside; playing the waiter at an inn table at midnight, half for the frolic, half to study character;
holding the hand and closing the eyes of his faithful
old servant, Billy Balmer, who had come from far to
die near him, or sitting by the bedside of an old

woman, long an inmate of his home, arranging her pillows with awkward but gentle hand or reading her favorite verses in the Bible; petting a hapless sparrow; pampering and feeding no less than sixty-two game cocks in his back yard, with a hospital for the invalids in an attic.

Twisting a whip from the fist of a brutal carter, who was cruelly beating his horse, and placing the wretched animal in better control than that of its owner, leading the venerable, raw-boned quadruped through the fashionable streets of Edinburgh, an act which required moral courage. And courage he never lacked in things great or small. A passionate lover of nature, a despiser of shams. "Intolerant to no one but quacks and cockneys," erratic, prejudiced, intense, affectionate, truthful, do you not see him? The brawny-chested, broad-shouldered, fire-eyed. lofty-browed, sunny-faced, sunny-hearted, Kit North! His name scarcely appears in our text-books on English literature. His works are not generally known in this country, but the few who do appreciate his power and versatility, his humor, pathos, satire, wit and tenderness, wisdom and eloquence, value him as a tried and intimate friend, and find in the "Noctes" an unfailing fountain of delight.

The Shepherd knew what he was talking about when he said to Christopher — "Listenin' to you, sir, is like lookin' into a *well*; at first ye think it clear, but no verra deep, but ye let drop in a peeble and what a length o' time ere the air-bells come up to the surface frae the profoond."

In Scotland he is remembered and read, not as Scott and Burns, but first in the rank just after them — remembered with affection, enthusiasm, and respect.

Look first at John Wilson as a beautiful child, full of life and fun, fond of angling when but a baby. He was only three years old when he rambled off one day, armed with a willow wand duly furnished with a thread line and crooked pin, to fish in a "wee burnie" of which he had taken note, away a good mile from home. Unknown to anyone, the adventurer sallied forth for a "solitary cast" to spend a day of delight by the rippling stream, with what success we find recorded in Fytte First of Christopher in his sporting jacket.

"A tug — a tug! With face ten times flushed and pale by turns ere you could count ten, he has at last strength in the agitation of his fear and joy to pull away at the monster, and there he lies in his beauty among the gowans and the greensward, for he has whapped him right over his head and far away — a fish a quarter of an ounce in weight, and, at the very least, two inches long! Off he flies on wings of wind to his father, mother, and sisters and brothers and cousins, and all the neighborhood, holding the fish aloft in both hands, still fearful of its escape, and like a genuine child of corruption, his eyes brighten at the first blush of cold blood on his small puny fingers. He carries about with him, upstairs and downstairs, his prey upon a plate, and will not wash his hands, for he exults in the silver scales adhering to the thumb-nail that scooped out the pin."

While the future Christopher was asserting himself out of doors, the " professor " was displaying his capacity in the nursery.

His sisters looked up to him, and admired and wondered, as standing upon a chair he would address them and the servants. One sermon he was often called on to repeat, with this text: " There was a fish, and it was a de'il o' a fish, and it was ill to its young anes." In this allegory he displayed pathos, humor, and oratorical power. He was also remarkable for his drawings, especially of animals.

A tiger, full of crouching life, just ready to spring, was exhibited by his mother to admiring guests.

This precocious boy, unlike many geniuses, was foremost in the playground, king of all sports, throwing his whole energy into either study or play, a favorite with everyone.

Always intensely susceptible to grief or gladness, his first real sorrow was the death of his sister. He was borne from her grave death-like, and wishing to die. And in his twelfth year he lost his father. " As he stood at the head of the grave and heard the dull earth rattling over the coffin, his emotions so overcame him that he fainted. His daughter remarks that this union of strength and sensitiveness suggests those blue-eyed and long-haired Norsemen, who made their songs amid the smiting of swords, swift of foot, strong of arm, skilled in love, ready in counsel, fierce to their enemies, tender and true to their friends.

At Glasgow University he showed the same passionate vehemence and tendency to extremes, in study, social life, poetry, music, wild escapade — yet never immoral nor dissipated. Such superabundant vitality is apt to be misunderstood by the commonplace majority to whom such ebullitions savor of intoxication or insanity or a lamentable eccentricity, but more of such individuality, independence, enthusiasm, and outdoor life would be an improvement to our race.

He kept a diary in college days, like himself, odd and queerly mixed. In one line, "Gave Archy my buckskins to clean"; in next, "Prize for the best specimen of the Socratic mode of reasoning given out in Logic"; again, "Called on my grandmother; went·to a sale of books; had a boxing-match of three rounds with Lloyd — *beat* him "; or, "ran three miles on the Paisley road for a wager against a chaise with Andrew Napier — *beat* them *both!*" In vacation, "Finished my poem on Slavery. Began an essay on the Faculty of Imagination. Stayed at home all day. Wrote on the Philosophy of the Stoics.

"For barley sugar, 6 pence.

" Began to learn the flute by myself.

" Prizes distributed, got three of them."

Sotheby said it was worth a journey from London to hear him translate a Greek chorus, and at a later day, the brawny Cumberland men called him " a verra bad un to lick."

" I trust I make myself understood," he once said to such a man, after knocking him down.

When a boy he won a bet by walking six miles in two minutes less than an hour. He was equally remarkable as a leaper, surpassing all competitors. He once jumped across the Cheswell, twenty-three feet clear, with a run of only a few yards, the greatest feat of this kind on record. Gen. Washington's greatest leap was but twenty-one feet. It is curious that Wilson's learned rival, Sir W. Hamilton, was also a noted leaper.

At Oxford he was the first boxer, leaper, cock-fighter, and runner among the students, but gained the Newdigate prize for poetry, and became so flaming a Radical that he would not allow a servant to black his shoes, but might be seen, the yellow-haired glorious savage, performing that interesting operation himself.

At that early period he strongly admired Wordsworth and wrote him a letter of extraordinary length, which the contemplative bard kindly answered. In after years he lost all patience with the diffuse dreary wastes that marred his longer poems. The bald simplicity of his childish doggerel when he was true to his own theories about poetry was too much for Wilson's sense of the ludicrous, and his over-mastering conceit caused this former favorite to dwindle to the proportions of a good and great old man, who, when he forget his creed, rose to sublimity. If all dared to express their honest opinions as did Wilson, we should find there had been a good deal of sham admiration about many of our beacon lights in literature, from Chaucer to Browning.

At college, too, there was an unfortunate love affair, a tangled net of adoration, hope, perplexity, mystification, and despair, a necessary experience apparently in a poet's career, from Spenser's Rosalind to Tennyson's Lillian.

After graduation in 1807, he built, all on the ground floor, a beautiful home in Westmoreland, which De Quincey describes in his glowing way. It was Wilson, by the way, who gave the name to the " Lake School." De Quincey was impressed by the humility and gravity with which Wilson spoke of himself, no tinge of arrogance in his manner, a refreshing contrast to the colossal conceit of his neighbors.

There were merry regattas on the Lake and merrier dances on shore. De Quincey says that Wilson was the best male dancer, not professional, he had ever seen, although he had never taken a lesson : and it was at a ball that he met his fate, Miss Jane Penny, a leading belle of the Lake country, rich, accomplished, and beautiful. And when he danced with her, which he did often, they attracted all eyes, and many stopped to watch them. They were often cheered as they entered a room, in mere admiration of their appearance.

> " So stately his form and so lovely her face,
> That never a hall such a galliard did grace."

Pretty Miss Jane seems for a time quite jealous of a bewitching widow to whom Wilson was attentive. She writes: " Mr. Wilson is flirting with a pretty little widow. She is generally admired by the male part of creation, but not by our sex. I don't know whether Mr. Wilson's attentions to her will end in a marriage, but I hope not — *for his sake.* I think he is deserving a very superior woman."

Most truly did he win one, secured in Miss Penny. It was an ideal companionship; one of unbroken happiness. He was married on the 11th of May, 1811, and wrote that morning to his most intimate friends of his wife, with these words :

" She is, in gentleness, innocence, sense, and feeling, surpassed by no woman, and has remained pure as from her Maker's hands. Surely, if I know myself I am not deficient in kindness and gentleness of nature. I will to my dying day love, honor, and worship her." This determination was most fully kept, for Wilson was a model of a lover and husband in one.

Thenceforth his life had a deeper purpose, and his home was a place of pure sunshine. There was no wedding tour, but they went at once to his cottage home.

During the first year of married life he published " The Isle of Palms." The sale was not gratifying. Of the four happy years that were passed in the cottage at Elleray, from 1811 to 1815, there is little to be told. The happiest families, like the happiest nations, have no history. Then came unlooked-for trouble. An uncle proved dishonest and treacherous, squandering Wilson's entire fortune, and ruined himself also. Wilson bore the blow bravely, and generously assisted to support this disgraced relative. He now had to leave his beloved sycamore-sheltered Elleray, going to Edinburgh to live with his mother, a stately, handsome old lady, who welcomed him and his family to her pleasant house in Queen street. In 1815, he was called to the bar, but that routine was impossible for him. He did sometimes get cases, but said laughingly afterward, "I did not know what the devil to do with them."

About the beginning of July, 1815, Mr. and Mrs. Wilson set out for a pedestrian tour through the Highlands, which was successfully accomplished, astonishing the villagers wherever they stopped by their striking appearance. One day she walked twenty-five miles. On their return they were quite the lions of Edinburgh. It was predicted that Mrs. Wilson would come back sunburnt, weather-beaten, and freckled. But such expectations were agreeably disappointed. One old lady who called immediately exclaimed: " Weel, I declare, she's come back bonnier than ever."

De Quincey often accompanied Wilson on these tramps. Their friendship was lifelong. Sheltered at the house one stormy night, the marvelous little man remained a year. He gave his daily instructions to the cook in his own peculiar phraseology and with the minuteness and prolixity which never left him. The good soul listened in silent awe, entirely over-powered, as he requested that his slice of rare mutton be cut in a "diagonal rather than a longitudinal form," but gave as her private opinion, "That bodie has an *aufu'* sicht o' words. My ain master would ha' ordered a hale table fu' in a little more than a haff o' his haun — and here's a' this claver about a bit mutton, nae bigger than a peni. Mr. De Quinshey would mak a gran' preacher — though I'm thinkin' that a hantle o' the folk would na ken what he was drivin' at." A sensible criticism on the convolu-tions and intricacies of the Opium Eater's arabesque style, certainly as valuable as the comments of Grant White's washerwoman on puzzling passages in Shakespeare.

The "City of the Plague," published next year (1816) was favorably criticised by Jeffrey, and Byron placed it among the great works of the age. But as a poet, Wilson will not live — strange to say; he was too soft and feminine in style; while as a word pain-ter he is almost unequaled.

His novels, though exquisite specimens of poetic prose, are overloaded with sentiment and emotion, and the characters far above the average of Scot-tish rural life, yet they were hailed with delight when they appeared, producing the same sensation as

George McDonald's first and best story, " The Annals
of a Quiet Neighborhood."

With the year 1817, begins Wilson's connection
with *Blackwood's Magazine.*

At that time Edinburgh was crowded with clever
men. most of them young,who felt that the *Tory* party,
to which they belonged, had been too loudly crowed
over by the Edinburgh *Review*, the oldest of the great
British quarterlies, originated by such men as Sydney
Smith, Francis Jeffrey, Henry Brougham, and Francis
Horner.   It was a tremendous power, with its light
flying artillery of wit, personality, and sarcasm.
Jeffrey was a critic to be feared and hated.   Wordsworth used to class Robespierre, Bonaparte, and
Jeffrey together as the three most formidable enemies of the human race who had appeared within his
remembrance.   Jeffrey had dared to say of his
" Excursion," " This will never do."

A rival magazine was needed, and Blackwood, the
bookseller, started one.   The first numbers were described as " dull and decent." This was not what was
wanted.   Blackwood dismissed his editors and obtained the services of James Hogg, who by his
" Queen's Wake " had just taken rank among the
first poets of Scotland, of Lockhart, Scott's son-in-
law, who for caustic criticism almost equaled Jeffrey,
Dr. Magrim, a witty and learned Irishman, John
Galt, the novelist, Robert Sym, the Timothy Tickler
of the " Noctes," and John Wilson.

Hogg contributed the famous Chaldee Manuscript, a literary rocket, a sharp satire upon the Whig party in biblical language. Grant White's " New Gospel of Peace" is closely like this. This was received with dismay, astonishment, wrath, there was a wild outcry through the city, and it was threatened to prosecute Mr. Blackwood "for a profane parody of the Bible," though we imagine the personalities distressed the accusers more than the profanity. He paid £1,000 in costs and damages, but Blackwood was looked for eagerly afterwards; and it was never deficient in spicy comments, audacious, lively, unjustified, unscrupulous, and witty.

At one time it was a habit to review in Blackwood books which had never been published, such as " Peter's Letters to his Kinsfolks." A Dr. Peter Morris was invented as the letter-writer. Lockhart, who had originated the joke, was forced to complete the letters as a third edition of the book. The author's name became well known, and the magazine gained much credit for having introduced Dr. Morris to the world.

In this new magazine the genius of Wilson found free scope. Like an athlete who never before had had room or occasion to display his powers, he now reveled in their exercise in an arena where the competitors were abundant and the onlookers eagerly interested. Month after month he poured fourth the exuberant current of his ideas on politics, poetry, philosophy, religion, art, books, men, and nature, with a freshness and force that seemed incapable of exhaustion and regardless of obstacles, dealing at first many a blow, which later he saw reason to repent. But the malignant attacks came from others, and he was never the editor, although the leading spirit.

Wilson and Lockhart were the most versatile of all the band, between them capable at any time of providing the whole contents of a number. There was a striking contrast in the outward aspect of these men. Wilson, so ruddy, off-hand, and cheery, Lockhart, with pale olive complexion, thin lips, expression sombre and severe, and haughty, super-cilious manner, a man who could give you a chill, or, as someone said after a dinner in Boston, "I sat next Edward Everett yesterday, and caught a severe cold." He was well depicted by Wilson through the mouth of the Shepherd (who was made to say so much he never thought of), as "the Oxford collegian wi' a pale face and a black toozy head, but an ei like an eagle's." The black-haired, Spanish-looking Oxonian, with that uncanny laugh of his, was a dangerous person to encounter in the field of letters. "I've sometimes thocht, Mr. North," says the Shepherd, "that ye were a wee feared for him yoursel, and used rather without kenning it to draw in your horns." In the Chaldee he was called "The Scor-pion." Wilson impaled a victim as he did a fish, as if he loved him; the other, cool, crafty, and lacking in compassion.

Wilson said of himself:

" We love to do our work by fits and starts. We hate to keep fiddling away, an hour or two at a time at one article for weeks. So off with our coat, and at it like a blacksmith. When we once get the way of it, hand over hip, we laugh at Vulcan and all his Cyclops. From nine of the morning till nine at night, we keep hammering away at the metal, iron or gold, till we produce a most beautiful article. A biscuit and a glass of Madeira, twice or thrice at the most, and then to a well-won dinner. In three days, gentle reader, have We, Christopher North, often produced a whole magazine — a most splendid number. For the next three weeks we were as idle as a desert, and as vast as an antre, and thus we go, alternately laboring like an ant, and relaxing in the sunny air, like a dragon-fly, enamored of extremes."

In its palmy days, Blackwood's Magazine realized an ideal which has never been surpassed. Credit should be given to Wilson who invited Bulwer to contribute, which invitation stimulated the creation of " The Caxtons and My Novel," Bulwer's best prose production. Wilson was the first of his party to appreciate Shelley, and to do justice to Byron ; paid the most eloquent tributes to Burns and to Dickens. Seldom have discrimination and imaginative luxuriance been so combined. The names of the contributors secured by him furnish a brilliant array. No periodical was ever more indebted to the efforts of one individual.

Let me give a few extracts to show his originality,

insight, and power. Some wise heads insist that literature should be studied, enjoyed, or reviewed without any connection with the life and habits of the author, but I agree fully with Wilson when he says:

"In reviewing, in particular what can be done without personality? Nothing, nothing. What are books that don't express the personal characters of their authors; and who can review books without reviewing those that wrote them.

" Can a man read La Fontaine without perceiving his personal good nature? Swift's personal ill-nature is quite as visible. Can a man read Burns without having the idea of a great and a bold man, or Barry Cornwall without the very uncomfortable feeling of a little man and a timid one? The whole of the talk about personality is cant.

" Look at our literature now, and it is all periodical together. A thousand daily, thrice a week, twice a week, weekly newspapers, a hundred monthlies, fifty quarterlies, and twenty-five annuals. No mouth looks up now and is not fed! On the contrary, we are in danger of being crammed; an empty head is as rare as an empty stomach; the whole day is one meal, one physical, moral, and intellectual feast; the public goes to bed with a periodical in her hand and falls asleep with it beneath her pillow.

" What blockhead thinks now of reading Milton or Pope or Gray? Paradise Lost *is* lost; it has gone to the devil. Pope's Epistles are returned to the dead-letter office; the age is too loyal for 'Ruin seize thee, ruthless king,' and the oldest inhabitant has forgotten 'the curfew tolls.'"

"The great charm o' conversation is being aff on ony wind that blaws. Pleasant conversation between friends is just like walking through a mountainous kintra, at every glen-mouth the winn blaws frae a different airt."

"*North*. I believe country congregations are, in general, very attentive.

"*Shepherd*. Ay, ay, Sir! If twa are sleepin' ten are wauken, and I seriously think that mair than ae half o' them thats sleepin' enter into the spirit o' the sermon. You see they a' hear the text and the introductory remarks and the heads, and fa'in asleep in a serious and solemn mood, they carry the sense alang in them; neither can they be said no to hear an accompanyin' soun', so that it wadna be just fair to assert that they lose the sermon they dinna listen to, for thochts and ideas and feelings keep floatin' down alang the streams o' silent thocht, and when they awaken at the "Amen," their minds, if no greatly instructed, hae been tranquilleezed; they join loudly in the ensuing psalm, and without remembering mony o' the words, carry hame the feek o' the discoorse and a' the peculiarities of the doctrine."

This is like the story of the dominie who, hearing from Sandy that he liked the Sabba day best of all, endeavored to draw him out, hoping for a compliment for his sermons. "Oh, yes. Sunday's the day for me, for then, you see, I gets into my clean claes, and goes to the kirk, and sits down in my pew, and shuts the door, and lays up my legs, and thinks o' nothin'."

"'The human heart is shaped like this table — a sort o' oval, and thus friends can be accommodated in the ane and at the ither without ony body pretendin' to ony precedence, and to the prevention o' a quarrel on *that* pint, atween *love* and *pride*."

"The joy of grief. That is a joy known but to the happy."

"*James*. The soul that can dream of past sorrows till they touch it with a pensive delight, can be suffering under no severe trouble."

" We idolize Genius to the neglect of the worship of Virtue. One truly good action performed is worth all that Shakespeare ever wrote."

"'That which in *real* life would be fulsome cannot breathe sweetly in fiction, for fiction is still a reflection of truth, and truth is sacred."

On Wordsworth.

North.

" Why, Tickler, many of the poets of our days are, with all their genius, a set of enormous spoons. Wordsworth walks about the woods like a great satyr, or rather, like the god Pan, and piping away upon his reed, sometimes most infernally out of tune. He thinks he is listening, at the very least, to music equal to that of the spheres, and that nobody can blow a note but himself." He pronounced the " Excursion " the worst poem of any character in the English language, and, in a rollicking series of rhymes on various authors, exclaimed :

Now here's to Will Wordsworth, so wise and so wordy,
And the sweet, simple hymns of his own hurdy-gurdy.
Who in vain blows the bellows of Milton's old organ,
While he *thinks* he could lull all the snakes on the Gorgon.

And, after a gallant and protracted rhapsody over the lady poets of the land, Mrs. Hemans, L. E., etc., he closes with :

"And what the devil, then, would you be at, with your great bawling He-Poets from the Lakes, who go round and round about, strutting upon nothing, like so many turkey-cocks gobbling, with a long, red pendant at their noses, and frightening away the fair and lovely swans as they glide down the waters of immortality?"

"The ' Noctes Ambrosianæ,' so unlike anything else that had appeared, delighted the reading world; and Wilson seemed a diffused Shakespeare, or Shakespeare in a hurry, with a printer's devil waiting at the door. Falstaff was, for a season, eclipsed by the 'Shepherd,' and Mercutio and Hamlet together had their glories darkened by the blended wit and wisdom, pathos and fancy, of 'Christopher North.' "

Stevenson said in an early essay, of the more perennial part of the " Noctes," " We have here, what is perhaps the most durable monument to Wilson's fame. We might class him as a Presbyterian Fawn.

It is a thousand pities that the 'Noctes Ambrosianæ' are now so little appreciated. Fashion is incalculable, but I cannot think they will be permanently
forgotten."

These papers breathe the very essence of the
Bacchanalian revel of clever men, yet a too literal
interpretation must not be given to their festivities.
There was a small and crushed-up-in-a-corner hostel-
rie by the name of " Ambrose's Inn," where the
friends occasionally met, but these dialogues were
written with prolonged toil in a rapid manner, and
upon no stronger inspiration than a chicken for dinner and a cup of tea.

This glorification of the delights of drinking
belongs to a Scotsman's patriotism, and a man should
no more be considered to endorse all that he writes
in that convivial strain than a poet when he sings of
love, wheret he Clorindas and Delias, from Horace
to Swinburne, are two-thirds of them ideal creations.

This is not an apology for what seems and is a
blot, but simply a statement of facts. " The Paradoxes
of Literature " is a fertile and startling theme.
Wilson's characters in the " Noctes " are equally
idealized.

Hogg was an interesting man and a rustic phe-
nomenon, but Christopher made Jamie his mouth-
piece, and the Ettrick Shepherd of the " Noctes " is
one of the most finished creations which dramatic
genius ever evoked. Some of Wilson's thoughts on
Life, Faith, Death, Immortality, given as the off-hand

talk of the Shepherd, are perfect — sermons without any effect of preaching, impressive, helpful, elevating — too long, unfortunately, for quotation.

Hogg's prose writings were inferior to his poetry. He seemed unconscious of the beauty of his pastoral description and imagery. When Jordan praised his verses highly, the honest Shepherd rejoined: "Surely ye're daft; its only joost true about the wee burdies and the cows at e'en, and the wild flowers, and the sunset, and clouds, and things, and the feelings they creat. A canna fathom what ye're making a' this fuss about. Its joost a plain description of what every body can see; there's nae grand poetry in it." The intimacy between these men was delightful. Wilson once walked fifty miles in one day to be present at a Burns dinner, to pay a glowing tribute to Hogg. The simple-hearted old fellow, who had not expected it in the least, could only stammer out a few broken words of thanks, his face flushed scarlet with feeling, his eyes brimful of tears.

A guest at the Burns dinner in 1816 recollects that, somewhat late in the evening, Wilson mounted on one of the tables, danced a pas-seul among the wine glasses and decanters without any fracture of the crystal, aud then descending, resumed his seat, with a ludicrous air of intense and philosophic gravity, as if, in fact, he had done nothing worthy of consideration or gratitude. He longed for the power to write a popular song, saying, "I know what it should be, but I cannot do it. If I could write one that would be sung in valley, hill, and plain, I should die happy. There is not a peasant in Scotland who does not know Burns' Songs."

We now come to an important event. In April, 1820, the chair of Moral Philosophy in the University of Edinburgh became vacant by the death of Dr. Brown. Sir William Hamilton, a whig, who was well fitted for the place, and John Wilson, a tory, offered themselves as candidates, and after a severe contest, Wilson was triumphantly elected. Apparently, a most unfit and incongruous appointment, if moral philosophy is the gate to theology, as Chalmers insisted, and his opponents represented him as a reveler and blasphemer, even attacking his private character, which was absolutely unassailable. " No doubt he was a humorist, and there was so little distinctively " moral " in the rollicking wit of Blackwood that the majority stood aghast at the fact of this magnificent mad-cap, this reckless, half-savage Titan of Literature, spirited into the throne of Philosophy! Scott was Wilson's firm supporter in this trying time, indignantly denying the charges brought.

The faithful Billy Balmer was the first to bring the news home. Mrs. Wilson writes: " He went yesterday morning and stayed near the scene of action till it was all over, and then came puffing down with a face of delight, to tell me that Master was ahead — a good deal ! "

Then came the tremendous tug of preparation.

It was the last of July. The class was to meet the
beginning of November, and 120 lectures must be
prepared. The loving wife writes: " Mr. W. is very
well, but as thin as a rat, and no wonder, he says it
will take him one month at least to make out a catalogue of the books he has to read through and con-
sult. I am perfectly appalled when I go into the
dining-room and see all the folios, quartos, and duo-
decimos with which it is literally filled, and the poor
culprit himself sitting in the midst, with a beard as
long and red as an adult carrot, for he has not shaved
for a fortnight." The opening of the session, Christopher's first appearance as a professor, was an
interesting occasion.

" The lecture-room was crowded to the ceiling,"
says an eye-witness. Such a collection of hard-
browed, scowling Scotsmen muttering over their
knot-sticks, I never saw. The professor entered
with a bold step and in profound silence. Everyone expected some propitious introduction of himself, but he began in a voice of thunder right into
the matter of his lecture, and kept up unflinchingly
and unhesitatingly without a pause a flow of rhetoric
such as his predecessors never delivered in the same
place. Those who came to scoff remained to praise.

There were always some people who believed
that he was nothing more than a splendid declaimer
and that his lectures contained more poetry than
philosophy. But those who studied with him knew
how false was this estimate. One of his class, speak-

ing of his thorough work, " There was a notion that
he was there ' Christopher North ' and nothing else ;
that you could get scraps of poetry, bits of sentiment,
flights of fancy, flashes of genius, and anything but
moral philosophy.   Nothing was further from the
truth.   In the very first lecture he cut into the *core*
of the subject, raised the question which has always
in this country been held to be the hardest and
deepest in science (the origin of the moral faculty),
and hammered at it through the greater part of the
session.   Even those who had a morbid appetite for
swallowing hard and angular masses of logic found
that the work here was quite stiff enough for any of
us.   It was not till his lectures on the Affections
and the Imagination that he wandered freely over a
more inviting field.

Yes, " Wilson imported into the old university a
prodigious accession of vital force.   No academical
automaton was he with pedantic tones grinding out
the same dry formulæ year by year.   No round-
shouldered, abstracted, bloodless recluse, utterly
ignorant of life outside a library, and with about as
much influence on his young audience as a mummy
in a museum, or a last year's fly pressed in some
musty encyclopedia — you have seen metaphysicians
who had scarcely more life. Wilson was intensely
human, and to young men whose hatred is hum-
drum, whose delight is truth, courage, mastery, he
was a daily inspiration.   So profuse was the imagery,
so brilliant the diction, so exciting the passion that

very dull must have been the clod that did not catch
fire. Under the spell many found themselves thinkers, poets, and workers. It is matter for lasting
regret that these lectures written on bits of papers
and the backs of envelopes were not preserved to
give solidity to his reputation.

" His appearance in the class-room is far easier to
remember than to forget. He strode into it with the
professor's gown hanging loosely on his arms, took a
comprehensive look over the mob of young faces,
laid down his watch, so as to be out of the reach of
his sledge-hammer fist, glanced at his notes, and
then, to the bewilderment of those who had never
heard him before, looked long and earnestly out of
the north window towards the spire of the old Tron
Kirk, until, having at last got his idea, he faced
round and uttered it, with eye and hand and voice
and soul and spirit, and bore the class along with
him. . .

"And occasionally in the finer frenzy of his more
imaginative passages, as when he spoke of Alexander, clay-cold at Babylon, with the world lying conquered round his tomb — or of the Highland hills
that pour the rage of cataracts adown their riven
cliffs — or of the human mind with its 'primeval
granitic truths,' the grand old face flushed with the
proud thought, and the eyes grew dim with tears,
and the magnificent frame quivered with a universal
emotion."

You see how his undying enthusiasm permeated

the minds of his audience. 'Tis a living power to-day. It was heart to heart as well as head to head, and his power was always the side of good in the lecture-room. But we must return to his literary life. In 1820, this announcement appeared in the book-lists: " In the Press — Lays from Fairy Land, by John Wilson, author of The Isle of Palms." This was never published.

> " Doth grief e'er sleep in a Fairy's breast?
> Are dirges sung in the land of Rest?
> Tell us, when a fairy dies
> Hath she funeral obsequies?
> Are all dreams there of woe and mirth
> That trouble and delight on earth?"

Lord Jeffrey said he was never tired of reading his description of a " Fairy's Funeral," which I will read:

" There it was, on a little river island, that once, whether sleeping or waking, we know not, we saw celebrated a fairy's funeral. First we heard small pipes playing, as if no bigger than hollow rushes that whisper to the night winds, and more piteous than aught that trills from earthly instrument was the scarcely audible dirge. It seemed to float over the stream, every foam-bell emitting a plaintive note, till the fairy anthem came floating over our couch, and then alighting without footsteps on the heather. The pattering of little feet was then heard, as if living creatures were arranging themselves in order, and then there was nothing but a more ordered hymn. The harmony was like the melting of musical dewdrops, and sung without words of sorrow and death.

"We opened our eyes, or rather sight came to them when closed, and dream was vision.

"Hundreds of creatures, no taller than the crest of the lapwing, and all hanging down their veiled heads, stood in a circle on a green plat among the rocks; and in the midst was a bier, framed, as it seemed, of flowers unknown to the Highland hills, and on the bier a fairy lying with uncovered face, pale as a lily and motionless as the snow. The dirge grew fainter and fainter, and then quite died away, when two of the creatures came from the circle and took their station, one at the head, the other at the foot of the bier. They sang alternate measures, not louder than the twittering of the awakened woodlark before it goes up the dewy air, but dolorous and full of the desolation of death. The flower-bier stirred, for the spot on which it lay sank slowly down, and in a few moments the greensward was as smooth as ever, the very dews glittering above the buried fairy. A cloud passed over the moon, and with a choral lament the funeral troops sailed duskily away, heard afar off, so still was the midnight solitude of the glen. Then the disenthralled river began to rejoice as before, through all her streams and falls, and at the sudden leaping of the waters and outbursting of the moon we awoke."

The home life of Wilson combined all that is best expressed in those words.

Wife, children, pets, play through many of his essays. His wife's favorite plant was the myrtle; we find it peeping out here and there in his writings. There, as everywhere, he was like no one else. On his library table, fishing rods found company with Shakespeare and Ben Jonson, Jeremy Taylor reposed near a tin box of barley sugar, bank notes were stuffed between books (he never could keep a purse), peeping out from the Fairy Queen were no end of delicately-dressed flies, and the sparrow hopping about, master of the situation. This little pet imagined itself the most important occupant of the room. It would nestle in his waistcoat, hop upon his shoulder, and seemed influenced by a constant association, for it grew in stature until it was alleged that the sparrow was gradually becoming an eagle.

His love for animals was intense, and his favorites were, occasionally, a trial to the rest of the family, as, when his daughter found he had made a nest for some young game-cocks in her trunk of party dresses which was stored in the attic.

He was unique in everything. When Professor Aytoun went to him to ask the hand of his daughter, Wilson scribbled on a bit of paper, " With compliments of the author," and, pinning this to the sleeve of the blushing girl, led her to her happy lover.

But death, relentless, inevitable, took the idolized wife suddenly, and the blow almost deprived Wilson of reason for a time, and his sorrow was lifelong. When he first met his class after her loss, he was to decide on the merits of various essays which had been sent in on competition for a prize. He bowed low, and, in as firm voice as he could command, apologized for not having examined the essays. "For," said he, "gentlemen, I could not see to read them in the darkness of the shadow of the valley of death." As he spoke, the tears rolled down his cheeks. He said no more, but waved his hand to his class, who stood up as he concluded and hurried out of the lecture room.

Years after, when lecturing on Memory, he described the way in which a long-widowed husband would look back on happier days. His warm eloquence held his audience enchained. At last, overpowered by his emotions, the old man stopped in mid career, and buried his head in his arms on the desk before him. For a minute, there was perfect stillness, but when Wilson again raised his head, and two big tears were seen rolling down his cheeks as he tried to go on, his voice was drowned in the loud cheers of the students.

And if ever there was a woman worthy to be sorrowed for through a lonely life, it was she. So opposite to the dazzling, impetuous spirit of her mate, in her beautiful gentleness and equanimity, and adapting herself so entirely to his tastes.

This trial brought his spiritual nature into fuller action, and the tone of his writings was noticeably higher, his rough ways softened to a marked degree.

His kindness to his grandchildren was beautiful. The very strength of his hand softened to gently caress the little child on his knee or clinging to his feet. A party in grandpa's room was such a treat. He would set the table with all sorts of goodies, then act as waiter and be ordered about in the most irreverent fashion. The greatest men have ever been the most simple in their home life, and Wilson did not think it beneath his dignity to play with Noah's ark, dolls, trumpets, and puzzles, to amuse the little folks, even going up stairs to the nursery for a forgotten toy, or coming down stairs with his daughter's baby clutched by the back of her long robe, very much as a cat carries a kitten.

Many daughters, from Fanny Burney, Lady Holland, Mary Dewey, Mrs. Lloyd, to Miss Bushnell, have been their father's biographers, a difficult task. Although we may not gain so just an idea of the character, who else could give the charming home pictures, the inner life, the little ways and daily habits that make one acquainted with the man. Mrs. Gordon says: "I would not, as a matter of taste, introduce an ordinary toilette to the attention of the reader, but with the professor this business was so like himself, so original, that it will amuse rather than offend. By fits and starts, the process of shaving was carried on — walking out of his dressing-room into the study, lathering his chin one moment, then standing the next to take a look at some fragment of a lecture, which would absorb his attention,

until the fact of being without a coat and having his
face covered with soap was entirely forgotten, then
his waistcoat was put on ; after that, perhaps, he had
a hunt among old letters and papers for the lecture
now lost which a minute before he had in his hand.
His watch was a great joke. In the first place he
seldom wore his own, which never by any chance
was right, or treated according to the natural properties of a watch. Many wonderful escapes this ornament had from fire, water, and sudden death. He
says : " We wound up our chronometer irregularly,
by fits and starts, thrice a day, perhaps, or once a
week, till it fell into an intermittent fever, grew
delirious, and gave up the ghost." He had a curious
way of mislaying things, even that broad-brimmed
hat of his sometimes went a missing, his snuff-box,
his gloves, his pocket-handkerchief, everything,
just at the moment he wished to be off to his class,
became invisible."

It is pleasant to record a pension of 300 pounds
from the Queen and a reconciliation with Jeffrey.
Wilson was quick-tempered, but never malignant,
and his character was beautifully softened by the
hand of time. The last years I do not like to dwell
upon — when the massive frame drooped sadly, and
the magnificent mind was clouded, and books were
opened only to be closed, their meaning gone for
him. The yellow locks were tinged with gray ;
" the old man of the lion heart and scepter crutch "
was fast passing away. In second childhood he went

back with the old delight of angling. For my last
picture see him propped up in bed absorbed with
the relics of a youthful passion. Taking out each
elegantly dressed fly from its little bunch, drawing
it with trembling hand along the white coverlet,
then replacing it in his pocketbook, he would tell of
the streams he used to haunt.

Paraylsis came in the spring of 1853, a blessed
release, and on Sunday, at midnight, his heart was
still. Writing of his dying hour years before, he said:
" May that hour find me in my weeping home, 'mid
the blest stillness of a Sabbath day; may none I
deeply love be then away."

An answered prayer. And if our dear ones can
return to guide us to the new life, his wife, I am
sure, was very near him, though unseen. Wilson
loved America, and wanted to visit us. After our
famous men, he desired to see Niagara; not unlike
Niagara himself. And how *he* could have described
it.

Some wise heads mourn that Wilson did not concentrate his genius, distinguish himself in one direction. He might have been the greatest preacher of
the age, or the greatest actor of the day, or a powerful parliamentary orator, or a marvelous dramatist.
He had powers that might make him in literature
the very first man of his generation. Masson compares him to a Goth, much of whose powers went to
waste, for want of stringent self-regulation.

Yes; but can you harness the lightning that

flashes in zigzag splendor on a summer night? Brilliant, fitful, fascinating, Wilson had to be himself, and those who know him best find no cause to grieve.

It is noticeable that in estimating or describing Wilson, there is a natural cumulation of epithets, and more compound words and compound adjectives coined for the occasion have been applied to him than any other character in literature.

Maginn, a witty but dissipated Irish genius of that time, gives this off-hand picture: " A corker, a racer, a six-bottler, a twenty-four tumblerer, an out-and-outer, a true, upright, knocking-down, poetical, prosaic, moral, professional, good-looking, honorable, straight-forward tory; a gipsy, a magician, a wit, a six-foot club man, an unflinching ultra in the worst of times. In what was he not great"? And irresistibly carried along, I exclaim: " Dreamer, doer, poet, philosopher, simple child, wisest patriarch," hospitable friend, husband-lover, doting father, boisterous wit, rollicking humorist, master of pathos, practical joker, sincere mourner, such was the man Christopher North. A Hercules Apollo, strong and immortally beautiful, whom, with all his faults and foibles, we stop to admire and stay to love.

THE OLD MIRACLE PLAYS.

This essay on the "Old Miracle Plays" was prepared for my New York friends when Salmi Morse was threatening to bring out a "Passion Play" in that city. As few have the time to look up the history of these plays from the beginning, the result of my researches may still be interesting. Remember that what seems to us irreverent was once true worship.

In the year 1633, when the village of Oberammergau was visited by a devastating plague, the Monks of Ettal induced the parish to make a vow "That in thankful devotion and for edifying contemplation, they would every ten years publicly represent the Passion of Jesus the Saviour of the World." Whereupon the parish was immediately freed from the pestilence.

We are all familiar with the "Passion Play," as represented with simplicity and reverence by these Bavarian peasants. We have had lectures and letters, stereopticon views, vivid word pictures from friends who have witnessed it, and books giving the entire performance, enriched with photographs of the actors, are familiar to many.

It is an entirely different matter to propose to reproduce with an entirely different motive this remnant of the middle ages in a modern theater. It would then become a blasphemous mummery — a spectacular sacrilege — a sin akin to that of Judas, and the clergy, the press, and the voice of the people forbade it. Studying the subject, I found an immense amount of material. In the Boston public library alone, there are 132 volumes on the " Miracle Plays " in various languages.

We might start with Thespis and his portable stage, 535 B. C. or at a still earlier date, but I do not intend to ransack Greece and Rome for a history of the drama, or discuss the vexed questions of the necessity for scenic representations in every age and race. We see children perpetually acting in their plays and the childhood of nations is like that of individuals. There always has been and always will be a longing for theatrical excitement ; we may say it is dangerous, wicked, must be put down ! People will still flock to a good comedy, will still take real pleasure in most heart-rending tragedies.

In country villages and hamlets, the good wives find food for this natural appetite in the woes of their neighbors. Romance and tragedy are as busy in the farmhouse as the palace, and these stories of sentiment and sorrow are made common property and satisfy the eager craving for excitement. Now and then a hopeful clergyman, or an enthusiastic but inexperienced playwright, or a woman ignorant of what she is talking about, and (for that reason talking all the louder) will say that the pulpit and theater must go hand in hand, and dream of not exactly combining, but running them on a double track. You can easily see how it *might* be done, if ministers would only study the actor's art of impressing and holding an audience (throwing in a few timely lessons in elocution), and the actors — etc., etc., but it will never be done.

Curious fact, that the drama started in the church, *religion*, in all countries, first excited dramatic representations; the acts are closely connected ; all blood relations — they began in worship. Family quarrels are invariably the most violent, which perhaps accounts for a part of the hostility between priests and actors.

Let me give here a bit from Monsieur Coguelius' book on " Actors and their Art."

" In the church the theater was born with mysteries and miracle plays, and our brothers of the ' Passion Play ' are the direct ancestors of the Theatre Francais.

" In those days, church and theater fraternized. The scenic directions prove it, heaven above with its different divisions parted off in true hierarchic order, and the awful gulf of hell yawning below.

" How does it happen that the church, so maternally inclined towards mysteries and miracle plays, has picked so bitter a quarrel with us since ?

" Actors have been canonized by the church ; the church refused to bury Moliere in consecrated ground. Now the church consents to bury us, perhaps with *pleasure.*"

Lecky, in his History of Rationalism, says that " Every one who considers the world as it really exists and not as it appears in the writings of ascetics or sentimentalists, must have convinced himself that in great towns where multitudes of men of all classes and characters are massed together, and where there are innumerable strangers separated from all domestic ties and occupations, public amusements of an exciting order are absolutely necessary," and refers to the drama as of immense importance in the intellectual history of mankind, one of the most conspicuous signs of a rising civilization, combining the three great influences of eloquence, poetry, and of painting, the seed-plot of poetry and romance.

" The church adopted the drama as her handmaid. Demanding that men should dispense with and despise the pleasures of the world, she must herself minister to the natural demands of humanity and provide attractions in her own domain."

The church (says Van Laun in his " History of French Literature ") was, in fact, the *club* of the middle ages, always open, peaceful, cheerful, and usually entertaining.

The majority of the people did not understand the language of prayer and hymn, their hearts must be reached through the bodily senses.

The first Christian drama was a *gesture*. It was by a succession of gestures that the priests illustrated and interpreted their dead-letter of devotion. On Ascension days a priest stood in his surplice on the outer gallery of the Notre Dame, and with outstretched arms represented the assumption of Christ into Heaven. On the feast of Pentecost a dove figured the presence of the Holy Ghost, whilst tongues of fire descended from the roof of the church. At Easter, three men dressed in white robes, with hoods on their heads, a silver flask of consecrated oil in their hands, interpreted the story of the three Marys proceeding to the sepulchre, whilst a fourth, in the form of an angel, announced to them the resurrection of the Lord. At Christmas, the infant Jesus was shown in his manger, the youngest choristers playing the parts of angels from the galleries.

Little by little, by gradual growth, came rich costumes, stage properties, till we see the full-fledged ecclesiastical drama, acted in church and at the church doors.

" The Mystery of Adam," the work of a priest in the 12th century, was one of the first to be played at the church porch. The scene opens showing the Saviour in an embroidered dalmatic; Adam, standing before him dressed in a red tunic, attentive to his commands; Eve, with bowed head, dressed in a long white robe, with a veil of spotless silk; Satan, in serpent's garb, crawled about the stage, and up the trunk of the forbidden tree. After our first parents' had been expelled from Paradise, Satan busies himself with sowing thistles and briers. When the dejected couple return and see the teasing work of their enemy they express their despair by rolling on the ground.

In another play, a German mystery, Cain and Abel are brought before the Lord by Adam to be examined as to their proficiency in the Lord's prayer. Abel, prompted by the Saviour, gets through respectably, but Cain, instigated by the devil, says the prayer backwards, and is flogged, after having received a severe cuff from his father, for not taking his hat off!

From the earliest times men have been accustomed to throw into dramatic forms the objects of their belief, and the pagan mysteries, which were essentially dramatic, retained their authority over the popular mind long after every other portion of the ancient worship was despised.

The first Biblical play on record is on Moses, and is the composition of a Jew named Ezekiel, who lived in the 2d century. They were written in Latin until the latter part of the 13th century, and were usually acted by priests in the churches. As they grew more popular they brought religion into disrepute by their indecency and irreverence. But in this form they prepared the way for the Reformation.

The first recorded development of the Miracle play was in France in the 11th century, but soon all German and Latin nations shared the same impulse.

At first, undertaken by the priests to instruct the people, but afterwards the people themselves took all but the most important parts.

Called "miracle" plays because they represented the miracles or narrated some wonder of the Christian faith, or any story in Scripture or the Apocrypha. Sometimes a whole town undertook a play, then a solemn trumpet-call summoned those who wished to join for the honor of Christ or the good of their souls. Each swore on pain of death to carefully study their role and not fail to appear. No entrance money was paid, but expenses made up by voluntary gifts.

Sometimes the performance was carried on from Creation to the Judgment and lasted for several days, one even twenty-five days, in the open air and fair weather.

But the miracle plays required a stage of three stories. The topmost Paradise, of course. In that were the Trinity, the saints, and angels.

It was carefully adorned with tapestry and shaded by green trees, which appeared to blossom and emit sweet odors.

Below was Hell. The opening and shutting of the mouth of an enormous dragon represented the jaws of Hell, or the dragon was painted on linen, with great open jaws, opened and shut by men, and a light behind to give the effect of flames, and one of the stage directors of long ago remarked that when the devil has carried off a soul, there shall be a great noise made with pans and kettles, so that it shall be heard without, also a great smoke shall be made.

In Germany, Paradise was generally at one end of the stage, slightly raised, while the devil had only a large cask, in and out of which he could spring, while another served as the mountain of the Temptation.

All the players came on the stage at once; even the ass and the cock which crowed for Peter had their places. Each actor was supposed to be invisible till he received his cue and stood forth. Each when he first appeared must state what he represented, and as the art of shifting scenes was unknown, a notice in large letters indicated here a hill and there a grove, etc.

The dress, at first the ordinary priest's gown, became fantastic to suit the people. The condemned souls were supposed to wear no clothes, but sometimes compromised or indicated the fact by wearing tight-fitting shirts.

The stage tricks were of the simplest order. In one play Judas was to be hanged in due form by Beelzebub.

"The devil must take care of the fastening and sit behind on the bar of the gallows. Judas was to carry concealed in his coat a blackbird and the entrails of some animal, so that when his coat was torn the effect should be impressive. Then both slid down to the lower regions on a slanted rope."

The miracle play was very seriously regarded by the actors as well as by the spectators. It was the custom before commencing that the whole troupe

kneeling on the stage should sing the hymn, " Veni
Creator Spiritus," either in Latin or their own language, and close with a Te Deum.

In France, as well as in Italy, it was on the
boards of private theatres that the first glimmering
of the drama appears. Voltaire, with an unusual fit
of charity, vindicated the scriptural dramas of this
early period from the charges of absurdity brought
against them, assuring us they were performed with
a solemnity not unworthy of their sacred subjects.

The priests became jealous of their showy competitors. Many of these miracle plays perished with
their age, many were burned in the monasteries
destroyed by Henry VIII, some remain amid the
dust of old libraries. Horace Walpole had a rare
collection at Strawberry Hill.

In Longland's Piers Ploughman's Crede, about
the middle of 14th century, we find two lines from a
friar :

> " We haunt no taverns, nor hobble about,
>   At markets and miracles we meddle us never."

Chaucer has many allusions to these religious
dramas, and he speaks of the wife of Bath amusing
herself with these fashionable diversions while her
husband is absent in London during Lent.

> " Therefore made I my visitations
>   To vigils and to processions,
>   To preachings eke, and to these pilgrimages,
>   To plays of miracles and to marriages,
>   And wore my gay scarlet giles."

As in Greek worship, we find mysterious awe and daring jest closely connected. Sharply defined contrasts were enjoyed by the people and the comic by-play, absolutely necessary during several days of solemn representation, took nothing from their devout spirit.

Much that we find objectionable is only a mode of expression to which we are not accustomed. A mediæval *naïvetté* or uncouthness which meant nothing wrong. So the devil at first a frightful being became at length a comic personage in satyr-like masquerade, and his associate, Vice, was a witty fool, behaving almost exactly like our clown of the modern circus.

As the excruciating hand-organ is all that is left as a type of minstrelsy, Harlequin and Punch and Judy are supposed to have had this origin.

The devil was usually represented with horns, a very wide mouth (by means of a mask), staring eyes, a large nose, a red beard, cloven feet, a tail, and furnished with a stout club. His appearance and manner excited both awe and mirth, which Hudson gives as the germs of tragedy and comedy. Sometimes he had a protean versatility of mind and person, so that he could walk abroad as "plain devil," scaring all he met, or steal into society as a prudent counselor, an Iago-like friend, a dashing beau, or whatever was best for his purpose.

No play now is complete unless the devil makes his entrée in the guise of a rough or a gentlemanly villain, or a snaky, seductive woman. Vice was a comic fool, full of mad pranks and saucy jokes. And we are all pretty much like Gossip Tattle's spouse in Ben Jonson's "Staple of News," who says, "My husband, Timothy Tattle, rest his poor soul, was wont to say there was no play without a fool and a devil in't; he was for the devil still, bless him! The devil for *his* money, he would say; I would fain see the devil."

Vice was a droll character accoutered with a long coat, a cap, a pair of ass's ears, and a dagger of lath. This buffoon used to make fun with the devil, and he had several trite expressions as, "I'll be with you in a trice," "Ah hah, boy, are you there?" And this was a great entertainment to the audience to see their old enemy so belabored in effigy. He was the devil's "vice" or prime minister, and this is what made him so saucy.

Of all the persons who figured in the miracle plays, Herod, the Slayer of the Innocents, was the greatest favorite. We hear of him from Chaucer, who says of the Parish clerk, Absalom:

> "Sometime, to show his lightness and maistrie,
> He plaieth Herode on a scaffold hie."

He was always represented as an immense swearer and braggart and swaggerer, ranting and raving up and down the stage, with furious bombast and profanity. In one of the Chester series he says:

> "For I am king of all mankind:
> I bid, I beat, I loose, I bind:

> I master the moon ! Take this in mind,
> That I am most of might,
> I am the greatest above degree,
> That is, that was, or ever shall be ;
> The sun it dare not shine on me,
> An I bid him go down."

And in one of the Coventry series:

> " Of beauty and of boldness I bear evermore the bell ;
>   Of main and of might, I master every man ;
>   I ding with my doughtiness the devil down to Hell ;
>   For both of heaven and of earth, I am king, certain."

Termagant, the supposed god of the Saracens, was another staple character in the miracle plays, also a great boaster, quarreller, killer, tamer of the universe, child of the earthquake, and the brother of death. That Shakespeare had suffered, as Hudson says, "under the monstrous din of these strutting and bellowing stage-thumpers is shown by Hamlet's remonstrance with the players :

> " O it offends me to the soul, to hear a robustious, periwig-pated fellow tear a passion to rags, to very tatters, to split the ears of the groundlings : I would have such a fellow whipped for o'erdoing Termagant ; it out-Herods Herod : pray you — avoid it."

We also find material for the rest of his speech, as the players were instructed to speak with dignity and appropriate gestures — neither to cut off or add a syllable, and to pronounce in a distinct manner.

Regarded from an artistic point of view, the English Miracle plays are the best, have greater anima-

13

tion and skill in action, essentially epic, and they give a good idea of the manners, customs, and degree of progress of the English at that time. And, as prayers were in an unknown tongue, sermons few, and printing uninvented, they furnished almost all the religious knowledge. They are divided into the Chester, Coventry, York, and Townely series, named from the towns where they originated. The mayor of York decreed that the solemn play of Corpus Christi should be played every year, that the procession should appear on the day of said feast, so that people being in the said city might have leisure to attend devoutly the matins, vespers, and other hours of the said feast. And that men of crafts and all other men that find torches come forth in array. This festival of Corpus Christi was instituted by Pope Urban IV, to support the doctrine of transub-stantiation. Here is a portion of the order of the pageants of the play of Corpus Christi :

Tanners. God the Father Almighty creating and forming the heavens, angels, and archangels, Lucifer, and the angels that fell with him into Hell.

Carde Makers. God the Father creating Adam of the slime of the earth, and making Eve of the rib, and inspiring them with the spirit of life.

Shipwrights. God foretelling Noah to make an ark of light wood.

The Chester plays consist of twenty-four dramas, and annually performed till 1577, each trade taking one theme, as,

The Deluge, by the Dyers.

Shepherds feeding their flocks by night.

Painters and Glaciers.

The Temptation, by the Butchers.

The Last Supper, by the Bakers.

The Descent into Hell, by the Cooks.

The Resurrection, by the Skinners.

The Ascension, by the Tailors.

Ezekiel, by the Clothiers.

Henry V was seen there with his retinue.   Queen Margaret came from Kilyngworth.

Fyshmongers and Mariners.   Noah in the ark with his wife and three children, and divers animals.

Bukbynders.   Abraham sacrificing his son Isaac, a ram, bush, and angel. . . . .

Lance Makers.   Judas hanging himself.

Weavers of Woolen.   Mary ascending with a multitude of angels.   Eight Apostles with Thomas preaching in the desert.

The accounts of the various guilds contain entries of sums paid for machinery, dresses, etc., throwing light on the way in which these pageants were represented: " Herod's crest of iron, faulchion for Herod, 2 spears ; a staff for the demon, God's coat of white leather, 6 skins; 2 mitres for Cayphas and Annas; 4 gowns and 4 swords for the tormentors ; poleage for Pilate's son."

In the expenses for 1490, verbatim, we find that even the spirit of God was sometimes represented on the stage in human figure, although usually depicted as a dove:

Item paide to the sprytt of God, xvi d.

   "   "   "   angelles, viii d.

   "   "   "   demon, xvi d.

pd to Fawston for hanging Judas, iiizd.

                  coc. croyng, iiizd.

Item for mendynge the develles cote.

To a peynter for peyntyng Herod's face.

New coats for the souls.

To black souls and white souls.

These pure and sinful souls were distinguished by black and white coats. How the "womes of conscience" played their parts I have failed to discover. Hell's mouth needed frequent repairs, and, on one occasion, mention is made of expenses consequent on the conflagration of hell itself. Some of the entries are droll enough, as

"Paid for mending the wind, ix d." The winds appear to have been worked by ropes.

"Paid for a new rope for the wind, 16 d."

We see again

"Paid for 15 pairs of angels' wings."

And

"Item paid for mending hell-mouth, and for keeping of fire at hell-mouth."

And in 1558

"Payd for setting the world of fire, v d.

"Item, a hat for Pilate."

"For mending the devil's head."

Suits were occasionally borrowed, as we learn:

" Item to reward Mistress Grymesby for lending of her gear for Pilates wife, 12 d."

From a few stage directions scattered here and there through the manuscripts of the mysteries now extant, it would appear that the stage machinery by which a part of the effect was produced, must have been elaborate, both ingenious and expensive. The collective paraphernalia of acting, the stage, actors, and stage machinery were called a pageant. The players received liberal wages; handsome young men took the part of women. Independent of a liberal allowance of food they consumed almost incredible quantities of beer at rehearsals, at intervals in performances, and every corner on the street where the pageant happened to stop.

Each guild had its own pageant, and performed its own play at its own expense. For instance, " The Hall of Lucifer," was always performed by tanners. Their stage, on a large wagon, was drawn early in the morning in front of the gates of the Abbey, then wheeled to the High Cross in front of the mayor's house, and so through the different streets. The wagons of the various guilds separated at the appointed places of exhibition, and every company or trade repeated its own play at all the important stations, so that the populace could see the grand display. These were performed at Easter, Whitsuntide, or Christmas.

These plays sometimes lasted eight days, and were announced some time before by a herald in what was called "The Proemium" or prologue, giving to each guild their task with earnest appeals to each to do their best, with "good speech, fine players, and apparel comely," ending:

> " A Sunday next, if that we may,
>   At VI of the belle, we gynne our play
>   In Noman town wherefore we pray
>   That God now be your spede.   AMEN."

THE PROEMIUM.

Reverende lordes and ladyes all,
That at this tyme here assembled bec,
By this messeinge understande you shall,
That some tymes there was mayor of this citie
Sir John Amvay, Knighte, who moste worthelye
Contented hymselfe to sett out in playe
The devise of one Dove Rondall, moonke of Chester Abbey.

This moonke, moonke-like in Scriptures well seen,
In storyes travelled with the beste sorte,
In pagentes set fourth apparently to all eyne,
The olde and newe Testament, with livelye comforth,
Interminglinge therewith, onely to make sporte,
Some thinges, not warranted by any weilt,
Which to gladd the hearers he woulde me'n to take yt.

This matter he abbrevited with playes twenty-four,
And every playe of the matter gave but a taste,
Leavinge for better learninge the scircumstance to accomplishe.
For all his proceedings maye appear to be in hasti,
Yet altogether unprofitable his labor he did not wasti,
For at this daye and ever he deserveth the fame
Which all monkes deserves, professinge that name.

This worthy Knighti Amvay, then mayor of this citie,
This order toke, as declare to you I shall,
That by twentye-four occupations, artes, craftes, or misterie
These pagentes shoulde be played, after breef rehearsall.
For every pagente, a cariage to be provyded withall ;
In which sorte, we porpose, this Whitsontyde,
Our pageantes into three partes to divide.

Nowe, you worshippfull tanners that of custome olde
The fall of Lucifer did set out,
Some writers awarrante your matter theirfore be boulde,
Ersletye to play the same to all the vorowtte.
                                    Your shew-let-bee
Good speech, fyne players, with appariell comelye,

Of the drapers you the wealthy companye
The creation of the worlde.   Adam and Eve,
According to your wealth, set out wealthilye
And howe Cayne his brother Abell, his life did bereave.

  . . . .

The good, symple water leaders and drawers of Dee
See that your ark in all poyntes be prepared ;
Of Noe and his children the wholl storye
And of the universall floude, by you shall be played.

  . . . .

Cappers and lynnen drapers, see that you forth bring,
In well decked order, that worthy storie,
Of Balaam and his asse, and of Balaak the king
Make the asse to speak and sett yt out livelye.

The sacred dramas at Coventry drew immense
multitudes, and the exhibitions were patronized by
royalty.

Henry V was seen there with his retinue.
Queen Margaret came from Killingworth, having

with her lords and ladies. Richard III honored the Corpus Christi plays, also Henry VII. Before the suppression of the monasteries, the Grey Friars of Coventry were celebrated for their exhibitions on Corpus Christi day, their pageants being acted with mighty state and reverence in theaters placed on wheels and drawn to all the important streets of the city.

Queen Elizabeth was particularly fond of pageants of all kinds and was often entertained by miracle plays.

Carew, a writer of her time, said that for representing the Scripture history they raised an amphitheater in some open field, with a diameter of 50 feet. The country people flock from all sides many miles off, to see and hear it; for they have therein devils and devices to delight the eye as the ear.

Yet all was not splendor and amusement in the lives of the mystery-players. The profession of an actor, even in those days, was a laborious one. The great parts, those that were the most ardently sought after, imposed a degree of toil and fatigue on those who accepted them whereof few men would be capable to-day. For instance, Christ, in certain of the passion plays had over 4,000 lines to recite, and the crucifixion on the stage, as was remarked, lasted as long as in the reality. The actor, suspended to the cross in a state of almost total nudity, recited in that situation some 300 or 400 lines. In 1437 the curé, Nicolle, while impersonating the

Saviour in a passion play, came near dying on the cross in good earnest, from sheer fatigue and exhaustion. In the same play the representative of Judas hung himself in such a realistic fashion that he became insensible, and was nearly dead when taken down, so that his fellow-actors were forced to "carry him into a neighboring spot, there to rub him with vinegar and other restoratives." Sometimes the parts, when of great length, were played by three or four actors each, and this was especially the case when the personage to be represented was shown at different stages of his or her career. Thus, three actors were often charged with the rôle of the Holy Virgin, one impersonating her as a child, another as a young girl, and the third as a woman of mature age.

The last miracle play represented in England was that of "Christ's Passion," in the reign of James 1st, on Good Friday, at night, at which there were thousands present.

The people of the Middle Ages from the very fact that their existence was more monotonous than that of the people of the present day, were all the more ready to seize an opportunity for amusement, and the solemn representations of the mysteries were among their most cherished enjoyments. The entrance of the king or queen into a town, the birth of a prince or princess, the court festivals, as well as the ecclesiastical solemnities, and the feasts of the church, were an excuse for these popular spectacles.

The representations, prepared a long time before-hand, were announced by the public crier, like the royal and municipal decrees, at the most frequented places of the town. The spectators, who did not have to pay anything for witnessing the play. did not seat themselves promiscuously, but each person according to his rank and station. The nobles or dignitaries occupied platforms, upon which, as the representations lasted a long time, they sometimes had their meals served, like the old Romans, upon the balconies of the amphitheater or circus. The lower classes occupied places. either seated or standing, upon the bare earth or the pavement, as the case might be, the men being to the right and the women to the left, the same as in church. The local clergy, in order to let their congregations have an opportunity of witnessing the whole spectacle, advanced or put back the hour of service. In fact. the fondness of the public for these spectacles was so great that the houses were left almost deserted. and armed watchmen paced the silent streets to protect the property of the inhabitants, while the represent-ation was taking place. No permanent theaters at that time.

Geo. McDonald finds a good deal of poetic worth scattered through these plays. and quotes a scene from the " Fall of Man."

Here are parts of Eve's lamentation when con-scious of the death that has laid hold upon her :

> " Alas that ever that speech was spoken
> That the false angel said unto me !
> Alas ! our maker's bidding is broken,
> For I have touched his own dear tree.
> Our fleshly eyes are all unlokyn,
> Naked for sin ourself we see ;
> That sorry apple that we have tokyn,
> To death hath brought my spouse and me."

When the voice of God is heard saying :

> " Adam, that with my hands I made,
> Where art thou now ?   What hast thou wrought ?"

Adam replies in two lines, containing the whole truth of man's spiritual condition ever since :

> " Ah Lord ! for sin our flowers do fade ;
> I hear thy voice, but I see thee nought."

Notice the quaint simplicity of the words of God to the woman :

> " Unwise woman, say me why
> That thou hast done this foul folly,
> And I made thee a great lady
> In Paradise for to play ?"

Eve laments bitterly, and at length offers her throat to her husband, praying him to strangle her :

> " Now stumble we on stalk and stone ;
> My wit away from me has gone ; .
> Writhe on to my neck-bone
> With hardness of thine hand."

Adam replies :

> " Wife, thy wit is not worth a rush ! "

The scene ends with these words from Eve:

> " Alas that ever we wrought this sin !
> Our bodily sustenance for to win,
> Ye must delve and I shall spin,
> In care to lead our life."

In the " Woman Taken in Sin " there is a remarkable tradition that each of the woman's accusers, Scribes and Pharisees, thought Jesus was writing his individual sins on the ground.

The Accuser—

> " Alas for sorrow mine heart doth bleed,
> All my sins yon man did write ;
> If that my fellows to them took heed,
> I cannot me from death acquite,
> I would I were hid somewhere out of sight,
> That men I should me nowhere see nor know,
> If I be taken I am aflyght,
> In mekyl shame I shall be throne."

Two volumes of the ancient Cornish drama exist, in Celtic dialect, once spoken in Cornwall, and of greater merit than all the other remains of the language taken together; its antiquity is its chief value.

Subjects, as usual :

The Beginning of the World.

Passion of Our Lord.

Resurrection.

Then God the Father shall go to heaven, and afterwards the devil, like a serpent, speaks to Eve in the tree of knowledge, and he says wickedly to Eve:

Eve, why dost thou not come near?
To speak with me and talk?
One thing which I know if thou knewest it,
It would amuse thee,
Forever thou wouldst laugh
      For joy and for mirth.
As thou camest into the world,
To heaven thou wouldst ascend.

Eve.

What thing can that be
Tell me directly.

Devi .

From heaven I come now,
Sweet Eve, to better thy condition.
The fruit of the tree of knowledge,
Eat, never make a difficulty.

Eve.

I am outside (puzzled) thinking
What I may do
As to plucking the apple
For fear of being deceived by thee.

At last she gathers the apple and carries it to
Adam, saying:

Adam, reach me thy hand:
Take that from me,
Quietly without blowing thy horn,
Eat it immediately.

Adam.

Speak to me, thou woman,
Where didst thou gather the fruit?
Was it of that same sort
Which was forbidden to us?

Eve.

When I was walking about
I heard on one side
An angel beginning to sing
Above me on the tree,
He did advise me
That I should gather fruit from it ;
Greater than God we should be,
Nor be troubled forever.

Adam.

Oh ! out upon thee, wicked woman.
That thou listenedst to him,
For he was an evil bird
Whom thou didst hear singing.
And will bring us to sorrow
Unless we do refrain.
Let every one think on the end of it
How it can end.

Eve.

Since thou wilt not believe,
Thou shalt lose my love
Ever whilst thou livest,
Here thou shalt not see me again.

Eve, rather than thou be angry,
I will do all as thou wishest,
Bring it to me immediately
And I will eat it.

Madam D. Arblay has an interesting account of
an interview with an entertaining Mr. Bryant, who,
after giving two or three amusing anecdotes such as
the comic slip-slops of the first Lord Baltimore who

said, "I have been upon a little excoriation to see a ship lanced, and there is not a finer going vessel upon the face of God's yearth ; you've no idiom how well it sailed," spoke next of the mysteries or origin of our theatrical entertainments, and repeated the plan and conduct of several of those strange compositions, in particular one he remembered which was called "Noah's Ark," and in which that patriarch and his sons, just previous to the deluge, made it all their delight to speed themselves into the ark *without* Mrs. Noah, whom they wished to escape ; but she surprised them just as they had embarked, and made so prodigious a racket against the door that after a long and violent contention she forced them to open it, and gained admission, having first contented them by being kept out till she was thoroughly wet to the skin. These most eccentric and unaccountable dramas filled up the chief of our conversation, and whether to consider them most with laughter, as ridiculous, or with horror, as blasphemous, remains a doubt I cannot well solve.

Noah is the type of a henpecked husband, and his wife of a loud-voiced shrew, in all the plays I have seen.

A CHESTER PLAY.

THE DELUGE.

Manne that I made, I will destroy ;
Beast, worme, and foule to flie,
For on earth they doe me noye
The folke yt is thereon.

For it harmes me so hartfullie
  The malyce now that can multiply,
That sore me greves, inwardlie,
  That ever I made manne.

Therefore, Noe, my servant free,
  That righteous man art, as I see,
A shipp sone thou shalt make the
  Of trees drye and light.

Destroyed all the world shall be
  Save thou, thy wife, thy sonnes three ;
And all their wives, also with the,
  Shall saved be for thy sake.

Noe.

Ah, Lord ! I thank the lowd and still,
That to me art in such will ;
And spares me and my house to spill,
  As now I and othlie find.
Thy bydding, Lord, I shall fulfill,
And never more the greeve, ne grill,
That suche grace has sent me till
  Among all mankinde.

Have done you men and women all ;
Helpe, for ought that may befall,
To worke this shipp, chamber and hall,
As God hath bydden us doe.

Sem.

Father, I am already bowne,
Anne axe I have, by my crowne,
As sharpe as any in all this towne,
For to goe thereto.

Ham.

I have a hatchet wonder kene,
To byte well, as may be seene
A better grounder, as I wene,
Is not in all this towne.

Japhet.

And I can well make a pyn,
And with this hammer knocke it in ;
Goe and worche, without more dyme,
And I am ready bowne.

Wife of Noah.

And we shall bring timber, too,
For women nothing els doe ;
Women be weak to undergoe,
Any great travayle.

Each of the wives offered to assist ; Japhet's most practical of the four, cried :

" And I will gather shippes here,
To make a fire for you in feere,
And for to dight your dynner,
Against you come in."

Noe.

Now, in the name of God, I will begin
To make the shippe that we shall in,
That we be ready for to swym
At the coming of the floode.
These boards I joyne together,
To keep us safe from the wedder,
That we may rome both hither and thider,
And safe be from this floode.
Of this tree will I have the mast,
Tyde with gables that will last ;
With a sayle yarde for each blaste,
And each thing in the kinde.

But now comes trouble, for Noah's wife is disinclined to enter.   Noah says:

> " Wife, in this castle we shall be keped,
>   My childer and thou would in leaped."

She answers:

" In faith, Noah, I had as lief thou had slipped for all thy frankish
          fare.
  For I will not doe after thy red."

Noe.

Good wife, doe as I the bydd.

Noah's Wife.

By Christ, not; or I see more neede,
Though thou stand all the day and rave.

Noe.

Lord, that women be crabbed, aye !
And never are meke, that dare I saye.
This is well sene by me to daye,
In witness of you each one.
Good wife, let be all this beere
That thou makes in this place here
For all they wene thou art master ;
And so thou art, by St. John.

Then God gives His commands for filling the ark, and adds:

Forty days and forty nightes,
Rayne shall fall for their unrightes,
And that I have made through my mighte,
Now thinke I to destroy.

Noah.

Lord, at youre byddinge I am bayne
Sith none other grace will gayne.
Hel will I fulfil fayne,
For gracious I the fynde.
A hundred wynters and twenty
This shipp making tarried have I.
If, through amendment, any mercye
Wolde fall unto mankinde.
Have done, you men and women all ;
Hye you, lest this water fall,
That each beast were in his stall,
And into ship broughte.
Of clean beasts seaven shall be,
Of unclean, two, this God bade me.
This flood is nye well may we see,
Therefore tarry you nought.

Shem.

Sir, here are lions, leopards in,
Horses, mares, oxen, and swyne,
Goates, calves, sheepe, and kine,
Here sitten thou may see.

Ham.

Camels, asses, men may find,
Buck, doe, harte, and hind,
And beastes of all manner kinde,
Here been, as thinks me.

Japhet.

Take here cats and dogs, too,
Otter, fox, fulmart, also ;
Hares, hopping gaylie, can yee
Have cowle hae for to eate.

> *Noah's Wife.*
>
> And here are beares, wolfes sett,
> Apes, owles, marmoset ;
> Weesells, squirrels, and ferret,
> Here they eaten their meate.
>
> *Wife of Shem.*
>
> Yet more beasts are in this house,
> Here catles maken in full crowse ;
> Here a ratten, here a mouse,
> They stand nye together.
>
> *Wife of Ham.*
>
> And here are fowles less and more,
> Hearns, cranes, and bittour,
> Swans, peacocks, have them before
> Meate for this wedder.
>
> *Wife of Japhet.*
>
> Here are cocks, kites, crowes,
> Rookes, ravens, many rowes,
> Cuckoos, curlews, whoso knows
> Each one in his kinde.
> And here are doves, diggs, drakes,
> Redshankes, running through the lakes ;
> And each fowle that ledden makes,
> In this ship men may find.

In the stage directions, the sons of Noah are enjoined to mention aloud the names of the animals which enter, a representation of which, painted on parchment, is to be carried by the actors.

Noah then speaks :

> " Wife, come in, why standes thou there ?
> Thou art ever forward that dare, I swear ;
> Come on God's half, tyme that were,
> For feare lest that we drown."

Noah's Wife.

Yea, Sir, set up your sail,
And row forth with evil heale,
For, without any fayle,
I will not out of this towne.
But I have my gossips every one.
One foot further I will not gone.
They shall not drown, by St. John !
And I may save their life.
They loved me full well, by Christ !
But thou will let them in thy chist ;
Else row forth, Noah, whither thou list,
And get thee a new wife.

Noah.

Shem, some loe thy mother is wraw ;
Forsooth, such another I do not know !

Shem.

Father, I shall set her in, I trow,
Without any fayle.
Mother, my father after thee send,
And bids thee into yonder ship wend.
Look up and see the wind,
For we be ready to sail.

Noah's Wife.

Son, go again to him and say,
I will not come therein to-day.

Noah.

Come in, wife, in twenty devill's way,
Or else stand without.

Ham.

Shall we *all* fetch her in ?

Noah.

Yea, sons, in Christ's blessings and mine,
I would you hied you betime,
For of this flood I am in doubt.

Japhet.

Mother, we pray you altogether,
For we are here, your childer,
Come into the ship for feare of the wedder,
For his love that you bought.

Noah's Wife.

That will I not for your call,
But if I have my gossips all.

Gossip.

The flood comes in full fleeting fast,
On every side it breadeth in hast,
For fear of drowning I am agast.
Good gossip, let me come in !
Or let us drink, or we depart,
For often times we have done soe ;
For at a time thou drinke a quart,
And so will I or that I go.

Shem.

In faith, mother, yet you shall,
Whether you will or not ! (Then he carries her in.)

Noah.

Welcome, wife, into this boat.

Noah's Wife.

And have thou that for thy note ?
                (And gives him a slap in the face.)

Noah.

Ah, marry ! this is hot.

A modern writer gives the following account of a performance, called " The Creation of the World," at a theater in Lisbon. On our entrance we found the theater nearly filled with well-dressed people, the front row of boxes full of ladies most superbly and tastefully dressed, their hair in braids and ornamented with a profusion of diamonds and artificial flowers, without caps, and, upon the whole, making a very brilliant appearance. . . . When the curtain drew up we saw the Eternal Father descend in a cloud with a long, white beard, with a great number of lights and angels around him. He then gave orders for the creation of the world. Over his head was drawn an equilateral-triangle as an emblem of the Trinity. The next scene presented us with the serpent tempting Eve to eat the apple and his infernal majesty (the prince of darkness) paid the most exaggerated enconiums to her beauty, in order to engage her to eat, which as soon as he had done and persuaded Adam to do the same, there came a most terrible storm of thunder and lightning with a dance of infernal spirits with the devil in the midst, dressed in black with scarlet stockings, and a gold-laced hat on his head. While the dance was performing, a voice from behind the scenes pronounced in a hoarse and solemn manner, the word " Jesus," on which the devils immediately vanished in a cloud of smoke.

After this, the Eternal Father descended in great wrath, without any attendant, and called for

Noah (who, bye the bye, we were much surprised to
see as we did not know before that he was at that
time in existence; however, appear he did), who,
when he appeared, the Eternal Father told him he
was sorry he had created such a set of ungrateful
scoundrels, and that, for their wickedness, he intended
to drown them altogether. Here, Noah interceded for
them, and at last, it was agreed that he should build
an ark, and he was ordered to go to the king's dock-
yard in Lisbon, and there he would see John Gon-
zalvez, the master builder, for he preferred him to
either the French or English builders (this produced
great applause). The Eternal Father then went up
to Heaven, and Noah to build his ark.

It was from such a play as this (called Adam and
Eve) that Milton, when he was in Italy, is said to
have taken the first hint for his " Paradise Lost."

In the play of " The Creation," as seen in Germany about 1783, light was produced by a stupid
looking Capuchin in full bottomed wig, and a brocade
morning gown worn over his own rusty dress, who,
groping peevishly about in the dark, pushed the tapestry right and left, disclosing a glimmer through
linen cloths from candles placed behind them. The
sea was created by pouring water on the stage, and
the land by mould thrown on. Angels were per-
sonated by girls and young priests in masquerade
costumes, with the wings of geese clumsily fastened
to their shoulders. These nondescript angels (celes-
tial poultry), as Coleridge would call them, actively

assisted the character in the flowered dressing gown in producing the sun, moon, and stars.

To represent the brute creation, cattle were driven on the stage, with a horse (well shod), and two pigs, with rings in their noses. Adam and Eve were even more grotesque, and an ill-trained mastiff with a big brass collar, regaled himself upon the beef bone which had done duty as the extracted rib. And the narrator of all this says that there was no laughter among the audience, but it was entered into most seriously, with credulity and reverence.

As a marked improvement on these ancient performances, the theater of Strasburg in 1816 exhibited scenes from the life of Christ from the best pictures of the great masters. Not a word was spoken, but music of the highest order, instrumental and vocal, added greatly to the impressiveness of the representation. Dr. Burney says, it is certain that the modern tragedy is taken from the mysteries, and that the Oratorio is only a mystery or morality in music. The Oratorio commenced with the priests of the Oratory, a brotherhood at Rome in 1540, who set sacred stories to music to draw young people to church, and shrewdly left one-half to be performed *after* the sermon, so that they gained many listeners.

Collier tells us that a miracle play is still exhibited at Gloucestershire at Christmas, with the characters of Herod, Beelzebub, etc. Victor Hugo, in the " Hunchback of Notre Dame," furnishes a vivid study of the performance of a miracle play in the middle ages, when they had lost their hold on the people. It was an utter failure. Madame Calderon De La Barca, wife of the Mexican consul, gives in the second volume of her interesting story of " Two Years in Mexico " an account of a religious drama performed on Good Friday at Coyohnacan (Cuyacan), evidently an imitation of the old miracle plays. She says at the close there was no drunkenness or quarrelling or confusion of any sort. An occasional hymn rising in the silence of the air, or the distant flashing of a hundred lights, alone gave notice that the funeral procession of the Saviour had not yet halted for the night; but there was no noise, not even mirth. Everything was conducted with a sobriety befitting the event that was celebrated.

We were told an anecdote concerning Simon, the Cyrenian, which is not bad. A man was taken up in one of the villages as a vagrant and desired by the justices to give an account of himself — to explain why he was always wandering about, and had no employment. The man, with the greatest indignation replied, " No employment. I am substitute Cyrenian at Cuyacan in the Holy Week ! "

Her husband prepared a series of critical treatises on the religious dramas of Spain.

The Tyrolese entertain a passionate love for the mimic art. In that chatty book, " Gadding with a Primitive People," I find that they still have a yearly " Passion Play," on a small scale and in a way that seems horridly irreverent to us. A large store was made Jehovah's throne, a few years since, and some boys kindled a fire and drove the actor down. In South Germany, Tyrol was undoubtedly the cradle of the mystery and miracle plays.

One of the most telling traits illustrating the age of these plays, and which it is difficult to rhyme with the strict religious sense peculiar to these people, is the seemingly irreligious intermingling of the most commonplace events of every-day life with sacred episodes and saintly personages. Ere we harshly criticise this feature, we must remember that the native looks upon it in quite a different light than we should — as a part of his belief.

The people, simple-hearted and full of reverent faith in the Bible, delighted in seeing the personages they had heard about in the churches, whose words they had so often heard, whose images they had devoutly contemplated.

Protestantism wrested from Faith a large share of her working material, and had little favor for a light treatment of solemn subjects.

And in the 15th century the miracles and mysteries were condemned and left behind by the new secular culture, which only smiled at the artless effort to portray supernatural events. Thenceforward the stage, which has for its office to typify the *world*, has been erected far apart from the *church*.

Says Hudson, " We can hardly do justice either to the authors or to the audiences of these religious comedies, there being an almost impassable gulf fixed between their thoughts and ours. They were really quite innocent of the evils which we see and feel in what was so entertaining to them."

John Stuart Mill speaks of "the childlike character of the religious sentiment of a rude people, who know terror, but not awe, and are often on the most intimate terms of familiarity with the objects of their adoration."

Those exhibitions, so rude and revolting to modern taste and decorum, were full of religion and honest delectation to the simple minds who witnessed them, and without doubt they contained the germ of that splendid dramatic growth with which the literature and life of England are now adorned.

Yet some deny any connection between the modern drama and miracle plays.

There is a close similarity between the Persian and the mediæval miracle play. It is the same thing sprung in the same soil, for the Parsees are true Aryan builders, and a real drama always sprouts where you find indigenous, unconscious building of the first order, which the Persian buildings from Persepolis to Hatra are.

Matthew Arnold has written of the "Persian Passion Play," enacted annually even now, "far away in that wonderful East, from which whatever airs of superiority Europe may justly give itself, all our religion has come, and where religion of some sort or other has still an empire over men's feelings such as it has nowhere else."

Ali, the Lion of God, Mahomet's young cousin, the first person who, after his wife, believed in him was assassinated. His two sons, Hassan and Hussein, also suffered in the same way at Kerbela, a tragedy so familiar to every Mahomedan, and to us so little known.

"O death!" cries the minstrel of Persia, "whom didst thou spare? Were even Hassan and Hussein, those footstools of the throne of God on the seventh heaven, spared by thee? *No*, thou madest them martyrs at Kerbela."

Gibbon tells us that the tombs of Ali and his sons have their yearly pilgrims and their tribute of enthusiastic mourning, and they have been made the subject of a national drama. The first ten days of the month of Mohassen, the anniversary of the martyrdom at Keebela, are given up to this excitement. Kings and people, everyone, is in mourning, and at night when the plays are not going on, processions keep passing, the air resounds with the beating of breasts and of litanies of O Hassan, Hussein, the most devoted mourners slashing their faces and bodies with knives, staining their white garments with blood.

It seems as if no one went to bed, and certainly no one who went to bed could sleep. Confraternities go in procession, with a black flag and torches, every man with his shirt torn open, and beating himself with the right hand on left shoulder in measured cadence to a canticle in honor of the martys.

Noisiest of all are the Berbers. One of their race having derided the family of Hassan in their affliction, they now expiate their crime by beating themselves with chains and pricking their arms and cheeks with needles. So we are carried back, on this old Asiatic soil, where beliefs and usages are heaped layer upon layer and ruin upon ruin, far past these martyrs, past Mahomedanism, past Christianity, to the priests of Baal, gashing themselves with knives, and to the worship of Adonis. The theaters for this sacred drama are numerous and multiplying. Some hold 300, some several thousand persons. At Ispahan the representations bring together more than 20,000 people. A vast walled parallelogram with brick platform or stage in center, and this surrounded by black poles, joined at top by horizontal rods from which hang colored lamps. An immense awning protects the audience. Upon rows of gigantic masts are hung tiger and panther skins to indicate the violent character of the scenes to be represented, also shields of steel and of hippopotamus skin, and flags and naked swords. A sea of color and splendor meets the eye all round. Woodwork and brickwork disappear under cushions, rich carpets, silk hangings, India muslin embroidered with silver and gold, shawls from Kerman and from Cashmere; there are lamps, lusters of colored crystal, mirrors, Bohemian and Venetian glass, porcelain vases of all degrees of magnitude, from China and from Europe, paintings in profusion everywhere, an Arabian night scene.

But there is a marked contrast in the poverty of scenic contrivance and stage illusion. A copper basin of water represents the Euphrates ; a heap of chopped straw in a corner is the sand of the desert of Kerbela. No attempt at proper costume. The power of the actors is in their genuine sense of the seriousness of the business they are engaged in, nothing stilted, false, or conventional. The children who appear are from the principal families of their city.

"It is touching to see," says Count Gobineau, "these little things of three or four years old, dressed in black gauze frocks with large sleeves, and on their heads small round black caps, embroidered with silver and gold, kneeling beside the body of the actor, who represents the martyr, embracing him and with their little hands covering themselves with chopped straw, for sand, in sign of grief."

In the travels "Through Persia by Caravan" the author says : "Once I showed a sketch of Kerbela to our servants and to a knot of bystanders, telling them what it represented. Immediately the picture was in danger. All wished to kiss it, to press it to their foreheads, and cried, ' Ah Hassan ! ' with an expression of deep regret, more true and tender in the ardor of sincerity than one expects to find uttered over a grave which has been closed for twelve centuries."

Matthew Arnold gives an interesting explanation of this lasting enthusiasm for these saintly, gentle, self-denying sufferers, which puts into the arid religion of Mahomet something of the tenderness, emotion, and sympathy which the formal Old Testament conception of righteousness received from the life and deeds of Christ and his followers. Could he wish for any sign more convincing that Christ was indeed the desire of all nations? So necessary is what Christianity contains, that a powerful successful religion arises without, and the missing virtue forces its way in. The martyrs of Kerbela held aloft to the eyes of millions of our race the lesson so loved by the sufferer of Calvary.

OUR EARLY NEWSPAPER WITS.

—

Just sixty minutes for a review of the clever men
who have made newspaper wit a thing to be grateful for. No time will be wasted in quoting the
hackneyed definitions of wit and humor that usually
preface or rather make two-thirds of articles on this
subject. James Parton says, that a lecture differs
from every other form of composition in this, that
so many points, distinctly stated and emphatically
made, must be given in an exceedingly limited time.
This will be my aim in bringing before you the
humorists of the press, selecting their best sayings
for your amusement. Seba Smith originated this
style of writing during the administration of Andrew
Jackson, assuming to be his special confidant, right-
hand man and occasional bedfellow, with an ill-
concealed envy of all other political favorites, and an
honest hankering after the presidential chair for
himself. His letters under the *nom de plume* of
Major Jack Downing, were declared by Lord
Brougham to be not merely humorous, but states-
manlike, and for quaintness and humor, originality,
and genius, unequalled since the writing of Hudibras.
They were published in book form in 1834, and are

now almost forgotten, but are still entertaining. In
the introduction he says: "I only wish I had gone
to school a little more when I was a boy, if I had my
letters now would make folks crawl all over; but if
I had been to school all my lifetime I know I never
could be able to write more honestly than I have. I
am sometimes puzzled most plaguidly to git words
to tell jest exactly what I think and what I know,
and when I git 'em, I don't know exactly how to
spell 'em, but so long as I git the sound I'll let other
folks git the sense out, pretty much as our old friend
down to Salem, who bilt a big ship to go to China,
he called her the '*Asha.*' Now there is sich a thing
as folks knowin' too much. All the larned ones was
puzzled to know who 'Asha' was, and they never
would-a-known to this day what it ment if the owner
of the ship hadn't tell'd 'em that China was in Asha.
'Oh! ah!' says the larned folks, 'we see now, but
that aint the way to spell it.' 'What!' says he, 'if
A-s-h-a don't spell Asha, what on earth does it spell?'
and that stumped 'em."

Here is a fair specimen of his style: "I and the
gineral have got things now pretty considerable
snug, and it is raly curious to see how much more
easy and simple all the public affairs go on, than they
did a spell ago when Mr. Adams was president. If
it wasn't for Congress meetin', we could jest go about
pretty much where we pleased, and keep things
strait too ; and I begin to think now with the gineral,
that arter all, there is no great shakes in managin

the affairs of the nation. We have, pretty much all on us, ben joggin' about now since last grass, and things are jest as strait and clear now as they was then. The gineral has nigh upon made up his mind that there is no use to have any more Congress. They only bother us; they wou'd do more good to stay at home and write letters to us, tellin' us what is goin' on among 'em at home. It would save a considerable sum of money, too; and I'm also sartain that there is a plaguy raft of fellows on wages that don't earn nothin'. We keep all the secretaries and the vice-president and some district attorneys and a good many more of our folks and Amos Kindle moving about, and they tell us jest how the cat jumps. And, as I said afore, if it wasn't for Congress meetin' once a year, we'd put the government in a one-horse wagon and go jest where we liked."

Mr. Van Buren, whose political nickname was "The Fox," a shrewd and politic, wily and wire-pulling man, is most admirably caricatured by the jolly major.

In a discussion of the lucky vice-president, the general says: "Well, Major, he *is* a plaguey curious critter, arter all; he'll make wheels turn sometimes right agin one another, yit he gits along, and when he lets his slice fall, or some one nocks it out of his hand, it always, somehow, falls butter side up."

"Well," says I, "Gineral, don't you know why?"

"Not exactly," says he, "Major."

"Well," says I, "I'll tell you, he butters both sides to once," says I.

On shaking hands with a crowd at Philadelphia: "There was such a stream of 'em coming in that the hall was full in a few minutes, and it was so jammed up around the door that they couldn't get out again if they were to die. So they had to knock out some of the windows and go out t'other way. The president shook hands with all his might an hour or two, till he got so tired he couldn't hardly stand it. I took hold and shook for him once in a while to help him along, but at last he got so tired he had to lay down on a soft bench, covered with cloth, and shake as well as he could; and when he couldn't shake, he'd nod to 'em as they come along. And at last, he got so beat out, he couldn't only wrinkle his forehead and wink. Then I kind of stood behind him, and reached my arm round under his, and shook for him for about half an hour as tight as I could spring. Then we concluded it was best to adjourn for that day."

Orpheus C. Kerr (Robt. H. Newell) and Petroleum Nasby (D. R. Locke) both followed in Jack's footsteps, with humorous letters full of hard hits at the weak places in political and army life, and Judge Haliburton, an English writer, better known as Sam Slick, contributed, in 1835, to a weekly newspaper in Nova Scotia, a series of articles satirizing the Yankee character that became extremely popular, but for originality and genuine fun, the palm must be given to the major.

Orpheus C. Kerr published three volumes of his letters from the army, rather tedious with the constant repetition of his pet phrase, "my boy." And 'tis hard to find anything that is not a trifle coarse.

WASHINGTON, D. C., June 15, 1861.

"The members of the Mackerel Brigade, now stationed on Arlington Heights to watch the movements of the Potomac, which is expected to rise shortly, desire me to thank the women of America for supplies of havelocks and other delicacies of the season just received. The havelocks, my boy, are rather roomy, and we took them for shirts at first; and the shirts are so narrow-minded that we took them for havelocks. If the women of America would manage to get a little less linen in the collars of the latter article, and a little more into the other departments of the graceful garments, there would be fewer colds in this division of the Grand Army.

"The havelocks, as I have said before, are roomy, very roomy, my boy. William Brown of Company B, regiment 5, put on one last night, when he went on sentry duty, and looked like a broomstick in a pillow-case for all the world. When the officer of the night came round and caught sight of William in his havelock, he was struck dumb with admiration for a moment; then he ejaculated: 'What a splendid moonbeam!' William made a movement and the sergeant came up. 'What *is* that white object?' says the officer to the sergeant. 'The young man which is William Brown,' says the sergeant. 'Thunder!' roars the officer, 'tell him to go to his tent and take off that night-gown.' 'You're mistaken,' says the sergeant, 'the sentry is William Brown in his havelock, which was made by the wimmen of America.'

" The shirts, too, are noble articles as far down as the collar. Captain Mortimer de Montague, one of the skirmish squad, put one on when he went to the President's reception, and the collar stood up so high that he couldn't put his cap on. His appearance at the White House was picturesque and interesting, and, as he entered the drawing room, General Scott remarked very feelingly, ' Ah! here comes one of our wounded heroes.' ' He's not wounded, General,' remarked an officer standing by. ' Then why is his head bandaged up so?' asked the venerable veteran. ' Oh,' says the officer, ' that's only one of the shirts made by the patriotic women of America.'"

And one more bit:

" I asked the general of the Mackerel Brigade the other day, what kind of a flower he thought would spring above my head when I rested in a soldier's sepulchre, and he said: ' A cabbage, my boy,' he said a cabbage."

We will now turn to Nasby, who was so popular during the war, and let him tell you of his ingenious scheme for inexpensive living:

" I hev invented a new carpit-bag for the espeshal yoose uv patriots and agitaters. It is made uv thin Injy rubber, with a frame that folds up into a small compass. Yoo take that carpit-bag and blow it up till it bulges out at the sides ez tho it wuz full of cloze and things, and walk into a lodging house and demand rooms with confidence. That carpit-bag bustin' with valyooables settles it. It looks solvent, and everything is in looks. Yoo stay on the strength uv that bag, and hev yoor meals sent to yoor room, and live fat. Presently, your landlady wants money, and commences to watch that carpit-bag. Yoo can't get out of the house with it, for that is her anker and her hope. Very good. Some evening yoo go to yoor room, let the wind out uv it, fold it up and put it in yoor coat pocket, and bid her good evening, telling her yoo shel be home early, and she may light the fire at ten, and the place that knowd yoo wunst knows yoo no more furever. The first dark place yoo come to yoo blow it up again, and go boldly into another house and establish yoorself in comfort ef not in luxury."

Abraham Lincoln used to find relief from the presence of the responsibilities which weighed upon his mind, in reading the droll witticisms of Nasby and Artemus Ward. When the great question of emancipation was under consideration, he once came into a cabinet meeting, chuckling over one of Nasby's letters from " Confederate Cross Roads," and insisted upon reading it before any business was done. Men of formal dignity like Salmon P. Chase and Edward M. Stanton were shocked at Lincoln's apparent levity at such a crisis; but he was, really, a sadder as well as a wiser man than they.

Artemus Ward (Charles F. Browne), who gained his first honors as a newspaper wit in the Cleveland *Plaindealer*, never sacrificed his friends for an epigram; he made you laugh and love him too. He seldom smiled in his lectures, no matter how absurd his statements. Many good people failed to see the comical in his performances. One old lady, accompanied by her serious-minded daughters, left the hall in the midst of his lecture saying: " It is too bad to laugh at that poor young man. He doesn't know what he is saying and ought to be sent to a lunatic asylum."

Others would survey this driest of droll men with looks of benevolent pity. It was his delight to puzzle. In the middle of his lecture he would hesitate, stop, and say solemnly, " Owing to a slight indisposition, we will now have an intermission of fifteen minutes." The audience were properly amazed, at the prospect of staring at vacancy for a quarter of an hour, when, rubbing his hands the lecturer would add, " but — ah — during the intermission I will go on with my lecture."

He once stated that the same lecture would be repeated in Constantinople — one week from date — and tickets for the round trip would be given to audience as they passed out! He observed that what he said had given pain to several, and he would then endeavor to explain his jokes.

Sometimes he would seem to forget his audience, and stand for several seconds gazing intently at his panorama. Then he would recover from this fit of abstraction and remark apologetically, "I am very fond of looking at my pictures." Imagine the effect, when, after such an interruption, he would point with his little riding whip to some nondescript quadrupeds which he had all along characterized as cows and remark, "Those animals are *horses* — I know they are because my artist says so. I had the picture two years before I discovered the fact. The artist came to me about six months ago and said, "It is useless to disguise it from you any longer, they are *horses*."

"The most celebrated artists of London are so delighted with this picture that they come every day to gaze at it. I wish you were nearer to it so you could see it better. I wish I could take it to your residences and let you see it by daylight. Some of the greatest artists in London come here every morning before daylight with *lanterns* to look at it. They say they never saw anything like it before — and they hope they never shall again."

He insisted that one of his earliest literary efforts was an essay sent to the Smithsonian Institute, but, strange to say, rejected on the theme, "Is cats to be trusted."

Some one speaking of Artemus called him a perfect steam factory of puns and a museum of American humor. His first lecture he called "The Babes in the Woods;" he had thought of naming it "My

Seven Grandmothers." It consisted of a wandering batch of comicalities, touching upon everything but the babes.

The next was entitled " Sixty Minutes in Africa." Behind him hung a large map of Africa, which region he said "abounded in various natural productions, such as reptiles and flowers. It produces the red rose, the white rose, and the neg--roes. Apropos of negroes, let me tell you a little story," and no further reference to Africa until the very close of the entertainment.

His experience as a showman is familiar, yet I never tire of his business letters, for instance —

"I'm moving *slowly* down to'rds your place. How *is* the show bizness in your place. My show at present consists of three moral bares, a kangeroo (an *amoosin* little raskal, 'twould make you laf yourself to deth to see the little cuss jump up and squeal), wax figgers of Genl. Washington, Genl. Taylor, John Bunyan, Captain Kidd, Dr. Webster, in the act of killing Parkman, beside several miscellayous moral wax statoos of celebrated pirates," etc. (after hinting strongly for a puff). And again: "If you say anything about my show say my snaiks is as harmliss as a new born Babe. What an interestin' study it is to see a zewological animal, like a snaik, under perfec' subjecshun! I am anxious to skewer your influence. I repeat in regard to them handbills that I shall get 'em struck off to your printin' offis. My perlitical sentiments agree with yourn exactly. I know they dew, because I never saw a man whose didn't."

It was Artemus who preferred bald-headed butter and considered absence of body a better thing than presence of mind in case of an accident.

Here is a characteristic story of the thin man engaged for a living skeleton, for a tour through Australia :

" He was the thinnest man I ever saw. He was a splendid skeleton. He didn't weigh anything scarcely, and I said to myself, the people of Australia will flock to see this tremendous curiosity. It is a long voyage, as you know, from New York to Melbourne, and, to my utter surprise, the skeleton had no sooner got out to sea than he commenced eating in the most horrible manner. He had never been on the ocean before, and he said it agreed with him. I thought so ! I never saw a man eat so much in my life. Beef, mutton, pork, he swallowed them all like a shark, and between meals he was often discovered behind barrels eating hard-boiled eggs ! The result was that when we reached Melbourne, this infamous skeleton weighed sixty-four pounds more than I did. I thought I was ruined — but I wasn't. I took him on to California — another very long voyage — and when I got to San Francisco I exhibited him as a fat man ! "

" People laugh at me," said Browne, " because of my eccentric sentences. There is no wit in the form of a well-rounded sentence. If I say ' Alexander conquered the world and sighed because he couldn't do so some more,' there is a funny mixture." You notice that a majority of his jokes depend upon a sudden change from a serious beginning to an absurd ending.

The character he created represents humor of an original type, yet he is said to have copied it from a living oddity ; as Denman Thompson gives a faithful imitation of a resident of "Swanzey" as Josh Whitcomb.   His success in England was largely due to the impression that he gave a clever caricature of an American backwoodsman or 'showman.   The celebrated wits on the staff of *Punch* used to frequent Egyptian Hall and roar at his solemn fun, vacant face, and inimitable drawl.   Mark Twain says " Artemus looked like a glove stretcher ; his hair red and brushed well forward at the sides reminded one of a divided flame.   His nose rambled on aggressively before him with all the strength and determination of a cow-catcher, while his red moustache, to follow out the simile, seemed not unlike the unfortunate cow."

Lieut. Derby, known as " John Phœnix " and " Squibob," was often deliciously droll.

His lectures on Astronomy, he frankly tells us, were originally prepared to be delivered before the Lowell Institute of Boston, Mass., but owing to the unexpected circumstance of the author's receiving no invitation to lecture before that institution, they were laid aside shortly after their completion.

He some time after did receive an invitation to lecture before the Vallecetos Literary and Scientific Institute, but on arriving at that place, he learned with deep regret that the only inhabitant had left a few days previous, having availed himself of the opportunity presented by a passing emigrant's horse, and that, in consequence, the opening of the Institute was indefinitely postponed.

But the lectures are full of original ideas. He says:

" Up to the time of a gentleman named Copernicus, who flourished about the middle of the fifteenth century, it was supposed by our stupid ancestors that the earth was the center of all creation, being a large, flat body, resting on a rock, which rested on another rock, and so on all the way down, and that the sun, planets, and immovable stars all revolved about it once in twenty-four hours.

But Co-Pernicus (who was a son of Daniel Pernicus, of the firm of Pernicus & Co., wool dealers, and who was named Co-Pernicus out of respect to his father's partners, soon set this matter to rights and started the idea of the present solar system.

The demonstration of this system in all its perfection was left to Isaac Newton (an English philosopher), who seeing an apple tumble down from a tree, was led to think thereon with such gravity that he finally discovered the attraction of gravitation, which proved to be the great law of nature that keeps everything in its place. Thus we see that as an apple originally brought sin and ignorance into the world, the same fruit proved thereafter the cause of vast knowledge and enlightenment, and indeed we may doubt whether any other fruit but an apple and a sour one at that, would have produced these grand results: for had the fallen fruit been a pear, an orange, or a peach tree, there is little doubt that Newton would have eaten it up and thought no more on the subject."

When the bill for a new chimney came in he exclaims: " Bills, bills, bills ! How *can* a man name his child William? The horrid idea of the partner of his joys and sorrows presenting him with a *Bill !* —and to have that Bill continually in the house, constantly running up and down stairs always unsettled !"

" Leaving San Francisco as the last line fell from the dock, and our noble steamer with a mighty throb and deep sigh, at bidding adieu to San Francisco, swung slowly round, the passengers crowded to the side to exchange a farewell salutation with their friends and acquaintances. 'Good-bye, Jones,' 'Goodbye, Brown,' 'God bless you old fellow, take care of yourself !' they shouted. Not seeing any one that I knew, and fearing the passengers might think I had no friends, I shouted 'Good-bye, Muggins,' and had the satisfaction of having a shabby man, much inebriated, reply as he swung his rimless hat, 'Good-bye, my brother.' Not particularly elated at this recognition, I tried it again, with, 'Good-bye, Colonel,' whereat thirty-four respectable gentlemen took off their hats, and I got down from the position that I had occupied on a camp stool, with much dignity.

"Away we sped down the bay, the captain standing on the wheel-house directing our course. 'Port, Port a little, Port,' he shouted. 'What's he a calling for?' inquired a youth of good-natured but unmistakable verdancy of appearance, of me. 'Port wine,' said I, 'and the storekeeper don't hear him, you'd better take him up some.' 'I will,' said Innocence; 'I've got a bottle of first-rate in my state room.' And he did, but soon returned with a particularly crest-fallen and sheepish appearance. 'Well, what did he say to you,' inquired I. 'Pointed at the notice on that tin,' said the poor fellow. 'Passengers not allowed on the wheel-house.' '*He* is, though, ain't he?' added my friend with a faint attempt at a smile, as the captain in an awful voice shouted, 'Starboard!' 'Is what?' said I, '*Loud on the wheel-house!*'"

Receiving a formal letter from the Secretary of War, inquiring "How far does the Tombigby run up?" he came near being cashiered for replying. "Dear sir, after a careful examination we find the Tombigby never did run up." They inquired if the *Santa Clara* could be dammed, and he replied he was certain it could, for he had been damning it ever since he came.

"The Squibob Papers," a second volume from Lieut. Derby, is enriched by comic illustrations from his own pen, which would convulse the most serious-minded audience, if they could only be enlarged and displayed.

"A Side Elevation of G. Washington *not* by Gilbert Stuart," adorns the first page. It was taken when the general was in the act of chewing tobacco, the left cheek is distended most absurdly, and the left eye is closed in a very wise wink.

In his famous "Fourth of July Oration," he follows the universal custom of inserting a full and complete biography of the immortal Washington and pays the following beautiful tribute to the memory of this greatest of men :

"George Washington was one of the most distinguished movers in the American Revolution. He was born of poor but honest parents at Genoa, in the year 1492. His mother was called the mother of Washington. He married, early in life, a widow lady, Mrs. Martha Custis, whom Prescott describes as the *cussidest* pretty woman south of Mason and Dixon's line.

"Young Washington commenced business as a county surveyor and was present in that character at a sham-fight, under General Braddock, when so many guns were fired that the whole body of militia were stunned by the explosion, and sate down to supper unable to hear a word that was said. This supper was afterwards alluded to as Braddock's deaf eat, and the simile, 'deaf as a Braddock,' subsequently vulgarized into 'deaf as a haddock,' had its rise from that circumstance.

"Washington commanded several troops during the Revolutionary War, and distinguished himself by fearlessly crossing the Delaware river, on ice of very inadequate thickness, to visit a family of Hessians of his acquaintance. He was passionately fond of green peas and string beans, and his favorite motto was: 'In time of peace prepare for war.'

"Washington died from exposure on the summit of Mount Vernon, in the year 1786, leaving behind him a name that will endure forever if posterity persist in calling their children after him to the same extent that has been fashionable."

Derby's skill as a philologist is again seen in his explanation of the word oration, which he declared had a military origin in a custom once prevalent among commanding officers and chaplains of making long and verbose addresses to the troops, which were stigmatized as "all talk and no rations," whence the word "noration" was modernized into oration.

In his own "noration" in his frantic rhapsody on the 4th of July he exclaims, "For on this day the great American eagle flaps her wings and soars aloft, until it makes your eyes sore to look at her, and looking down upon her myriads of free and enlightened children she screams, 'E Pluribus Unum!' which may be freely interpreted, 'Ain't I some?'

and myriads of freemen answer back with joyous shout:

"'You are Punkins!'"

His account of the meeting of the Massachusetts Dental Association or "three hundred tewth carpenters," with the motto on their banner, "A long pull, a strong pull, and a pull altogether," is peculiarly rich.

"There was the elegant city practitioner, with shiny hat and straw-colored gloves, side by side with the gentleman from the country who hauls a man all over the floor for two hours, and gives him the worth of his money."

One of the many toasts was, "The Woodcock, emblem of dentistry, he picks up his living from the holes, and passes in a precious long bill."

Other interesting exercises were gone through with.

A hackman passing by on his carriage was placed under the influence of chloroform, all his teeth extracted without pain, and an entire new and elegant set put in their place, all in forty-two seconds. His appearance was wonderfully improved. "I have never seen 300 dentists together before, and I don't believe anybody else ever did, but I consider it a pleasing and an imposing spectacle, and would suggest that the next time they meet they shall make an excursion which shall combine business with pleasure, and all go down together and remove the snags from the mouth of the Mississippi."

Derby at thirty years old shared with Artemus Ward the fame of being the greatest American humorist. One of his pranks sent him to San Diego. Jefferson Davis had asked the army officers who had served in Mexico to submit designs for a new service uniform. Derby responded with a series of clever drawings, one of which represented a cavalry man with an orange stuck on his cap as a pompon, explaining that it looked as well as the ordinary pompon, and in case the wearer grew tired or thirsty he could take it off and suck it.

Another device was an iron hook on the seat of the trousers. It could be put through a saddle ring so that no amount of hard riding could dislodge a horseman. In the infantry service these hooks might be used to carry camp kettles on a march and in battle, the file closers could use a ringed pole to advantage in catching men who had started to run away. Davis was so angry at this irreverence that he ordered the young officer to a hot and dusty place of exile. Seeing the sign while in Washington, "Ladies Depository," he made a futile effort to deposit his wife while he went around the corner to — see — a man.

We come next to Mortimer Thompson, famous twenty years ago, the author of " Doesticks," " What He Says," " The Elephant Club," " Pluribustah," etc. He wrote a capital take-off on the successful vendors of quack medicines, at the time when

Townsend's Sarsaparilla was the favorite beverage for bilious invalids.

"As I, too, desire to have a mansion on Fifth Avenue, like the Medical Worthy of Sarsaparilla memory, and wished like him to be able to build a patent medicine palace, with a private chapel under the back stairs, and conservatory down cellar. I cast about me for some means whereby the requisite cash might be reputably accumulated.

"Emulous of the deathly notoriety which has been acquired by the medicinal worthies just mentioned, I also resolved to achieve a name and a fortune in the same reputable and honest manner. Bought a gallon of tar, a cake of beeswax, and a firkin of lard, and in twenty-one hours I presented to the world the first batch of 'Doestick's Patent, Self-Acting, Four-Horse Power Balsam,' designed to cure all diseases of mind, body, or estate, to give strength to the weak, money to the poor, bread and butter to the hungry, boots to the barefoot, decency to blackguards, and common sense to the Know-Nothings. It acts physically, morally, mentally, psychologically, physiologically, and geologically, and it is intended to make our sublunary sphere a blissful paradise, to which Heaven itself shall be but a side-show."

TESTIMONIALS.

" DEAR SIR — The land composing my farm has hitherto been so poor that a Scotchman couldn't get his living off it, and so stony that we had to slice·

our potatoes and plant them edgeways; but hearing of your balsam, I put some on the corner of a ten-acre lot, surrounded by a rail fence, and in the morning I found the rocks had entirely disappeared, a neat stone wall encircled the field, and the rails were split into ovenwood and piled up symmetrically in my back yard.

" Put half an ounce into the middle of a huckleberry swamp. In two days it was cleared off, planted with corn and pumpkins, and had a row of peach tress in full bloom through the middle."

I give one more from a member of the senior class in a Western college :

"MY DEAR DOCTOR — [You know I attended medical lectures half a winter, and once assisted in getting a crooked needle out of a baby's leg, so I understand perfectly well the theory and practice of medicine, and the *Doctor* is perfectly legitimate under the Prussian system.] By the incessant study required in this establishment I had become worn down so thin that I was obliged to put on an overcoat to cast a shadow, but accidentally hearing of your Balsam, I obtained a quantity, and, in obedience to the homeopathic principles of this institution, took an infinitesimal dose only; in four days I measured one hundred and eighty-two inches round the waist; could chop eleven cords of hickory wood in two hours and a half, and, on a bet, carried a yoke of oxen two miles and a quarter in my left hand, my right being tied behind me, and if anyone doubts the fact, the oxen are still to be seen.

"About two weeks after this I had the pleasure of participating in a gunpowder explosion, on which occasion my arms and legs were scattered over the village, and my mangled remains pretty equally distributed throughout the entire country.

"Under these circumstances my life was despaired of, and my classmates had bought a pine coffin, and borrowed whole shirts to attend the funeral in, when the invincible power of your four-horse power balsam (which I happened to have in my vest pocket) suddenly brought together the scattered pieces of my body — collected my limbs from the rural districts, put new life into my shattered frame, and I was restored, uninjured, to my friends, with a new set of double teeth."

The Boston *Post* originated the "Funny Column," in which every local sheet now indulges. It was there that Saxe published his famous epigrams and B. P. Shillaber made himself famous by quotations from Mrs. Partington. One or two "oracular pearls" from the lips of this popular old lady must be given. Taken together they lose their lustre and she becomes a tedious old party, with the effort for the wrong word disagreeably obvious. Even *Ike*, forever plaguing the cat and doing some absurd thing to neatly end the paragraph never seems like a real boy.

"Widow Bedott" and "Josiah Allen's wife" are

actual persons. You laugh at them and with them, while this blundering dame seems simply a mouth-piece for Shillaber. But let us listen to her verbal contortions for a moment:

"Entered at the Custom House," said Mrs. Partington, pondering on the expression, "I don't see how the vessels ever got in: but I am glad that the collector cleared 'em right out again. It will learn them better manners next time, I think."

"Now go to meeting, dear," said Mrs. P., as Isaac stood smoothing his hair, preparatory to going out on Sunday. He looked down at his new shoes and a thought of the green fields made him sigh. A fishing-line hung out of one pocket, which Mrs. Partington didn't see.

"Where shall I go to?" asked Ike. Since the old lady had given up her seat in the Old North Church she had no stated place of worship. "Go," replied she sublimely, as she pulled down his jacket behind, "Go — anywheres, where the gospel is dispensed with."

"Ah, yes," said Mrs. Partington, some years ago, as she watched the military pass by on the 22d of February, "Ah, yes, Washington is dead, and the worst of it is his mantel-piece hasn't fallen upon any living man!"

There are women in real life who say better things of this sort. I remember an old lady who at an evening party said of a passing belle, "Why, she's a perfect paragram of a young lady!" "I think you mean parallelogram," suggested a friend. Upon which she replied with a look of withering superiority, " I said parallelogram, Mr. Tenney."

Occasionally, there is more of Shillaber than Partington, as in this remark : " There must be some sort of kin between poets and pullets, for they both are always chanting their lays." Shillaber has written good poetry, but will always be thought of as a blundering, kind-hearted old dame, with large spectacles on her beaming face and a small rogue at her side. He felt this himself and said he made a mistake in appearing as a lecturer, because the public wanted only Mrs. Partington. He says pathetically, " George William Curtis said long ago, that when one has managed to stand on his head successfully, the public wishes to see how he did it, but he must continue to stand on his head or they will be disappointed. I found this to be true. Partington was the cry. Partington was on the big posters at the corners of the streets. Partington was the theme of the lyceum presidents in introduction. I had stood on my head for fun, but here, in sober earnest, I could not make a mountebank of myself.

" Artemus Ward wrote me from Cleveland : ' Come out here like an old woman and sing a comic song, and you will carry the town.' The best I could give them were a few pleasant and mild lectures of excellent morals and of unexceptionable tone, but they desired Partington, and I confess to the folly, now, when I need it, of abandoning a fortune, right within my very grasp, because I would not yield and leaving the field at its very threshold."

Mrs. Partington is not an original creation, but is a reproduction of Smollett's Tabitha Bramble, Sheridan's Mrs. Malaprop, and Theodore Hook's Mrs. Ramsbottom, all of them much better, however.

The name was suggested by an anecdote related by Sydney Smith in a speech at Taunton in 1831. He said: "I do not mean to be disrespectful, but the attempt of the lords to stop the progress of reform reminds me very forcibly of the great storm of Sidmouth, and the conduct of the excellent Mrs. Partington on that occasion. In the winter of 1824, there set in a great flood upon that town; the tide rose to an incredible height; the waves rushed in upon the houses and everything was threatened with destruction. In the midst of this sublime storm Dame Partington, who lived upon the beach, was seen at the door of her house, with mop and pattens, trundling her mop and squeezing out the salt water and vigorously pushing away the Atlantic ocean. The Atlantic was roused. Mrs. Partington's spirit was up, but I need not tell you that the contest was unequal. The Atlantic Ocean beat Mrs. Partington. She was excellent at a slop or a puddle, but she should not have meddled with a tempest."

As a brilliant journalist and versatile genius none can rank higher than George D. Prentice — a politician and poet, an able lawyer, author, statesman, editor, wit, and a success in all. Bryant said: "I have never known anyone in editorial life who equaled him in the energetic and industrious use of his powers. Of the vastness of those powers, very few are able to take the measure."

In that just, discriminating, and worthy memorial of George D. Prentice, delivered before the General Assembly of Kentucky by Mr. Henry Watterson, and for which every friend and admirer of George D. Prentice is his debtor, Mr. Watterson says: "I found in London that his fame is exceeded by that of no newspaper writer; but the journalists of Paris, where there is still nothing but personal journalism, considered him a few years ago as the solitary journalist of genius among us. His sarcasms have often got into Charivari." He was, without question, the most popular and influential newspaper writer of whom we have any record. The author of the letters of Junius was popular and potent, but his reign, compared with that of Mr. Prentice, was very brief. His career was that of a shooting meteor which vanished rapidly. The career of Mr. Prentice was that of a fixed luminary, steadily and serenely shedding its light through a long series of years. His style, for success in his objects, was preëminently superior to that of any other newspaper writer. There are qualities of newspaper literature in which he was surpassed, but I have never known his equal in the power to seize the public mind and to imbue it with his own convictions. The secret of his success was his gleaming, penetrating style; his

brief, concentrated humor or pungent wit and sarcasm, which was easily understood and housed in the
memory. His versatility was as wonderful as any
other element of his perfections as a paragraphist.
He never repeated himself, nor did he need to borrow from others. In these gifts, for such they seemed
to be, in his long career as a journalist, he had no
equal, even among the strong and able men who
measured weapons with him."

He could strike with a rapier or a bludgeon, and
there was little mercy for editors who attacked him.
One opposed a pet plan of his in a long and labored
leader headed "More Villainy Afoot." The only
notice taken by Prentice of this was a brief item.
" We regret to see that Mr. So-and-so has lost his
horse."

When another grandly remarked of a certain
question, ".Let others take the responsibility, *we
wash our hands of it."* he responded, " Washing
your hands is an operation that will do you no manner of harm. Please think of your *face* at the same
time."

And here are some of his lighter sallies :

An English writer says, in his advice to young
married women, " that their mother Eve married a
gardener." It might be added "that the gardener
in consequence of the match lost his situation."

" About the only person that we ever heard of
that wasn't spoiled by being *lionized* was a Jew
named Daniel."

" We suppose there can be no disputing that the first *Ark*-tic expedition was got up by Noah."

"An author, ridiculing the idea of ghosts, asks how a dead man can get into a locked room. ' Probably, with a skeleton key.' "

" ' My dear wife, I wish you would try to keep your temper.' ' My dear husband, I wish you would try to get rid of yours.' "

" ' I'll bet my ears,' said an angry husband. ' Indeed, dear, you shouldn't carry betting to such *lengths*.' "

"The Cincinnati representative in Congress boasts that he can bring an argument to a pint as quick as any other man. He can bring a quart to a pint a good deal quicker."

" A female correspondent suggests a condition on which she will give us a kiss. We feel in duty bound to say, that kissing is a thing that at every proper opportunity, we set our face against."

His ready wit never failed him. Bill Nye gives this illustration :

The old *Journal* office used to be the stamping ground of many southern men more or less known, who liked to hear the veteran journalist tell a story or warm up a presumptuous young man for lunch. Among those who frequented the *Journal* office was Will S. Hays, the song writer.

Coming into Mr. Prentice's office one day in that free and easy way of his, he sat down on one chair, with his feet in another, and jamming his hat on the back of his head, said, without consulting Mr. Prentice's leisure :

" Seen my last song, George ? "

Mr. Prentice ceased writing, sighed heavily, and, looking up sadly and reproachfully at the young man, said :

" I hope so, Billy."

His common sense was as remarkable as his brilliancy.

" Men and women who read a great many light and superficial works will have a mere mass of crude and worthless knowledge, unless they also read books filled with stern, strong, hard thought. The birds have to pick up pebble stones to aid the digestion of the softer contents of their caws."

We are indebted to the friendly biographer and editor of Mr. Prentice's poems, John J. Piatt, for this extract from a letter written by Mr. Prentice :

" I rejoice, my little friend, that you are a believer. For my own part, I have no doubt either of the truths of Christianity or of the momentous and infinite importance of those truths. I hear a thousand things from the pulpit that make me smile, yet I would rather be a Christian of the very humblest order of intellect than the most gloriously-gifted infidel that ever blazed like a comet through the atmosphere of earth."

Henry R. Shaw, Josh Billings, who as Eli Perkins expressed it, wore his hair in a court train over his collar, gained a wide notoriety as writer and lecturer.   He failed several times in business, turned harlequin at forty-five, took the public by storm and made a large fortune as a comic paragraphist, lecturer, and maker of Alminax and apothegms.   How quaint and irresistible is his Essay on Rats :

"Rats originally cum from Norway, and I wish they had originally stayed there.   They are about as uncalled for as a pain in the small of the back. They can be domesticated dredful eazy, that is, as far as gittin' in cupboards and eatin' cheese and knawing pie is concerned.   The best way to domesticate them that I ever saw, is tew surround them gently with a steel trap; you can reason with them then to great advantage.   I scrpose there is between 50 and 60 millions of rats in Ameriky (I quote now entirely from memory), and I don't suppose there is a single necessary rat in the whole lot.   This shows at a glance how many waste rats there is."

A few of his terse sayings will show the wisdom of the joker: "When a feller gets a goin' down hill, it dus seem as tho everything had been greased for the okashun."

"I don't insist upon pedigree for a man or horse. If a horse kan trot fast the pedigree is all right; if he kan't, I wouldn't give a shilling a yard for his pedigree."

"It is dredful easy to be a phool.   A man kan be one and not know it.   Fust appearances are ced to be everything.   I don't put all my faith into this sayin.

I think oysters and klams, for instance, will bear looking into."

This union of strong common sense, keen wit, outrageous orthography is seldom tiresome. The success of his writings has brought numerous competitors into the field who seem to imagine that, if the spelling is only bad enough, the absence of wit and sense will not be noticed, not understanding that the peculiar spelling is an ingenious method of evading either pretension or an assumption of intellectual acuteness.

Horace Greeley denounced the modern humorist who thrives on bad spelling.

Samuel L. Clemens, the irrepressible Mark Twain, is best in long narratives. The tidal wave of laughter that rose from the reading of " Innocents Abroad," spread over two continents.

The London *World*, in publishing a series of penportraits of " Celebrities at Home," devoted one paper to " Mark Twain at Hartford," describing him as surrounded by every object which wealth and taste can procure, the prince of entertainers, the center of a delightful circle of friends.

It would be easy to resolve Mr. Clemens' methods of rousing a laugh into a few general formulas such as solemn misstatement and specific exaggeration. For instance, speaking of New England weather, he said : " In the spring I've counted 136 different kinds of weather inside of 24 hours." If he had said, " I have counted a great many different kinds of weather, no one would have smiled. The wit lies in the definiteness of the exaggeration. Alas! after an analysis of the method, the wit eludes us. Wit can never be captured nor defined. Mr. Clemens named one of his dogs " Joseph Cook," because, as he said, there are some things about that dog he can't understand, depths in that dog's nature which he fails to fathom. He says of a cat's midnight serenade that he doesn't mind the noise, it's their sickening grammar that distresses him. Mark Twain has a natural drawl. Artemus Ward assumed his to surprise and hold his audience.

Mark Twain tells us in his valuable appendix to " A Tramp Abroad," all about the German journals which have neither " editorials," " personals," nor " funny paragraphs ; " no " rumors," no abuse of public officials, no rehash of cold sermons, no weather items.

Once a week the German daily of the highest class lightens up its heavy columns with a profound *an abysmal* book criticism ; a criticism which carries you down, down, down, into the scientific bowels of the subject ; sometimes it gives you a gay and chipper essay about ancient Grecian funeral customs, or the ancient Egyptian methods of tarring a mummy, or the reasons for believing that some of the peoples who existed before the flood did not approve of cats.

These matters can be handled in such a way as to make a person lowspirited.

The German humorous papers are beautifully

printed, and the illustrations finely drawn and deliciously funny. So generally are the two or three terse sentences which accompany the picture. I remember one where a most dilapidated tramp is ruefully contemplating some coins which lie in his open palm. He says: " Well, begging is getting played out. Only about 5 marks, $1.25, for the whole day, many an *official* who makes more." And a picture of a commercial traveler who is about to unroll his samples.

Merchant (pettishly) — " No, *don't*. I don't want to buy anything."

Drummer — " If you please, I was only going to show you — "

Merchant — " But I don't wish to see them."

Drummer (after a pause, pleadingly) — " But do you mind letting *me* look at them? I havn't seen them for three weeks ! ! "

Brander Matthews considers Mr. Clemens our greatest humorist, also one of the masters of English prose, one of the foremost story-tellers of the world, with the gift of swift narrative, with the certain grasp of human nature, with a rare power of presenting character at a passionate crisis, yet usually set down as only a funny man or a newspaper humorist. He has more humor than any one else of his generation.

Charles H. Webb, known as " John Paul," has written much in the way of newspaper wit, exceedingly droll and dry, quite unlike his predecessors,

17

and is, besides, a writer of pleasant verses and burlesques on several novels. These were tremen-
dously funny, seizing on the weak points of each and
making them doubly ridiculous. He is a quiet,
homely man, with red hair and a stutter as delicious
as was Lamb's hesitancy in getting off a joke, his
blue eyes often saying more than his tongue. His
letters from Saratoga, the South, abroad, are capital
and unique. He says, "I did not take after my
father, but it was an ecstatic satisfaction to reflect
how often that worthy gentleman took after me!

"Never shall it be said by me that I put my
hand to the plough and turned back; never shall it
be said that I put hand to a plough at all, unless
a plough should chase me upstairs into the privacy
of my bedroom, and then I should only put hand to
it for the purpose of throwing it out of the window.
The beauty of the farmer's life was never very clear
to me."

Autograph albums are sufficiently trying when
you are urged to record some sweet sentiment and
display your bad penmanship on poor paper, but
"mental photographs" are an added agony. The
truth is tame in answering these conundrums and
your struggle to be witty and original is depressing
in the extreme. Even Mr. Webb made some stupid
efforts, but one or two answers are comical, for
instance :

"What is your favorite object in Nature? Two
Bowers."

" Hour in the day?   Bed time."

"Gem?   Jemima."

"Style of beauty?   A round figure."

" What book (not religious) would you part with last?   My pocket-book."

" Where would you live?   In clover."

" What is your aim in life?   Amiability."

" What is your motto?   When you must —you'd better."

" Max Adeler," Charles H. Clark of the Philadelphia *Bulletin*, objected to being ranked among the professional humorists, as his life is earnest and full of serious work, but as his humor is among the most rollicking and grotesque that has ever appeared in this country, we cannot afford to leave him out. Both his books, " Out of the Hurly-Burly," and " Elbow Room " are extremely popular, 5,000 copies of the latter selling in London within a month after its appearance.

He is not a paragraphist, but prefers to throw his droll fun into the form of sustained narrative.

He dedicates " Elbow Room " to that delicious yet unconscious humorist, " The Intelligent Compositor," who transformed " Filtration is sometimes accomplished with the assistance of albumen," into " Flirtation is sometimes accomplished with the resistance of aldermen "; made me inquire, " Where are the dead, the *varnished* dead"; also for this sentence, " A comet swept o'er the heavens with its trailing skirt," substituted, " A count slept in the hay-mow in a traveling shirt."

Such talent is wonderful and awful.   His obituary notices in " Hurly-Burly," in that chapter entitled. "Trouble in the Sanctum," have been quoted all over the land.   Imagine the surprise of a bereaved mother on finding this tribute to her darling :

> " O bury Bartholomew out in the woods,
>   In a beautiful hole in the ground,
>   Where the bumble-bees buzz and the woodpeckers sing,
>   And the straddle-bugs tumble around,
>   So that in winter when the snow and the slush,
>   Have covered his last little bed,
>   His brother Artemas can go out with Sam,
>   And visit the place, with his sled."

Or picture the feelings of the estimable family of Mr. McGlue as they read :

> " The death angel smote Alexander McGlue,
>   And gave him protracted repose,
>   He wore a checked shirt and a No. 9 shoe,
>   And he had a pink wart on his nose.
>   No doubt he is happier dwelling in space,
>   Over there on the evergreen shore.
>   His friends are informed that his funeral takes place
>   Precisely at quarter past four."

The brother's indignant protestations as to the absolute freedom of Alexander's face from warts of any sort, particularly the pink variety, must be read to be appreciated.

There is a wide difference of opinion as to the merits of Eli Perkins (Melville D. Landon).   Some pronounce him incomparably funny, others make all manner of fun of him and his writings, others think him a disagreeable Paul Pry at Saratoga, where no one is safe from his pen.

At any rate he has the art of making money, knows nothing of the sorrow of "broad grins under narrow circumstances," and draws large crowds to his lectures.

He states that the first composition he ever wrote ran about thus: "A eel is a fish with its tail all the way up to his ears. Never fool with powder. Eli Perkins."

This, he says, was the only original poetry he ever wrote, and it was composed by another feller.

His "Saratoga in 1901," published first in *Commercial Advertiser*," and is full of facts and gossip and lively description chronicling the anecdotes and *bon mots* of others in a generous way. He asks them why a table is in the subjunctive mood and answers: " Because it's would (wood) or should be," and affirms that Saratoga reminds him constantly of home, " because its the dearest spot on earth."

On one of his big posters the other day was seen, after the subject and testimonials from the press, the comfortable assurance that Eli would surely be there at such a date, and underneath his telegram :

"I shall be on hand. I invariably attend my own lectures."

Every once in a while a new "funny man" appears. It is not so long ago since people were inquiring "Who's that fellow on the Danbury

News?"   His descriptions of the absurd complications connected with such household afflictions as cleaning house, and putting up stoves, and hanging out clothes in winter time, in a sleety rain, or a man's delirious attempts to sew on a button when his wife's hand is disabled, or to drive a refractory hen into a coop, or a cow out of the garden, are side-splitting; fine illustrations of the "total depravity of inanimate objects" and "the perversity of things in general."   His special peculiarity is the effective use of the word "that;" "that horse" or "that boy" sounding much more comical than "the boy" or "the horse."   His news items are capital in their way, such as "A King St. man's name is so long he can knock down apples with it," or, "A Danbury agriculturist has put a bundle of straw upon his barn because straws show which way the wind blows."

He is good in such a paragraph as this:

"We can never tell exactly where we lose our umbrellas.   It is singular how gently an umbrella unclasps itself from the tendrils of our mind and floats out into the filmy distance of nothingness."

Mr. Bailey is, however, at his very best in detailing a family squabble over some ludicrous trouble, as a bureau drawer that won't be managed.

"The man who will invent a bureau drawer which will move out and in without a hitch, will not only secure a fortune, but will attain to an eminence in history not second, perhaps, to the greatest warriors.

There is nothing, perhaps (always excepting a stove pipe), that will so exasperate a man as a bureau drawer which will not shut. It is a deceptive article. It will start off all right, then it pauses at one end, while the other swings in as far as it can. It is the custom to throw the whole weight of the person against the end which sticks. If any one has succeeded in closing a drawer by so doing, he will confer a favor by sending his address to this office.

"Mrs. Holcomb was trying to shut a bureau drawer Saturday morning; but it was an abortive effort. Finally she burst into tears. Then Mr. Holcomb told her to stand aside and see him do it. 'You see,' observed Mr. Holcomb, with quiet dignity, 'that the drawer is all awry. Now, anybody but a woman would see at once, that to move a drawer standing in that position would be impossible. I now bring this other end even with the other, so, then I take hold of both knobs and with an equal pressure from each hand, the drawer moves easily in. See?' The dreadful thing moved readily forward for a distance of nearly two inches, then it stopped abruptly!"

"'Ah!' observed Mrs. Holcomb, beginning to look happy again. Mr. Holcomb very properly made no response to this ungenerous expression; but he gently worked each end of the drawer to and fro, but without success.

"Then he pulled the drawer all out, adjusted it properly, and started it carefully back; it moved as if it were on oiled wheels.

" Mr. Holcomb smiled.

" Then it stopped.

" Mr. Holcomb looked solemn.

" ' Perhaps you haven't got the ends adjusted,' suggested the happy Mrs. Holcomb.

" Mr. Holcomb made no reply, were it not for an increased flush in his face it might have been doubted if he heard the remark at all. He pushed harder at the drawer than was apparent to her, but it didn't move. He tried to bring it back again; but it would not come.

" ' What dumb fool put this drawer together, I'd like to know?' he snapped out.

" She made no reply, but she felt that she had not known such happiness since the day she stood before the altar with him, with orange blossoms in her hair.

" ' I'd like to know what in thunder you've been doing to this drawer, Jane Holcomb,' he jerked out.

" ' I haven't done anything to it,' she replied.

" ' I know better,' he asserted.

" ' Well, know what you please, for all I care,' she sympathizingly retorted. The cords swelled up on his neck and the corners of his mouth grew white.

" ' Are you sure you have got everything out of here you want,' he finally asked, with a desperate effort to appear composed.

" ' O! that's what you are stopping for, is it? But you needn't; I have got what I wanted; you can shut it right up.'

" He grew redder in the face and set his teeth

firmly together, and put all his strength to the obdurate drawer, while a hard look gleamed in his eye.

" But it did not move.

" He pushed harder and groaned.

" ' I'm afraid you havn't got the ends adjusted,' she maliciously suggested.

" ' I'll shut that drawer or I'll know the reason of it,' he shouted, and he jumped up and gave it a passionate kick.

" ' *O, my !* ' she exclaimed.

" He dropped on his knees again, and grabbed hold of the knobs, and pushed at them with all his might.   But it didn't move.

" ' Why in heaven's name don't you open the window?   Do you want to smother me,' he cried.

" It was warm, dreadfully warm.   The perspiration stood in great drops on his face or ran down into his neck.   The birds sang merrily outside the door, and the glad sunshine lay in golden sheets on the earth ; but he didn't notice them.   He would have given five dollars if he had not touched the accursed bureau ; he would have given ten if he had never been born.   He threw all his weight on both knobs, it moved, then it went to its place with a suddenness that threw him from his balance and brought his burning face against the bureau with force enough to skin his nose and fill his eyes with water to a degree that was blinding.   Then he went out on the back stoop and sat there for an hour scowling at the scenery."

Mr. Bailey described constitutional irritability in a peculiar manner. His only object was to cause laughter, but the utility of his work was presently seen to be outrunning his intentions. With the exception of some fine descriptive writing in his letters from England, he seems to have shown little earnestness of purpose. But he has admirably ridiculed a serious defect of human nature. Undoubtedly, many a passionate man who has been ready to shriek with rage at some small pin-point of a circumstance, has suddenly caught the ridiculous impression of the affair, and subsided from his high-strung condition into one of laughter. This is absolute gain. Spinoza has demonstrated that in the condition of cheerfulness we are nearer real existence — live more — than in a condition of pain, which causes a lessening of our existence through reason.

Mr. Lanigan of the New York *World* has published there a series of inimitable fables, quite eclipsing Æsop with his cynical moral, and these unique fables are illustrated by Church, so that the pictures are as good as the text:

THE KIND-HEARTED SHE-ELEPHANT.

A kind-hearted She-Elephant, while walking through the Jungle where the Spicy Breezes blow soft o'er Ceylon's Isle, heedlessly set foot upon a Partridge, which she crushed to death within a few inches of the Nest containing its Callow Brood. "Poor little things!" said the generous Mammoth, "I have been a Mother myself, and my affection shall atone for the Fatal Consequences of my Neglect." So saying, she sat down upon the Orphaned Birds.

Moral.—The above Teaches us What Home is Without a Mother; also, that it is not every Person who should be intrusted with the Care of an Orphan Asylum.

The Lion and the Insurance Agent.

An Insurance Agent happening to meet a Lion, asked him if he would insure his Life. "No," responded the Monarch of the Forest with a resounding Roar, "nor yours." Thus saying he tore the unhappy Man to pieces, and fed on his damaged Cheek and other more penetrable Portions.

Moral.— There is such a Thing as being instant out of Season.

The Grasshopper and the Ant.

A Frivolous Grasshopper, having spent the Summer in Mirth and Revelry, went on the Approach of the inclement Winter to the Ant, and implored it of its charity to stake him. "You had better go to your Uncle," replied the prudent Ant; had you imitated my Forethought and deposited your Funds in a Savings Bank you would not now be compelled to regard your Duster in the light of an Ulster." Thus saying, the virtuous Ant retired, and read in the Papers next morning that the Savings Bank where he had deposited his Funds had suspended.

Moral.— Dum Vivimus, Vivamus.

The Two Turkeys.

An Honest Farmer once led his two Turkeys into his Granary and told them to eat, drink, and be merry. One of these Turkeys was wise and one foolish. The foolish Bird at once indulged excessively in the Pleasures of the Stable, unsuspicious of the Future, but the wiser Fowl, in order that he might not be fattened and slaughtered, fasted continually, mortified his Flesh and devoted himself to gloomy Reflections upon the brevity of Life. When Thanksgiving approached, the Honest Farmer killed both

Turkeys, and by placing a Rock in the interior of the Prudent Turkey made him weigh more than his plumper Brother.

Moral.— As we Travel through Life, Let us Live by the Way.

Burdette is one of the best of our popular paragraphists. Banter, badinage, burlesque, irony, verse, repartee, narrative, and lecture, from quiet humor to the wildest buffoonery, he is at home in all, a man of daring fun and extreme versatility.

"The body of a tramp was found beside a haystack out in Sac County one day last week, nearly devoured by rats. As Æsop remarked, 'Mus — et rusticus.'"

From the *Hawkeye Humorist:*

"Woman is a natural traveler. It is a study to see her start off on a trip by herself. She comes down to the depot in an express wagon three hours before train time. She insists on sitting on her trunk out on the platform, to keep it from being stolen. She picks up her reticule, fan, parasol, lunch-basket, small pot with a house plant in it, shawl, paper bag of candy, bouquet, (she never travels without one), small tumbler and extra veil, and chases hysterically after every switch engine that goes by, under the impression that it is her train. Her voice trembles as she presents herself at the restaurant and tries to buy a ticket, and she knocks with the handle of her parasol on the door of the old disused tool-house, in vain hopes that the baggage-man will come out and check her trunk.

She asks everybody in the depot and on the platform when the train will start, and where it will stand, and, looking straight at the great clock, asks: 'What time is it now?' She sees with terror the baggage-man shy her trunk into a car where two men are smoking instead of locking it up by itself in a large, strong, brown car, with 'Bad order shops' chalked on the side, which she has long ago determined to be the baggage car, as the only safe one in sight. Although the first at the depot she is the last to get her ticket, and once on the car she sits to the end of her journey in an agony of apprehension that she has got on the wrong train, and will be landed at some strange station, put in a close carriage, drugged and murdered, and to every last male passenger who walks down the aisle she stands up and presents her ticket which she invariably carries in her hand. She finally recognizes her waiting friends on the platform, leaves the car in a burst of gratitude, and the train is ten miles away before she remembers that her reticule, fan, parasol, lunch-basket, verbena, shawl, candy, tumbler, veil, and bouquet are on the car-seat, where she left them or at the depot in Peoria, for the life of her she can't tell which."

I have the good fortune to know, as friends, many of the wits of the New York press; among them, Mr. Alden, who delighted his friends with his "Sixth Column Fancies" and "Shooting Stars" in the Daily *Times*, Mr. Croffut, author of the "Cumedietta of

Deseret," the Bourbon ballads, and for several years
connected with the *Graphic*, and known widely by
his witty doggerel and "Graphicalities." This doggerel is, perhaps, too funny, but it is Croffut's and
shall go in.

"WHY IS A—?"

" Willie, here's a conundrum — Why's a—"
   Then, as she stammered and paused to think,
He cried, " Shoot it off ! Whoop 'er up, 'Liza !
   Bet y' I'll guess it quicker'n wink."

" Wait, Impatience ! Give me a minute—"
   She pleaded, then said : " What crime is a tar —"
And stuck once more. "There's a good joke in it !"
   She added, while he, " How slow you are !"

Again she began, " What crime does a sailor,
   In a soldier's quarters taken sick,
Resemble? Now, then, you noisy railer !
   Just guess it ! Give us the answer quick !"

He guessed three weeks, and didn't get nigh it :
   Ate fish to strengthen his phosphoric brain ;
Set all his ingenious friends to try it ;
   Then got shampooed, and went at it again.

At last he gave up, and she told the answer :
   " A sailor took sick in such a place, Will,
Is like an attempt to murder a man, sir !
   You see he's a salt within tent took ill !"

A shriek like the whoop of a Sioux he uttered,
   Then fell in a swoon. They poulticed his head ;
In a week they saw that his pulse still fluttered ;
   In a month they bolstered him up in bed.

The doctor sought Eliza to tell her,
  " Your William is crazy ; observe that grin ;*
His mind still wanders ; you'll kill that feller
  'F you ever conundrum to him agin !"

W. A. C.

Such clippings or sippings of American punch would prove a pleasant beverage in a dull day. Take, for instance, this soliloquy from a little paper in Arkansas :

" Some of our exchanges are publishing a curious item to the effect, that a horse in Iowa pulled the plug out of the bunghole of a barrel for the purpose of slaking his thirst. We do not see anything extraordinary in the occurrence. Now, if the horse had pulled the barrel out of the bunghole and slaked his thirst with the plug, or if the barrel had pulled the bunghole out of the horse and slaked its thirst with the plug, or if the barrel had pulled the bunghole out of the plug and slaked its thirst with the horse, or if the plug had pulled the horse out of the barrel and slaked its thirst with the bunghole, or if the bunghole had pulled the thirst out of the horse and slaked the plug with the barrel, or if the barrel had pulled the horse out of the bunghole and plugged its thirst with the slake, it might be worth while to make a fuss about it."

To personate folly a writer must appear foolish. If he represents the ludicrous in life, he must often play the buffoon, which, by the way, is a very difficult part, and is generally given a higher place on the stage than heavy tragedy. Gravity, owl-like gravity, is often a badge of mediocrity.

Comic journalism did not thrive at first in the United States. The people were too serious; life was too earnest to stop to smile over a purely amusing paper. But *Puck*, *Life*, *The Judge*, and a half dozen other funny sheets now manage to keep a strong hold on the public. Hudson said, sometime ago: "Our people don't want their wit on a separate dish. No one can always be funny. Weekly drafts, like a run on a bank, tend to exhaust them." There are other newspaper wits that should be mentioned, as Halleck and Drake in their famous "Croaker" papers; Joseph Neal with his "Charcoal sketches"; Lewis Gaylord Clark of the "Knickerbocker" Magazine; and later, Will M. Carleton and Charles Follen Adams, best known by his perfect poem of "Leedle Yacob Strauss"; but writing comical verses all the time that appeal to the heart, while they raise a smile.

Wit, humor that is full of absurd exaggerations, and fun of an essentially American type, bubble up spontaneously all over our country as freely as the oil wells of Pennsylvania. Even the religious weeklies have now a funny column, and some of the paragraphs in our best dailies sparkle with wit that deserves a longer life.

The humor of the newspapers is a natural and wholesome product of our national development. We are a nation of newspaper readers. The daily and weekly journals reflect every phase of our busy progressive life, and aim to keep pace with, if not to direct the intellectual growth of the people. A column which presents the current wit and humor of the day has become an essential department of every good paper. From the harrowing details of a railroad accident on the first page, and from the scarcely less depressing editorial struggle with the tariff question, we turn with restful relief to the grotesque wit of Bill Nye or the commonsense humor of Bob Burdette.

In the string of paragraphs clipped from the funny columns all over the land, there is material for a surer "Elixir of Life" than can ever be educed from pulverized rabbit or solution of French Guinea Pig.

Let us not forget the pioneers in this good work, rough and coarse, but individual and interesting, they are not surpassed by their successors.

The special characteristics of American humor can be traced back to the dry maxims and shrewd sense of Benjamin Franklin when the habits of our people were simpler and the scope of the press narrower. A good joke or story found no means of general circulation, unless through the humble medium of the traveling clown or negro minstrel. Even in the enterprising newspaper of the present day there appears now and then some weather-beaten pleasantry, which, to the boy of forty years ago, is suggestive of the burnt cork of the minstrel or the cap and bells of the circus clown, now almost crowded

18

out of the arena by better things. In the rush and worry of modern life the humorist has found a larger field; many brilliant names have been added to the roll of newspaper wits, but those first in the field have never been eclipsed.

MADAME DE GENLIS.

Only France, that land of fascinating women and phenomenal individualities, could have produced a Madame de Genlis. Brilliant, yet tedious; sensible, absurd; amiable, resentful; eccentric, conventional; the author of nearly one hundred volumes — sober works on education, and worldly novels of very questionable influence, poems and history, biography and botany, natural history and etiquette, religion and malicious scandal; alternating between court and convent for nearly a century; adored and hated; praised and vindicated; regarded as a saint and sinner; a shameless *intriguante* and a French Hannah More! Was she not a captivating bundle of opposite qualities? I cannot claim genius for my heroine, nor a large amount of the piety and prudery she professed; but as the Governor of Princes (for Governor she would be called) while a most successful writer for children, when stories for children were almost unknown; as a popular novelist; as an extraordinary and entertaining person, whose life affords both amusement and instruction — she is a marked character, a power in her day, a type of the ancient nobility of France; as regards her social life, of a vanity that was at once sublime and ridiculous.

She was born on the 25th of January, 1746, on a little estate in Burgundy, such a puny infant that it was not thought worth while to dress her; so she was sewed up in a down pillow, and the atom was laid in an armchair, to struggle with life or die. In a few moments the corpulent mayor, almost blind, came to pay his visit of congratulation, and separating the huge flaps of his overcoat, was just about to sit down in that very chair when the nurse screamed and pulled him away. And in her Memoirs she remarks, with her usual conceit: " It was not the good nurse who saved me; no, it was God himself, acting by her instrumentality. He had given me a mission upon earth, which he decreed should be fulfilled."

She had the usual joys, sorrows, and hair-breadth 'scapes of childhood — was nearly drowned at eighteen months — soon after tumbled into the kitchen fire — had a dangerous fall at five — but bore a charmed life.

Her father had purchased a large estate, beautifully situated. Its chateau resembled those described by Mrs. Radcliffe; ancient and tumbledown, with old towers and immense courtyards, on the opposite side of the Loire, near the famous Abbey of Sept-Font's, where perpetual silence reigned; and her father, when the children were too noisy in their evening games, would propose they should play here the holy fathers of Sept-Font, which changed the riotous frolic into peaceful pantomime.

When the little girl was six years old her mother took her to Paris to visit an aunt, and she describes graphically the horrors to which she was subjected, in order to be made stylish and graceful. She had two teeth pulled out, was squeezed into stiff corsets, which pinched her terribly, her feet were imprisoned in tight shoes, so that she could not take a step without pain, three or four thousand curl papers (this is *her* estimate) were used to twist her hair, and she wore, for the first time, a hoop. Then, in order to get rid of her country attitudes, she had an iron collar put round her neck ; and as the unfortunate little tot squinted slightly, she was obliged to wear goggles four hours each day, and was, besides, forbidden to run, jump, or ask questions! Paris was anything but a paradise to her then ; but soon came the great ceremony of her public baptism, after which (loaded with candies and playthings) she was taken to the opera, and life looked bright again. She was, she tells us, " a child of remarkable sweetness of disposition."

The next great event was her being received as a Canoness of the noble chapter of St. Alix, as an honorary novitiate ; the Grand Prior having discerned the "aureole of moral grandeur upon her youthful brow." This dignity confers the title of Countess. Madame la Comtesse de Lancy was conducted in pomp to the church, a consecrated ring placed on her finger, and she was decorated with the signs of the order.

Her education was almost totally neglected, for her governess had, as she expresses it, " nothing of profane knowledge "; so history and other serious studies were soon abandoned, and she was never taught to write at all. Her mother was busy with society and her own interests, and never saw her except at meals. Her father, a handsome man, fond of music and philosophy and hunting, seemed only anxious to conquer her womanish antipathies to mice and toads and spiders, he insisted on her taming a mouse, and frequently obliged her to catch spiders with her fingers and hold toads in her hands, but never succeeded in removing the aversion.

At eight Felicité dictated romances and comedies to Mademoiselle de Mars, when she did not know how to form a single letter; and she remarks: " Even in the reveries of my infancy there was a foundation of love, of glory, and of virtue, which in a child must be thought remarkable." Her brother, she says, was far from being so brilliant and remarkable a child as she was !

A fondness for music and for teaching was inborn. She used to get out of her window by a rope, and, sliding down to the terrace, gather the boys of the village about her to teach them the little she knew — poetry she had committed to memory, and bits from the Catechism. In after years she was ambitious to officiate as schoolma'am in general to all France, and felt abundantly able to fill the position.

In 1755 her father, of whom we hear little, went to Paris and remained eighteen months. Her mother resolved to prepare a *fête* to celebrate his return, and composed a comedietta in the pastoral style, in which the pretty daughter took the part of Love. Tragedies were also performed, and we imagine the fashionable wife was more anxious to enliven the dull monotony of the country than to honor her husband, whose long absence was endured with great composure. As Iphigenia, Felicité was gorgeously arrayed in cherry silk and silver, trimmed with sables : but her costume as Cupid was so becoming that she wore it regularly. The wings were suppressed on Sundays, and she adopted a red riding-hood cloak : but during the week she rambled and danced over the fields with a short rose-colored dress trimmed with lace and artificial flowers, blue wings, long hair floating, quiver on shoulder, and bow in hand : and this chronic masquerade was indulged in for nearly a year. This alone was enough to tinge her whole life with romance. Her talent for acting was always remarkable.

Her next attire was a regular boy's dress, and she took daily lessons in fencing, as in dancing. She praises her own agility, grace, and musical skill at this age, and also declares that she could read character from the face with unerring instinct. She delighted in building air-castles, figuring for herself

an extraordinary and brilliant destiny, with persecu-
tions and reverses of fortune no stranger than those
which actually occurred.

Lovers came while she was in short dresses, and
kept coming in crowds till she was quite an old lady
— she, of course, always surprised, always cool and
cruel, with often fatal effect. "I was but eleven
years old," she writes, "and small of my age, when
I inspired the first passion — at least, the first *avowed*
passion — quite unconsciously. I even felt shocked,
grieved, when the son of one Pinat, an apothecary,
proclaimed a devotion which he could no longer conceal, in verses glowing with a Sappho's fire. If
there was no other proof of the distraction of mind,
the delirium of love, with which Louis Pinat was
afflicted, it would be manifest in the fact that he had
overlooked the impassable gulf which must ever
separate noblemen and apothecaries." She advised
him to leave that part of the country before the
mischief already done was irremediable. He yielded
and departed for Paris. Another, conscious of the
hopeless disparity in years, sought safety in flight,
and ultimately succeeded in banishing her image
from his memory. A young and promising lawyer
was the next victim; refused, he at first contemplated suicide, but changed his mind, and emigrated
to St. Domingo. Poor Baron de Zeolachen, Colonel
of Swiss Guards and eighty years of age, fell hopelessly in love with the irresistible maiden; she was

inexorable as ever, and "his days" (records his destroyer) " were shortened."

The next winter was spent in Paris, and she remembers listening to Marmontel as he read his tale of " The Self-styled Philosopher " to her aunt, little thinking that the quiet girl in the corner would one day be one of his severest critics and rouse his bitter enmity. She now began to compose verses very creditable for a child. One gentleman thought them wonderful, copied several to show to his friends, and presented the poetess with a copy of Rousseau's Odes and Sacred Poems (a French lyric poet, not to be confounded with Jean Jacques). One of the little red morocco volumes was always in her pocket; she committed all to memory, and recited them with great expression. The giver urged her to read constantly, but this was impossible, as her aunt was a woman of the world and had few books; but she succeeded in procuring the libretto of a Gascon opera, and had fallen asleep while reading in bed; the candle set fire to the curtains, and her mother, stealing in with a pleasant surprise — an elegant bracelet, with her miniature set in opals and emeralds, which she intended to put on her arm — found the chamber full of suffocating smoke, and in ten minutes later the unconscious prodigy would have been lost to the world.

Her father, after some despairing struggles against adverse fate, sold his marquisate and chateau to meet the demands of creditors, and went to St.

Domingo, hoping to reëstablish his fortune by a speculation in sugar. Failing in this, he was taken prisoner by an English ship when returning to France, and carried to Launceton, where he formed an intimacy with a fellow-prisoner — Comte de Genlis, a younger son of a noble French family, who had served in the navy in the East Indies. Being powerfully connected at the French Court, the Count was soon exchanged; and returning to Paris, procured the liberation of M. Ducrest, who lived but a short time afterward.

Felicité and her mother had been visitors at the country house of a rich old gentleman, eccentric and benevolent, who was, to quote from Madame's memoirs, "enchanted with the little talents I possessed, and said often with a profound sigh in looking at me, 'What a pity that she is but thirteen!'" She played wonderfully on harp and guitar, and sang and danced like a professional. It is said that Mademoiselle Ducrest supported herself at this time by giving lessons on the harp, which was eminently creditable. In the French *Biographic Universelle*, which devotes many pages to her career, it is said that she danced and played at the houses of her friends, with a charge for admission : she does not mention either fact herself. Lovers again pleaded their suits. One old fellow wooed her with a huge packet sent by his valet, containing his genealogy at full length. She liked best a rich and handsome widower of twenty-six, but was determined to marry no one but a man of quality and belonging to the Court. She says frankly, that she had received so much praise that vanity had become her ruling motive. She does say : " In spite of all the praises with which I was loaded, I was ill at ease in these brilliant parties, and I discovered two things : first, that one ought not to enter into the great world, but when one can be on a footing with others as to dress ; and secondly, that if it had not been for my talents these persons would have had no wish to invite me."

But the coming man with all the requisite qualifications is almost here. Her father, who carried everywhere with him a box, on which was the portrait of his daughter playing the harp, had shown her picture to the brave young soldier, already decorated with the cross of St. Louis. To him he read her bright letters, and those of her mother, full of praise for her many accomplishments, and glowing accounts of social success. Genlis was about to be married to a lady possessed of 40,000 francs a year. But he was genuinely in love. The mother and daughter had retired to a convent after the father's death, and thither the Count followed them, and was soon married secretly and at midnight. It was a union with love on one side, pure ambition on the other. His rich relatives were angry and disgusted, and refused to see either for some years.

When he was ordered to join his regiment, the bride, only fifteen, was placed in a convent, where her vivacity and irrepressible love of excitement were constantly bubbling over in wild pranks with the staid old nuns; running about the corridors at night in strange disguises, sometimes attired as the devil himself, with horns on her merry head, and her pretty face blackened. Or she would steal into the cells of deaf old sisters, and paint their withered cheeks with rouge, or patch them for mutual surprise, when they rose for matins, and many a dance was given in her apartments, music being provided by an aged fiddler. Her mornings were devoted to music and reading, and long letters to her mother and her husband. Little plays were composed in honor of a visit from her mother, from which she continued to get a great deal of fun, allotting the different characters in a most inappropriate and ridiculous way, and persuading the duped performers that they were irresistible. Indeed, one old creature who acted as her maid, gray-haired, with bad complexion, and minus two front teeth, was induced to appear as a shepherdess, with a short white petticoat bordered with bright ribbon, and wearing on one side of her head a jaunty little straw hat decked with flowers. Extolled extravagantly for her acting and graces, she received it all with amazing credulity, and when the naughty instigator of all this mischief proposed that this becoming and appropriate costume be worn constantly, the humbugged fright consented, and paraded about with a crook, to the delight of all observers.

The school-girlish Madame was so happy at the

convent, that when her husband came to take her to their home at Genlis, she pleaded for one month more, " and was much surprised at receiving a dry and decided refusal " — which is a very Frenchy picture.

Her practical jokes in her own house were exquisitely ludicrous in conception and admirably carried out, and her vagaries of conduct must have caused much astonishment to her more commonplace neighbors. With her sister-in-law, both dressed as peasant women, she went about buying milk, and they then indulged in the luxury of a bath in milk, the surface strewn with rose leaves. She once lost her way on purpose while on a wild boar hunt, just for an adventure, hoping to find a mysterious castle, with inmates full of wit and courtesy eager to detain her as their guest. After galloping for three hours, very hungry, and no castle in view, she found that, like Goldsmith's matron in "She Stoops to Conquer," she was nearer home than she supposed. She had given her husband a great fright and received a severe scolding. When laughed at as a fine lady at a picnic on account of her embroidered white slippers, she swallowed a live fish to prove that she was not dainty.

But now she began to study in earnest. Education she had none; as for history, she was so ignorant she did not know where to begin, and never had heard of geometry; she at first had no guide in her reading. But she was determined to lose no oppor-

tunity of learning; it was her plan throughout life
to ask explanations of what she did not understand;
and she kept a commonplace book by her and wrote
in it each day. These three habits would make any
young lady well-informed.

She gained some idea of field labor and of garden-
ing, went to see cider made, visited the houses of the
village tradesmen where they were at work — the
carpenter, weaver, basket-maker, etc.— and constantly practised medicine at Genlis in partnership
with the village barber — a wise physician — confin-
ing her prescriptions to simple drinks and nourish-
ing broths, moderating the barber's rage for emetics,
and bled the peasants, giving thirty *sous* after each
bleeding. As was natural, she soon had a great number of patients, all anxious to be bled. Phlebotomy
was the rage until the Count complained of the expense of this treatment. With all this she learned
the game of billiards, and painted flowers and prac-
ticed on some musical instrument every day. She
played well on half a dozen — was a performer on
the bag-pipe, besides harp, guitar, violin, harpischord,
and organ.

She had real genius for entertaining her friends,
and on one occasion planned a quadrille called the
Proverbs, in which each couple formed a proverb by
their costume, while the figures also represented a
proverb, " Run backwards before you leap." She
composed the air herself. Unfortunately for the
success of this novel diversion, some envious gen-

tlemen who were not invited to join the dance sent
a Savoyard dressed as a cat into their midst, creating
a great excitement. *His* proverb was, " Beware of
waking a sleeping cat."

With the birth of her daughter Caroline, the
young mother became more serious, and her first
real work was, " Reflections of a Mother Twenty
Years of Age." This manuscript was lost, but many
of its thoughts were transferred to her book, " Adèle
and Théodore," which was translated into English
by Misses Edgeworth and Holcroft. Soon after her
twentieth birthday, she was presented at court by
the stately uncle and aunt of her husband, now completely reconciled.

Her eight volumes of autobiography, written
after she was eighty, although absurd from her constant habit of self-adulation, are full of interesting
sketches of distinguished men and women, and
illustrate the history and social life of a century
agone. In these recollections she confesses everyone's faults — but her own. The second volume
opens with a ludicrous mistake of hers in regard to
Rousseau. Prenéle, a famous comic actor of that day,
who could imitate Rousseau to the life, confides to
Count de Genlis his intention of calling on Madame
as the eccentric philosopher. The little lady was
told of the coming joke, when, strange to say, both
gentlemen forgot all about it; and when she heard
that Rousseau was anxious to make her acquaintance, and hear her play on the harp, she was in

great glee, received the actor with a merry laugh, sang several of Rousseau's songs with careless ease, and urged him to come next day to dine. It was not till his departure that the misunderstanding was explained. Then her husband had his turn of laughing immoderately; and it was decided that the great man should never know her mistake.

In speaking of his works, he said: " I am not a Catholic, but no one has spoken of the gospel with more conviction and feeling." He talked admirably of music, and was a real connoisseur, yet his own compositions were not good. His sole means of subsistence was copying music, which he did with singular skill. He must have been extremely unreasonable and immensely conceited. One evening when Madame de Genlis had the loan of a grated box, with private staircase, at the opera, she persuaded Rousseau to go with them. He said that he carefully avoided showing himself in public, but consented. On entering the box he would not allow the grate to be put down, saying he was sure Madame would not like it. She was too prettily dressed to remain hidden, and as she insisted, he actually held it up, saying he would conceal himself behind her. In a moment he put his head forward, on purpose to be seen, and again and again, till several persons called out, " There is Rousseau!" and the cry passed through the house, but no applause. He left as soon as the curtain fell, in a furious and implacable state, really enraged to think he had not

produced a sensation ; but asserting that he would
never see Madame again, as she had taken him there
to be shown off, as wild beasts are exhibited at a fair.
And she really never met him again. The Marchioness of Pompadour having succeeded in putting
Voltaire and others at her feet, tried, as she said, to
tame Rosseau ; but a letter she received from him
disgusted her from making any more advances.
" He is an owl," said she one day to Madame de
Mirepoix. " Yes," said the Maréchale, " but he is
Minerva's."

At twenty-four Madame de Genlis was made a
lady of honor in the household of the Duc de
Chartres, afterwards Duke of Orleans, known during
the Revolution as Egalitè, a profligate patron and
dangerous mischief-maker. The society of the
Palais Royal was of course the best in Paris, and
Madame de Genlis was a great favorite with all the
gentlemen, and with the ladies who were not
envious. But she kept up her studies with marvelous enthusiasm, always making extracts as she read.
She persuaded the Duchess of Chartres to learn
geography, and even taught her to spell, afterwards
giving her lessons in history and mythology. She
had also her secretary writing her notes and letters.
Still, she kept up her own embroidery, painting, and
music. She kept up her practice on the harp and
instruments, and collected a fine cabinet of shells,
minerals, and stones, which was afterwards confiscated and sold for the benefit of the nation ; and she

continued to write comedies. Was there ever such
a versatile and busy woman ?

When Glück went to Paris to have his operas
performed, he completely bewitched Madame de
Genlis, who was such an enthusiastic musician.
She went to all the rehearsals, and every evening to
the opera, and had Glück and other famous performers come to her *soirées* twice a week. She sang
for them, and played his overtures on the harp; but
at last felt that "music, Glück, and the opera had
acquired too great a power over her." So she made
a resolution never again to go to opera or theater,
and she kept her vow faithfully, great as was the
sacrifice. She makes this frank comment: "I sincerely wish now that religion had been my motive
in this, but it was only the taste for study and the
pride of being distinguished."

She now took up the study of the English language, and avers that she could read the poets easily
in five months. Determined never to lose any time,
she would read in the coach while traveling, and
carried one of her little books of extracts in her
pocket to read in odd moments. In traveling, she
would lead into conversation anyone she met who
could teach her anything, and then write down what
she had collected. Having heard that one gentleman had written in a few years four quarto volumes
by employing the ten or fifteen minutes before his
wife came to dinner, she copied one thousand verses
from various authors while waiting for the Duchesse

de Chartres, who was always a quarter of an hour late. It was a curious and valuable collection, beginning with the oldest poetry known in France. She went often to the Jardin des Plantes and the Cabinet of Natural History, and met there Buffon, who became an intimate friend.

In 1774, Louis XV died, and the unfortunate Louis XVI was king. The next year Madame de Genlis spent in traveling. While at Geneva she visited Voltaire; she had from a child disliked him for his infidel sentiments, but still desired his admiration. "It was the custom for ladies to become agitated, grow pale, and even to faint on seeing Voltaire; they threw themselves into his arms, stammered and wept and adored."

This was the etiquette of a presentation at Ferney, so that ordinary courtesy seemed almost a slight. But Voltaire, perceiving her perplexity, kissed her little hand, and the agony was over. She writes: "During the whole time of dinner Voltaire was far from agreeable. He seemed always in a passion with his servants, crying out to them with such strength of lungs that I often started involuntarily." But it was the result of habit, and the servants did not mind it in the least. He gave her a drive through the village to see the houses he had built and the benevolent establishments founded by him. Such gross flattery as he had received had spoiled him. He regarded himself as an oracle, and could not brook contradiction or criticism. Imagine, then,

his feelings when reduced to absolute subjection by
a page whom he had vexed. "When Frederick the
Great made short excursions he often asked Voltaire
to accompany him. On one of these trips Voltaire
was alone in a post-chaise following the royal carriage. A young page whom Voltaire had severely
scolded, as he thought unjustly, resolved to be
revenged; accordingly, when he was sent in advance
to have horses ready, he told all the post-masters
and postilions that the king had an old monkey, of
which he was so very fond that he delighted in
dressing him up like a person belonging to the
court, and that he always took this animal with him;
that the monkey cared for no one but the king, and
was extremely mischievous; and that, therefore, if
he attempted to get out of the chaise, they must prevent him. After receiving this notice all the servants of the different post-houses, whenever Voltaire
attempted to leave his carriage, opposed his exit,
and when he thrust out his hand to open the door,
he always received two or three sharp blows with a
stick upon his fingers, followed by shouts of laughter.
Voltaire, who did not understand a word of German,
could not demand an explanation of these singular
proceedings; his fury became extreme, but it only
served to redouble the gayety of the post-masters,
and a large crowd constantly assembled, in consequence of the page's report, to see 'the king's
monkey' and to hoot at him. What completed the
anger of Voltaire was that the king thought the

trick so good that he refused to punish the inventor; so the vengeance of the young page was complete."

Madame de Genlis's first book was a collection of her plays and poems, published entirely for the benefit of a noble man, who was most unjustly imprisoned for life if he did not pay a much larger sum than he or his friends could raise. One gentleman, unknown to her, but touched by the generous effort, paid three thousand francs for one copy; the others sold so well that in six days all were gone, with a clear profit of forty-six thousand francs. The injured party accepted the sum, the prisoner was set free. This work was translated into all the modern languages, and the Empress of Russia had a version made with Russian text opposite the French.

And now comes a very marked change. The Duc and Duchesse de Chartres proposed that Madame de Genlis take the entire charge of the instruction of their children. With her mania for teaching, and the honor of being offered a position which the wisest men of the realm desired and coveted — which Fénelon had filled in another reign — she could not refuse the offer. M. de Genlis, who had not accompanied her to Paris, being informed of the Duke's proposition, demurred, and requested his wife to join him in the country. She refused to do so, and they never saw each other again. It is necessary just here to allude to the shadow on Madame's character in her supposed intimacy with the Duke. Her affected unconsciousness of any

scandal and her display of prudery is in strange contrast to the convictions of the public. The Queen,
prejudiced by the complaints of the wife, excluded
her from the opportunities of display at court which
she would have gloried in, and she never could
obtain either a private or public audience. After
accepting the position she at once left the Palais
Royal, and retired to a pavilion built on her own
plan at the Convent Belle Chasse. She was then
thirty-one. She gave up dancing and rouge, then
universally worn. With her usual frankness (on all
subjects but one) she says: " It is singular that
though I had always possessed religious sentiments,
all the sacrifices of a *dévotée* which I have made have
have not been inspired by religion; and this is a
reflection which afflicts me." She gave up rouge,
because she had said it would be no sacrifice to her,
and no one seemed to believe her; so she made a
bet with the Duke that she would renounce rouge
on the 25th of January, 1776, and kept her word.

Now began her earnest life-work with the four
children of the Duke, a daughter and three boys, the
eldest being Louis Philippe, afterward King of
France. Like Madame de Maintenon, she was
extremely practical — a model housewife — and with
an eye to every detail, settling the accounts daily,
while everything was rendered useful as a means of
education. The tapestry of the princess's room was
painted in oil, and on a blue ground were represented busts of the seven kings of Rome, and the

emperors and empresses down to Constantine the
Great. Over the doors were historical scenes. The
staircases were covered with maps, which could be
taken down for lessons. Even the fire-screens,
hand-screens, and tops of the doors had lessons engraved on them; while in letters of gold, over the
grate which shut them out from the world, were
these words of Addison, taken from the *Spectator* :
" True happiness is of a retired nature, and an enemy
to pomp and noise." Her own daughters, two
beautiful girls, were educated with the Prince's
family.

During the first eighteen months in this sheltered
retreat she published several volumes of her Theater
of Education, all highly praised by the press and
critics of that time. Madame d'Epinay was especially delighted, and urged a visit. Here she met
Saint Lambert and Madame du Deffand.

She was now thoroughly in her element, and led,
as she says, a delicious life. She was the first governess or tutor of princes in France who taught the
languages by means of conversation. There was an
English and Italian maid, and the little princesses
had an English child for a playmate ; one of the
valets was a well-educated German, another Italian,
and the princes were given a good teacher of English. They now removed to St. Leu, a charming
residence, with a fine park. A small garden was laid
out for each of her pupils, and they dug in the dirt
like ordinary children, and planted flowers and veg-

etables.   A botanist and chemist were attached to the house, also a teacher of drawing.   A theater was built, where the children played pantomimes and her own pieces.   She says: " In the winter at Paris I had a turning machine put into my ante-chamber, and in recreation hours all the children, as well as myself, learned to turn.   I thus acquired, with them, all the trades in which strength is not required; making, for instance, pocket-books and morocco portfolios, which looked as well as those of English manufacture." They also made baskets, tapes, ribbons, gauze, pasteboard, and plans in relief, artificial flowers, gratings for libraries in brass wire, marbled paper, gilt frames, all sorts of work in hair, and even tried their hands at wigs, and the boys learnt cabinet-making. The Duke of Valois, with the aid of his brother, made a large press and a table with drawers for a poor peasant woman of St. Leu. This was their amusement. " Beside their palace of the five orders of architecture, which they could build and take down at pleasure, I made them make various tools and utensils, the interior of a laboratory, with retorts, crucibles, and alembics, and the interior of a cabinet of natural history. These were afterwards displayed in the gallery of the Palais Royal, and have since been placed in the Louvre. I was very proud to see the public admire the playthings I had invented for my pupils." The princes were taught to swim and row, and the Duke of Orleans bought an estate by the sea, where six months were passed studying shells, fishes, and sea-plants, and learning in a practical way about ships. During one winter they were taken to a hospital, to dress the wounds of the poor.

Then her husband inherited a large estate, 100,000 francs a year. He urged his wife to leave her pupils and return to him ; but ambition, and sincere attachment to the children, and self-love carried the day, and she refused, which was afterwards a deep grief to her. In her words : " In spite of the arguments of M. de Genlis, I persisted in a resolution which has cost me dear. If I had fulfilled my real duty, which was to rejoin him, especially when he desired and entreated it so earnestly, I might easily have induced him to leave France ; we should have lived comfortably in a foreign land, and he would not have perished on a scaffold ! This terrible reflection causes me eternal remorse ; since his death it never leaves me."

The assembly of the French Academy in 1783 gave the " Prize of Utility " to Madame d'Epinay's " Conversations of Emilia " in preference to Madame de Genlis's " Adèle and Théodore," a manual of education — a matter of intense surprise to the latter ; but she consoled herself by attributing the decision to her having spoken too favorably of religion and too lightly of philosophy. " But how," says Grimm, " could the vengeance of philosophy wound the high piety of our illustrious governess ? Can she who renounces the toilet, rouge, and all the pleasures, all the vanities of life, still regret its frivolous and pro-

fane laurels?"   The Duchess of Grammont said with
her usual frankness that she was overjoyed at the
success of Madame d Epinay, because she hoped that
Madame de Genlis would die with envy, which would
be an excellent thing; or that she would revenge
herself by a good satire, which would be good again;
and lastly, because she wished all the world to perceive, what she had for some time suspected, the
Academy to be falling into dotage.

At Belle Chasse an intimacy was formed with
Madame Necker. She made the first visit, bringing
her daughter, then sixteen. Madame de Genlis never
liked Madame de Stael. This is her first criticism:
"This young lady was not pretty, but she was very
animated, and though she spoke a deal too much, she
spoke cleverly." Madame Necker had educated her
on a poor plan, permitting her to pass much of her
time in her *salon*, among the crowd of *beaux esprits*
who were constantly to be found there, while the
young miss discussed with them on love and the
passions. The solitude of her chamber and a few
good books would have been more to her advantage.
She learned to talk fast and much, without any reflection, and has written in the same manner. She
had read little, and all her knowledge was superficial.
She had collected in her works not the result of
sound reading, but an infinite number of recollections and incoherent conversations. Madame Necker
was a virtuous, calm, reserved person, without any
fancy. She was studied in all she did, and arranged

beforehand a part for all situations. The Chevalier
de Chastellux picked up a little book while waiting
for Madame Necker to appear — as he was too early
for dinner — and found a careful preparation of her
subjects for conversation during the dinner. His
own name caught his eye, and he read: " I must talk
to the Chevalier de Chastellux about Public Happiness and Agatha " — two of his works. All were to
be complimented in some skillful way. The dinner
was peculiarly enjoyable to the amused chevalier, as
he saw that Madame repeated word for word the remarks in her book. Madame de Genlis, throughout
her memoirs, gives the idea that Madame de Stael
was a failure, but that if she had been allowed to edu-
cate her, it would have been vastly different, saying :
" I have often regretted sincerely that she had not
been my daughter or my pupil. I should then have
given her good literary principles, just ideas, and
unaffected manners. With such an education, joined
to her own talents and generous mind, she would
have been an accomplished person, and the first
female author of our day."

A short time before the Revolution, in 1785, she
visited England, and was received, by her own account, with unusual honor, which she writes of as
frankly as of her failings. She says : " No woman is
allowed to enter the House of Commons, but that
assembly, by a special order, invited me to be present at one of the debates. I was not allowed to introduce any other woman." This was one of Sheridan's

practical jokes. "Tragedy was not played in the summer, yet, in honor to me, Hamlet was performed at one of the theaters. An account of all these things was inserted in the English newspapers, with the most complimentary notices of myself. There appeared also in the journals an infinite number of verses in my honor. I received many marks of interest and esteem from the most distinguished persons in England ; among others, Fox, Sheridan, the Duchess of Devonshire, Mr. Burke, and Miss Burney. The Prince of Wales invited me to an entertainment, and the Queen invited me to Windsor. This was a great distinction, for she never received foreigners there. Lord Mansfield, the celebrated English judge, requested permission to visit me. Mr. Horace Walpole invited me to breakfast in his Gothic priory."

"I read a great many English works, and was struck with the absurd contempt which the writers of this country affect for other nations. With what injustice have they criticised our literature, at the same time they were stealing from or copying our writers ! How are we represented on the English stage ? The French are always treated there as weak fops, and what seems still more singular, as cowards. Let us compare this with the generous good feeling of our authors, who have so highly praised English writers and the English nation."

Walpole writes : "I will read no more of Rousseau ; his Confessions disgusted me beyond any book I ever opened. His Hen — the schoolmistress, Mad-

ame de Genlis —-is arrived in London. I nauseate
her, too ; the eggs of education that he and she both
laid could not be hatched till the chickens were ready
to die of old age. I revere genius, I have a dear
friendship for common sense ; I have a partiality for
professed nonsense ; but I abhor extravagance, that
is given for the quintessence of sense, and affectation
that pretends to be philosophy." But when he met
her, the prejudice vanished, and he says : " Her person is agreeable, and she seems to have been pretty.
Her conversation is natural and reasonable, not pre-
cisive and affected, and searching to be eloquent, as
I had expected." But he joins with other men in
ridiculing the office she held. " The Duc de Chartres has made Madame de Genlis governess of his
children. Why should not Madame de Schwellen-
berg be governess to our prince, and Bishop Hurd
wet nurse ? "

In Fanny Burney's Diary (1785) there are many
allusions to Madame de Genlis. She speaks of her at
first as the " sweetest and most accomplished French
woman she ever met with," and is, for a long time,
completely charmed ; but tales, true or false, were so
often forced into her unwilling ears, that she says :
" Notwithstanding the most ardent admiration of her
talents, and a zest yet greater for her engaging
society and elegantly lively and winning manners, I
yet dared no longer come within the precincts of her
fascinating allurements."

The biographer of Burke, describing Madame de

Genlis's visit to Butler's Court (1792) gives an unpleasant anecdote : "Her great ambition was to do, or be thought to do, everything ; to possess a *universal* genius both in mind and mechanical powers beyond the attainments of her own or even the other sex. A ring which she wore, of very curious, indeed, exquisite workmanship, having attracted the notice of Sir Joshua Reynolds, he inquired by what good fortune it had come into her possession, and received for answer that it was executed by herself. Sir Joshua stared, but made no reply. "I have done with her," said he, the first time he was alone with Mr. Burke afterwards. "To have the assurance to tell *me* such a tale ! Why, my dear sir, it is an *antique ;* no living artist in Europe can equal it."

She carried back and introduced into France, where it was unknown, the moss rose, as Pope introduced the weeping willow into England by planting some shoots which were sent him with a basket of figs.

Soon after her return the Revolution began, and her life was full of troubles — charges of sympathy with the Liberals, and serious danger from association with the children of the Duchess of Orleans, whom she was accused of estranging from their mother.

To all these attacks she pleaded " Not guilty," and wrote a book to prove it, insisting that she was at all times a Royalist. From her account, you judge her to be peculiarly conscientious and pure, resisting all admirers, and looking with severity upon damaged reputation. She was either a hypocrite or grossly slandered. Let us give her the benefit of the doubt.

Her husband, who fearlessly expressed himself opposed to the execution of the king, was punished on the scaffold. The Duke, also, was killed. After Madame de Genlis had wandered about with Mademoiselle d'Orleans for a year or two, the princess was recalled, and her lonely governess went to Berlin, where she gave lessons in literature, and designed patterns for a print factory, and wrote novels, thus supporting herself very comfortably. She said she knew fifty-two trades by which she could earn her living. Talleyrand, also an *emigré* with Madame de Stael, writing to her from Philadelphia, says of America: "This country is a place where honest men may prosper, though not, to be sure, quite so well as rogues, who, as may be expected, have many advantages on their side." She remained in exile for nine years. At Hamburg she received a visit from Klopstock, who talked at her steadily for three hours, mostly of himself, and retired highly pleased with her conversational ability.

In Paris, when she was allowed to return, in 1801, everything had strangely, sadly altered. She said: "Everything seemed new to me. I felt like a stranger who stops at every step to look around. I could scarcely recognize the streets, of which all the names were changed. I found philosophers substituted for saints. I saw passing hackney coaches,

which I recognized as the confiscated carriages of
my friends; and in walking, I saw on the stalls books
which bore on their bindings the coats of arms of
my acquaintances, and in shops their portraits exhibited for sale. Three-fourths of the unfortunate
nobles whom these pictures represented had been
guillotined, and the rest, despoiled of everything,
were wandering in foreign lands. Even the language was changed. The Bureaux d'Esprit, ridiculed by those who were envious or unable to rival
them, such as the Hotel de Rambouillet, were gone
forever. Suppers were no longer in fashion, for our
customs had changed as well as the language. Formerly, the ladies, after dinner was over, rose and
left the table, in order to wash their mouths; the
gentlemen went into an ante-chamber for the same
purpose. Now-a-days, this part of our toilette is performed at table in many houses, where Frenchmen,
seated by the side of ladies, wash their hands and
spit into a bowl. This spectacle would have been
truly astonishing to their grandfathers and grandmothers."

As she was seriously in need of money, she
wrote the " Romance de La Vallière." This story
was greatly liked. Napoleon, who was inordinately
fond of novel-reading, read it through without stopping, and was affected by it even to tears. It went
through eighteen editions, and brought the age of
Louis XIV into fashion. Sir James McIntosh said,
" It is surely a most fascinating book." Some

months after this success, "Madam de Maintenon" appeared. Fontanes, in his letter acknowledging the receipt of this book, closes by saying: "I doubt, even in an age more worthy of you, whether the Mesdames de Sevigné and La Fayette would have pardoned you for surpassing them. It is true that the La Rochefoucaulds, the La Fontaines, and the La Bruyéres would have been at your feet, but where are they at this day?"

Then followed novels and plays thick as the leaves of Vallambrosa. The Emperor now requested from Madame de Genlis a letter once a fortnight on "politics, finance, literature, and morals," as well as on any other subjects that might occur to her. He allotted to her handsome apartments in the Arsenal, and a pension of six thousand francs. After telling her readers how highly these letters were valued by the first consul, she adds, "It was not my fault if he did not become religious."

The Queen of Naples desired her as governess for her family. She did not accept the position, but was granted a pension of three thousand francs by the Queen, who admired her greatly. In consideration of this compliment, Madame de Genlis prepared a written course of history and literature, as a guide for the Queen's children.

Her drawing-room was crowded every evening during the winter of 1812. Lady Morgan was often seen there, fascinating all with her sparkling manner, warmth of heart, and good nature — not beautiful,

but always attractive. Madame Recamier was a constant visitor. She is usually spoken of as a beautiful
lay figure, or a soulless coquette, so that it is pleasant to hear a better opinion from one who knew her
well, and who was peculiarly quick to notice defects.
She says: " The more I conversed with her, the
more talent and interest I found in her conversation.
Had she not been so handsome and so celebrated for
her person, she would be ranked amongst the most
accomplished women of society. The world never
grants but one species of renown, and only lavishes
its praise for one darling quality. If Madame
Recamier had not been so *beautiful*, every one would
have praised the accuracy and discrimination of her
mind; *no one listens with more attention* (an important
trait where you wish to charm), for she feels and
comprehends everything. The delicacy of her sentiments gives an inexpressible charm to that of her
mind. Her opinions on every subject indirectly
connected with morals are never calculated before-
hand, and are extremely accurate. They are the
free, happy emanations of a pure and feeling heart.
Notwithstanding all the troubles and misfortunes
with which her life has been checkered, there is so
much sweetness in her temper, so much calmness in
her heart and conscience, that she has preserved
nearly all the fairness of her complexion, and all the
charming appearance of her early youth. The round
of pleasure in which she has lived has rendered her
completely unable to apply herself to serious occu-

pations. Disgusted with frivolous amusements of every kind, tired of trifling, she now only gives herself up to them through habits of idleness ; but she is a proof that it is the most disagreeable situation anyone can be placed in who possesses judgment and talents. In her most intimate chats she rarely speaks of herself, for the interests of her life have never been but relative. She has long possessed friends, who are deservedly devoted to her, in elevated stations, but has never profited herself by her influence with them, although always suggesting beneficent plans for others. There does not exist a woman who has rendered more services than she without cabal or intrigue, and there is not one who, after the loss of a great fortune, has possessed more dignity under reverses."

The remaining years of this long and busy life were spent in publishing a number of volumes--- so many that it would be fatiguing even to enumerate the titles — in entertaining her friends, and in attacking the new ideas of the philosophers. At one time, in the winter of 1820, she was writing five books at the same time.

It is not strange that she was always looking back regretfully to the good old times, when cultivated women queened it in their *salons*, and politics were kept out of general conversation. She says:

" Our profound thinkers, our great statesmen, are continually talking with contempt of the ' frivolity ' of the seventeenth and first half of the eighteenth

century. It is said again and again that society is
no longer 'frivolous.' Alas! it is true, and it is a
great misfortune, in my opinion. There is a great
pleasure in being able to argue well in a serious conversation, or to talk trifles gracefully in a select
private party; and the French, in former times,
seemed to have the exclusive privilege of wielding
this double power with success. Previous to this
horrid period, where impiety, licentiousness, and
pride run mad combined to give birth to all the
scenes we have witnessed, the frivolity of the French
was not a national defect. It was, on the contrary,
the preserver against pedantry, affectation, and a
thousand ridiculous and dangerous pretensions. It
was found where it ought to be to form the charm
of society, in the conversations of men of the world,
in letters, and the gayest amusements. It excluded
from our parties a positive and dogmatic spirit,
metaphysical discussions, politics, and dissertations;
and was, in its turn, excluded from important affairs
and serious works. Men never thought more profoundly or wrote more elegantly and correctly than
when society was adorned by the most amiable
frivolity, which was nothing else but a relaxation of
mind, and a gaiety full of wit, feeling, and grace.
Were we to expunge from the letters of Madame de
Sevigné everything that is frivolous, we should take
away their principal charm.

"Such was frivolity amongst us in the times of

old. The following incident will show what modern politeness is:

"Towards the end of June, 1821, I dined with thirteen persons, amongst whom were four peers, four marshals of France, and three generals; among the peers there were two dukes. Before dinner they were in their own way very polite to me, and I had no trouble in taking my share of the conversation at dinner, for the peers on either side spoke of nothing but politics, and addressed their conversation to gentlemen at the other end of the table. We returned to the drawing-room after dinner, and at the moment I was sitting down I saw with surprise that all the dukes and peers had *escaped* from me; each of them took hold of an armchair, dragged it after him, approached his neighbor, and thus formed a circle in the middle of the room. I was thus left quite alone, with a semicircle of backs turned towards me. To be sure, I saw the faces of the other half of the party. I thought at first they had seated themselves so to play at those little games that require such an arrangement, but it was no such thing; it was solely for the purpose of discussing the most difficult questions of state policy. Everyone became a noisy orator, bawled out his opinions, interrupted his neighbor, quarreled and talked till he got hoarse; they must all have been in a precious state of perspiration. It was a correct picture of the Chamber of Deputies — in fact, it was a great deal worse, for there was no president. I

had a great mind to play the part of one, and to call
them to order, but I had no bell, and my feeble voice
could not have been heard. This clamor and confusion lasted for more than an hour and a half, when
I left the drawing-room, delighted with having
received the first lesson of the new customs of
society, and the new code of French gallantry—of
that politeness which has rendered us so celebrated
throughout Europe. I confess that down to this
moment I had very inadequate notions of all these
things.

"I now met with women who naturally hated all
kinds of interesting or witty conversation, because
they could take no share in it; tittle tattle, or
scandal, formed all their talk; they had produced a
coolness among all their husbands' friends by their
insipidity, their dryness, and their aptness to take
offense — the ordinary defect of women who want
talent and education. The most of these persons,
ridiculously vain, reckoned their reciprocal visits,
and bid (as it were) for a courtesy; they were always
on the *qui vive!* always uneasy with regard to the
manner in which they were treated, without knowing positively how they ought to be treated; so that
they were generally irritating themselves by imag-
inary failures in politeness and ideal impertinences!"

Youth and charm lingered with this inscrutable
little woman until the very last. At eighty she had
perfect health, required no glasses—hearing as
good as at twenty, memory and mental faculties

unimpaired. The novel which is now most read of all her works is " Mademoiselle de Clermont." " Belisarius " was written simply to outdo Marmontel, who had published a book on the same subject. She revived in France the " Historical Novel," much in the style of Madame Mühlbach. Like Ruskin, who has planned more than seventy works which he wants to give the world before he leaves it, she closes her " Memoirs " with a hint of a dozen more books which she hopes to publish. She had many chimerical plans, such as the attempt to purify history and philosophy by omitting everything irreverent. skeptical, or untrue ; just as some in our day indulge the delusion that the drama would still be attractive if raised to the moral standard of the church. In short, she embraced the entire *Cosmos* in her schemes of reform, and wondered that all thinkers did not turn round and follow meekly in her train. In the long sketch of her in the " Universal Biography of France," they say : " The world was by her divided into two parts — her friends and her enemies. or rather, those who *admired her* and those who *criticised*." Her " Memoirs " were an apology, a compilation, selections from her works, a collection of anecdotes — in a word, they are anything but memoirs. Call them what you will, they are full of interest to this day.

A more conceited woman never lived, and her frankness in quoting her various compliments, poetical tributes. and constant conquests is weak but amusing. She felt herself capable of gracing any position, of instructing and guiding any who came in her path ; no subject so abstruse or profound that she could not master it ; no one escaped her criticism, yet she always spoke of herself as thoroughly impartial, never malicious, abused by critics, robbed by plagiarists. As the instructor of Louis Philippe she deserves great honor. You remember that during his exile he supported himself by teaching, rising at half-past four and walking miles to teach the higher mathematics in a Swiss college. When a civic crown was presented to him for saving a man from drowning, he wrote at once to his old teacher: "Without you, what should I have been?"

Her works were wonderfully popular in their day. By the way, it is a curious fact that W. S. Gilbert, author of the irresistible "Bab Ballads," and "Pygmalion and Galatea," to say nothing of "Pinafore," borrowed wholesale from Madame de Genlis's "Tale of an Old Castle" for his "Palace of Truth," which is so much admired. It is little more than a paraphrase of her story.

She had a slight, graceful figure, was rather *petite*, with curling brown hair and "soft, spiritual eyes." But her *nose* was her pride. Its praise had been sung by several of her admirers. In her seventieth year she stumbled over a trunk, broke two teeth, scratched her face in three places, and broke that beautiful nose — that nose so delicate, so perfect in outline. Her wailings over this calamity and her rhapsodic reminiscence of her nose as it used to be, are serio-comic in the extreme.

Her last days were rather sad ; her means were reduced, old friends gone, the glory of her nose among the things that were; yet Mrs. Opie, who called upon her in her last year, speaks of her as a really pretty and lively little old woman. She was found dead December, 1830 — the last morning of the year — aged eighty-four.

Men have reviewed her life and writings with great severity. In the " Quarterly " for 1826 we find this sentence : " If we may be allowed thus to express ourselves, we should say Madame de Genlis has a very large portion of a very small mind, and that portion is particularly active. Her intellectual arse-nal is boundlessly stored with sparrow-shot." In her eighty-third year she expressed the opinion that the value set upon the opinions of old women is the sur-est, if not the only, test of the moral, religious, and intellectual state of a country ; and in the " Suppers of the Maréchale de Luxembourg," gives a picture of society under this government ! This, of course, made her ridiculous, and reviewers were merciless. Yet Miss Kavanaugh says in her sketch : " No woman who has written so much, has written so well." St. Beuve says of her: " She was above everything an author, and would certainly have invented writing, if it had not appeared before her time. Her acquire-ments made her a living encyclopedia, which prided itself on being the rival antagonist of all other ency-

clopedias. But she was the most gracious and gallant of pedagogues. Very beautiful, very fascinating when she chose, knowing the strength and the
weak points of each one, and knowing how to cast
her spell of enchantment upon you, she became cold
and indifferent when you did not respond to her enthusiasm; of an infinite grace when admired, she
was hard and severe when one dared to disagree or
failed to please."

To judge her impartially she must not be taken
from the circle where she lived. She wrote for the
luxurious *habitués* of palaces and *salons*. Let me
quote a few of her good thoughts:

"Constant and varied occupation is much more
powerful than amusements in dispelling sorrow and
anxiety."

"There are but two suffrages worthy of desire by
a feeling and upright heart; one's own conscience,
and the voice of friendship."

"Virtue may be acquired, but goodness is a gift
of nature."

"A man declares his love, a woman confesses
hers."

"Evil-speaking always spoils the manners of a
woman."

"With the exception of the loss by death of those
we love, almost all our misfortunes and sorrows are
in part our own fault."

"Let musical teachers be given to those young
ladies only who have a musical voice and ear, and a

feeling for music ; let drawing be taught to those only who have a taste for the art, and the number of amateurs would be diminished ; and we should no longer meet with that crowd of women with trifling acquirements and high pretensions, which throws so much ennui over the surface of society."

" Criticism at the present day is nothing but a continual system of sneering and ridicule, more or less witty and more or less worn out ; such a continual shower of irony becomes monotonous."

" Sleep, which flies from luxury and indolence, is the sure reward of real fatigue."

" Men of letters have an actually existing superiority over female authors that is perfectly evident and indisputable. All the works of women put into one scale will not weigh some fine pages of Bossuet or Pascal, some scenes of Corneille, Racine, or Molière : but it must not be concluded from this that the mental constitution of women is inferior to that of men. Genius is composed of all the qualities they are admitted to possess, and which they may be endowed with in the highest degree — fancy, sensibility, and elevation of soul. The want of study and education having at all times kept women apart from the career of literature, they have shown their greatness of soul, not by describing historical facts in their writings, or by bringing forth ingenious fictions of fancy ; but by real actions they have done better than describe, and have often by their conduct furnished the models of sublime heroism. No woman

in her writing has described the lofty soul of Cornelia; what matters it, since Cornelia is not an imag-
inary being?"

French women of that early period, always excepting Madame de Sevigné, seem to be either fanatics
or flirts. We fear our eccentric friend is no exception; yet it is difficult to read her own story and not
believe in her innocence. Madame always ended
with a moral. In imitation, we regret that her character and talents were ruined by excessive vanity.
This fault led her into a dangerous position, and
kept her there; it shadowed every virtue, every accomplishment, and makes us not unwilling to say
good-bye to Countess de Genlis, Jack-of-all-trades,
Paragon of Perfection, " *Gouverneur du Roi.*"

ARE WOMEN WITTY?

ANTITHESES IN CRITICISM.

"Women have more wit than humor."—*Oliver Wendell Holmes.*

"Women have more humor than wit."—*John Boyle O'Reilly.*

"Women are not witty, I am sorry."—*John Boyle O'Reilly.*

"Humor is the rarest of qualities in women."—*Richard Grant White.*

It is best not to indulge in too positive statements when wishing to convince. So I ask the question, "Are women witty?" hoping that my readers will give a hearty verdict in the affirmative. Even this gentle interrogative has roused many a sneering reply, much adverse criticism, and one superior cynic inquires with a patronizing air if Miss Sanborn has never heard of Hood and Hook, Curran, Sheridan, etc., and what we women have to compare with their brilliancy, as if a modest plea for a recognition of woman's wit and humor argued ignorance of those immortals or any desire to belittle their fame.

From time immemorial, men have declared with owl-like solemnity and about as much wisdom, that women have no sense of humor, no capacity for wit, no woman's name in any collection of humorous poetry, epigrams, or repartees, until the last two years. In Mason's "Masterpieces of Humor" lately published by Putnam, women are represented for the first time. And special tributes are now given occasionally, as in a recent eclectic Sarah Orne Jewett is said to "possess genuine humor, the humor of Lamb and of Hood; the humor which is likely to bring a tear to the eye as well as a smile to the lips."

I wish to own that Pope recognized the quality in woman and acknowledged it several times, as:

> " Her tongue bewitched as oddly as her eyes,
> Less wit than mimic, more a wit than wise ! "

But search magazines from the earliest to the latest. You find at regular intervals heavy articles on wit and humor, with hackneyed definitions of these undefinable and elusive qualities, illustrations oft quoted, but no woman's name. And more than half of the wit of the past consists of hits at women, and satire on their faults and foibles.

" Why," says Stinson Jarvis, or Jarvis Stinson, in an open letter to the *Century*, " Why, in literature are there no female humorists?"

Why, in the name of common sense and common perception, does he fail to see that both humorous and witty women *abound* in America?

He answers his own question. " Is it not because our sister has been so far compelled by nature to make idols and because she is too much in earnest over her devotion to lapse into what would seem to be frivolity? If, in spite of all her effort, some other power throws her idols down, or, if they throw themselves down, she may become bitter or sad or savage or religious, but never humorous!"

I will give a few words written to me last week from an editor of one of the most important New York dailies to show the general impression of cultivated men:

"I used to think that there were no humorists of the female sex, but one day in *Puck*, Madeline Bridges, in the course of a colloquy between desert nomads, made one of them ask the other to 'come in out of the simoon,' as we in American slang ask people 'to come in out of the wet.' Whereupon I concluded that a sense of humor did exist in the feminine mind." How absurdly ignorant, conceited, and patronizing.

John Kendrick Bangs in a recent lecture indulges in the old slur about woman's utter lack of wit.

You naturally remember him as the author of "The Idiot Club!"

But women are waking up to reciprocal courtesies, and enjoy satirizing some of the many assailable characteristics of men as:

Geo. Eliot.— "I'm not denyin' the women are foolish; God Almighty made 'em to match the men."

Mrs. Phelps Ward.— "As a rule, a man can't cultivate his mustache and his talents impartially."

Mrs. Phelps Ward.— "No men are so fussy about

what they eat as those who think their brains the biggest part of them."

Rose Terry Cooke.—"Marryin' a man ain't like settin' alongside of him nights and hearin' him talk pretty; that's the fust prayer. There's lots an' lots o' meetin' after that!"

A lady once told me she could always know when she had taken too much wine at dinner—her husband's jokes began to seem funny!

From Ouida.—"A man is never so honest as when he speaks well of himself."

Lucretia Mott's humorous comment when she entered a room where her husband and his brother Richard were sitting, both of them remarkable for their taciturnity and reticence: "I thought you must both be here—it was so still!"

A wealthy *parvenu* lately gave the church which he attends two tablets of stone, with the Ten Commandments engraved upon them; whereupon a witty lady member of the church remarked that his reason for giving away the Commandments was that he couldn't keep them.

Recall the usual themes for a man's jokes, in print or in the home.

The poor mother-in-law! Is she to be forever traduced and roared over in barroom, theater, the club, and at stag dinners? From the time of Adam, who is supposed to have congratulated himself that he had none, that feeble joke has been tottering down the ages. Entire plays are based on it, and cultivated audiences crowd our best theaters to see a popular company, skilled in interpreting Shakespeare, rushing wildly round the stage, several stars in assumed hysterics or convulsions; while the mother-in-law, an unreasonable tyrant and virago, chases long-suffering sons-in-law around the room, striking them over the head with an umbrella, or slapping their faces like a modern fish-wife. This is uproariously applauded, and the morning papers report " A Brilliant Hit." " Instantaneous Success." " Peals of Laughter." The earliest attempts at dramatic representation were not more exaggerated and absurd. In fact, the scolding of Noah's wife in the Chester Miracle Play is more truly humorous.

As this much abused and vilified woman too often supports the son-in-law, or acts as nurse, cook, and general servant with willing affection and devotion for his entire family, this seems more cruel than comical. A man seldom gives this relative any credit for humor. Let us honor the *one* who acknowledged the wit of his mother-in-law! He says: " A few weeks after my son had swallowed a penny, she wrote to inquire, 'Has Ernest got over his *financial difficulties* yet?'"

How tired we are of the mouldy jokes on the new bonnet, seal-skin sack, mortality caused by young wife's attempts at cooking, shoes several sizes too small, sleeves or hats as many sizes too large, the big feet of Chicago girls, the gum-chewing at Vassar, and the frigid bean-devourer of Boston, also the mythical ice-cream fiend.

Prohibit vulgarity, profanity, flings at our sex, and the loudly vaunted wit of the past shrinks surprisingly.

With men the most irresistible humor often lies on the dangerous border-line between humor and vulgarity, while the humor of cultivated women, delicate and subtle, effervescent and evanescent, is more difficult to catch and preserve, like the seaweed in Emerson's "Each and All."

One eminent authority allows that there have been two really witty women in England: Lady Montagu and Catherine Fanshawe. We all know the former as letter-writer, converser, beauty, philanthropist, gossip, traveler, and wit, and perhaps all will recall the same sarcastic sentence: "There is but one reason I am glad I am a woman: I shall never have to marry one."

Miss Fanshawe was not only witty, but was known as an artist, a poet, and a thoroughly delightful woman. "Never running the risk of giving a moment's pain to anyone," a difficult attainment for ordinary mortals; still more so for a wit. Too many acting on the principle, "If you cannot speak evil" of a person — *do not speak of him!*

The enigma on the letter H ascribed to Byron and printed in various editions of his poems, was written by this versatile woman. She composed capital charades in verse, a fashionable pastime then.

When the Regents' Park was first laid out she
parodied the two well-known lines from Pope's
" Elegy on an Unfortunate Lady : "

> " Here shall the spring its earliest sweets bestow,
>   Here the first roses of the year shall blow."

in this fashion, only altering one word in first
line, one letter in second :

> " Here shall the spring its earliest *coughs* bestow,
>   Here the first *noses* of the year shall blow."

English women do not equal the French as wits,
but we can instance Lady Blessington, Jane Austen,
Fanny Burney, Jane Taylor, Hannah More, Mary
Ferrier, Mary Russell Mitford, Mrs. Carlyle,
Madame Mohl, Lady Ashburton, Mrs. Grote,
George Eliot, and many more.

We even have a veritable witticism from the
Queen. Hearing of the grace and agility of a pretty
Scotch lassie who had danced a sword dance most
cleverly for some of her officers she commanded the
same diversion for herself and was equally entertained. At the close of the brilliant performance
the girl advanced and courtesied profoundly.
" What can I do for you ? " asked her majesty.

" Give me the head of Gladstone," said the modern Herodias.

" I would gladly do that, my dear, but he lost it
some years since."

Princess Maud of Wales, like her father, the
Prince of Wales, dearly loves a joke, and is inclined

to be witty and facetious at all times. Some of the best current puns in London are attributed to the Princess Maud, just as fugitive jokes are yet credited to Abraham Lincoln.

Miss Havergal, who is known by her noble life work and volumes of devotional verses, was not devoid of genuine humor. When reading her interesting memoirs I copied a rhyme about Bores, which will appeal to all.

> " People of every age and class,
>   Under review appeared to pass,
>   Specimens, too, in greatest variety,
>   Of every sort of bores in society,
>   Boorish bores and bores polite,
>   People who stay too late at night,
>   People who make long morning calls,
>   People who think of nothing but balls,
>   People who never a move will make,
>   People who never a hint will take,
>   Strong-minded bores and weak-minded, too,
>   Masculine, feminine, not a few,
>   People who borrow books to lose,
>   People who will not wipe their shoes,
>   People who keep your mind on the rack,
>   Lest some pussy escape from the sack,
>   Over-stupid and over-clever,
>   People who seem to talk forever,
>   People who mutter and people who drawl,
>   People who will not talk at all.
>   Old pianos that rattle and jingle,
>   Or Broadwood Grands that make your ears tingle,
>   With polka and waltzes four hours a day,
>   All barrel organs whatever they play,

All German bands that won't play in tune,
People who practice too late or too soon,
Contraltos that groan and sopranos that squall,
Bassos that bellow and tenors that bawl."

And so on. The list is too long to quote entire, for bores, like the poor, we always have with us!

By the way, Eliza Leslie said : " Avoid giving invitations to bores. They will come without."

Lady Blessington may not have been pre-eminently witty, but said some good things as, " When the Sun shines on you, you see your friends. It requires sunshine to be seen by them to advantage." " Friends are the thermometers by which we may judge the temperature of our own fortunes." Her biographer speaks of her sallies of wit in her early happy days. Unlike Mad. de Stael, from whose torrent-like monologue men fled as for their lives, she seldom engrossed the conversation ; never dogmatised or played the learned lady. Brilliant thoughts were thrown off by her with the utmost ease. One *bon mot* followed another without pause or effort, and best of all, while her wit and humor were producing their desired effect, she would take care, by an apt word or gesture to draw out the persons who were best fitted to thrive in society, giving a chance to all — a give-and-take mode of interchange, sure to make a woman popular and essential for the would-be leader of a salon.

Louis Napoleon, after his election to the presidency of the French republic, did not invite Lady

Blessington to the Tuileries, although he had often been entertained by her in London. Meeting her one day, he inquired if she expected to remain long in Paris. To which her cool reply was: "And you?"

Of a very awkward man coming into the room, Mrs. Montague once whispered to Sir William Pepys: "There is a man who would give one of his hands to know what to do with the other."

She wrote many sparkling poems or verses for the showy, superficial annals then so popular.

After spraining her ankle severely and made painfully lame, Miss Cobbe says: "I went to drive in Regent's Park, and came rather late into the drawing room full of company, supported by what my maid called my best crutches. The servant did not know me and announced 'Miss Cobble.' I corrected her loudly enough for the guests to hear in that moment of pause: "No! Miss Hobble.'"

Lord Houghton's sister was often annoyed at her brother's indiscriminate hospitality. "Do you remember, my dear," he asked her at dinner one day, "whether that famous scoundrel X. was hanged or acquitted?" "He must have been hanged, or you would have had him to dinner long ago," replied the lady.

Mrs. Asquith has a ready wit and nimble tongue, and fears no one. She was the life of the celebrated yachting party given at Copenhagen, when Mr. Gladstone met the Czar. Upon her return to London, she convulsed society with her word pictures of

Mr. Gladstone who wanted to talk all the time, and Lord Tennyson who thought no entertainment so delightful as reading his own poetry, the two holding forth to rival, but constantly decreasing, companies at opposite ends of the ship.

Among French women, the only difficulty is to select from a host. Think of Madame du Deffaud, blind, old, bitter, but admired. Helvetius was blamed in her presence for having made selfishness the supreme motive of human action. " Bah ! " said she, " he has only revealed every one's secret."

When someone complained that Voltaire " had not much invention," she exclaimed, " What more can you ask? He has invented history."

Madame de Stael's reply to the diplomat, who, sitting between herself and Madame Recamier, said : " Here I am between wit and beauty." " Yes, and without possessing either."

Madame de Sevigné writes : " One loves so much to talk of one's self that one never tires of a tête-à-tête with a lover for years. That is the reason for confession. It is for the pleasure of talking of one's self, even though speaking evil." The phrase " After us the deluge," has been given to Madame de Pompadour. Marie Antoinette's milliner ought to be remembered for her epigram — " Nothing is new that has not been forgotten." Sophie Arnould, a fascinating French actress, about 1744, was noted for her wit, so much so that Arsène Houssaye has preserved her *bon mots* in a volume called *Arnouldiana*, which

will compare with anything of its kind in the French
language. For a dozen years prior to the Revolution, Sophie Arnould was a queen of society, as well
as art, and in her elegant salon she held a brilliant
court, where distinguished men were proud to pay
homage to her beauty and genius.

Benjamin Franklin said he nowhere found such
pleasure and such wit as with her. Poets sang her
praises, artists were eager for her portrait. " What
are you thinking of?" she said to Bernard in one of
his abstracted moods, " I was talking to myself," he
replied. " Be careful," she said, "you gossip with a
flatterer."

To a physician whom she met with a gun: " Ah,
Doctor, you are afraid of your professional resources
failing?"

A beautiful but brainless woman complained of
the persistency of her lovers: " You have only to
open your mouth and speak, to get rid of their im-
portunities." Being told that a Capuchin monk had
been devoured by rats, she exclaimed with an expressive shrug: " Poor beasts! their hunger must
have been something terrible! "

I come with pride and delight to the witty women
of our own country, beginning at Boston, with Helen
Bell, Rufus Choate's brilliant daughter, who made
that remark quoted without credit by Emerson. " To
a woman, the consciousness of being well dressed
gave a sense of tranquility which religion failed to
bestow."

Julia Ward Howe is undeniably witty.   Her con-
currence with a dilapidated bachelor, who retained
little but his conceit, was excellent.   He said : " It is
time now for me to settle down as a married man,
but I want so much ; I want youth, health, wealth, of
course ; beauty, grace — "   " Yes," she interrupted
sympathetically, " You poor man, you do want them
all."

Of a conceited young man airing his disbelief at
length in a magazine article, she said : " Charles evidently thinks he has invented Atheism."   After
dining with a certain family noted for their chilling
manners and lofty exclusiveness, she hurried to the
house of a jolly friend, and seating herself before the
glowing fire, sought to regain a natural warmth, explaining, " I have spent three hours with the Mer de
Glace, the Tete Noir, and the Yung Frau, and am
nearly frozen."

Pathos and humor as twins are exemplified by
her tearful horror over the panorama of Gettysburg,
and then urged by Mrs. Livermore to dine with her,
saying : " O no! my dear, its quarter past two, and
Mr. Howe will be wild if he does not get — not his
burg — but get his dinner."

Think of many other witty Boston women : Lucretia Hale with her inimitable Peterkin Family, her
sister Susan with her flashing repartee and genuine
epigrams, Mrs. Phelps Ward, Sarah Orne Jewett,
Abby Morton Diaz, Mrs. Maria Porter.

It was Mrs. Oliver Wendell Holmes, Jr., who said

that the Cunard steamer *Oregon* committed suicide to avoid being put on that company's Boston line.

Miss Hale recently sent me some economic aphorisms to keep my spirits up: "One swallow does not make a summer, neither does one scholar pay the dressmaker's bill." "There are no birds in last year's nest, but last winter's bonnet may bear another flower."

Charlotte Fiske Bates, formerly of Cambridge, excels in epigrams, quatrains, and short humorous poems.

There is much genuine humor among the women journalists of Boston, although they make no pretensions to wit, and do not seem to know how truly they possess it. "Do you live on the Back Bay?" said a lady the other day to Miss Jenkins, so well known by her "Chatterer" column in the *Herald* and whose home is on a narrow little street up town. "Rather, the small of the Back Bay," she answered instantly. Marion Howard Brazier spoke in one of her letters of a woman who had been married for fifty-six years and had never missed lighting the kitchen fire, and added thoughtfully: "Her husband must be the most extraordinary fire-escape on record."

While on a visit in Quebec, our driver said he carried a Boston woman and party up into the citadel court, and there pointed out the small brass cannon, saying: "This we captured from you at Bunker Hill." She quickly replied, "Ah, well, never mind, we have the hill."

A very "fresh" young man lately made the acquaintance of a young lady from Boston, to whom he proceeded to pour out a long story of some adventure in which he had played the hero. His listener was much surprised. "Did you really do that?" she asked. "I done it," answered the proud young man, and he began forthwith upon another long narrative, more startling even than the first. The Boston woman again expressed her polite surprise. "Yes," said the fellow, with an inflation of the chest, "that's what I done." A third story followed, with another "I done it," and then the Boston girl remarked: "Do you know, you remind me so strongly of Banquo's ghost?" "You mean the ghost in Shakespeare's play?" "Yes." "And why?" "Why, don't you remember that Macbeth said to him, 'Thou canst not say I did it?'" The young man could not imagine why everybody laughed.

Reading this lecture in towns near Boston, I asked for instances of humor among their women, and secured several. A minister's wife disliked living in one of these suburban places, giving as her reason that it had the *quiet* of the grave without its *peace.* Another woman said: "If I am ever tried for my life, I do hope I can have a jury of my own family, for they would never agree." And a young girl hunting in vain for the box of hard boiled eggs provided for a picnic, and harder yet, failing to find them, exclaimed: "Those eggs must have been mislaid."

The first wife of Mr. Higginson was a noted wit. Many of her sayings are preserved in his novels. In New York we count the witty women by tens: Mary Mapes Dodge, Mrs. Runkle, Mrs. Botta, Mrs. Alice Wellington Rollins, Mrs. Lizzie Champney, Mrs. Terhune (Marion Harland), Mary D. Brine, Josephine Pollard, Mrs. E. T. Corbett, Mrs. Victor, Mary Kyle Dallas, and Kate Douglass Wiggins Riggs, who will count two-score at least. In Brooklyn, Caroline B. LeRow, Frances Lee Pratt, Ella Kirk, and a dozen more. I would like to illustrate by extracts from their work. Marietta Holley belongs to New York state. Her Samantha Allen and Betsey Bobbet convulsed the continent. She is constantly solicited for humorous articles and more funny books, until she is well-nigh killed. Men, I mean publishers, find that women's wit puts much money in their pockets. As they rattle the gold and caressingly count the bills from twentieth editions, do they still think of 'women as sad, crushed, sentimental, hero-adoring geese, who can't see the humorous side? Octave Thanet is most decidedly humorous. Phoebe Cary has been called " the wittiest woman in America." She parodied Whittier's exquisite Maud Muller. I recall four pithy lines :

<blockquote>
" We're apt to fuss and fret
About the one we didn't get ;
But we needn't make such an awful fuss
If the one we didn't want didn't get us."
</blockquote>

Barnum asked her one evening what was her favorite brand of champagne? " We *drink* Heidseik, but we keep *Mum.*" Another day he reported the marriage of his skeleton man and the fat woman. She said instantly, " I suppose they loved through thick and thin."

Fanny Fern must not be forgotten, nor Aunt Fanny Barrows, nor Margaret Undergrift. The Misses Wilder of Brooklyn had a great reputation for ready wit. Once, when the Misses Wilder, both being at that time not yet engaged, proposed to have a screen to separate their parlors, a young gentleman was asked to suggest a motto to embroider on the screen. He replied: " For many have called but few have chosen." Miss Maud Wilder retorted on the instant: " No, we will put on, for your special benefit, ' Be not faithless but be leaving.'" I will give two verses from Maud, now Mrs. Goodwin:

> Carved in the old Cathedral
>   Where the wise men service said,
> Just over the old oak pulpit,
>   Is a monkey, scratching his head.
>
> But to-day, in our high church pulpits,
>   The case is reversed ; instead,
> 'Tis the monkey reads the service,
>   And the wise man scratches his head.

The driver for Mrs. Kemble and her coaching parties at Lenox said: " If I could have bottled up the sparkle, the wit and humor evolved in those excursions, I could have made a book to be read by everybody, but it would be too difficult now to reproduce it. If you have read Miss Sedgwick and heard Mrs. Kemble and Miss Cushman, you can possibly imagine what must have been its character. Miss C. said, I could drive the slowest and get there the quickest of any man she ever knew."

It was Fanny Kemble who spoke of some one as "single as a stray glove." Mrs. Child, describing adornments of a room, speaks of a vase of flowers done in water colors, looking sickly and straggling about as if they were only neighbors-in-law; and Ophelia with a quantity of "carrotty" hair which is thrown over three or four rheumatic trees, and one foot ankle-deep in water, as if she were going to see which she liked best, hanging or drowning.

Rose Terry Cooke possessed both wit and humor, and they shone in her sketches of New England characters, and in her daily conversation. I remember she spoke to me of some one as a "decayed gentlewoman," but quickly added, "not offensively so."

In Washington think of Gail Hamilton, Kate Field, Julia Schayer, and Grace Greenwood. Grace Greenwood makes capital puns, and has said a thousand witty things, as when she said of a genuine type of the old New England Yankee, "He looks as if the Lord had made him and then *pinched* him."

Some lady was describing an unfortunate man who had tumbled awkwardly about in getting into

an omnibus, grabbing at ladies' knees for support, as
" a perfect savage." "Of the Pawnee tribe, doubtless," said Grace. She used to be a chronic punster,
and is one of the best raconteurs in America. She,
doubtless, inherited her wit from her mother. She
says, that on coming into the breakfast room on a
winter's morning, she saw her mother in a shawl of
brilliant hue, and cried out, " See the scarlet woman ! "
Her mother rose and with a mocking bow responded,
" Yes, and the mother of abominations." This reminds me of Talmage's youngest daughter who was
fond of evening gaieties and often slept late in consequence. Coming down about nine o'clock, she met
her parent's stern gaze, and received the depressing
greeting : "Good morning, daughter of sin." " Morning, Father," was her response.

In Philadelphia, Miss Louise Stockton displays a
quaint humor almost equal to her brother Frank.

In Chicago I consider Mrs. Clinton Locke and
Sarah Hackett Stevens among their wittiest women.
Mrs. Locke is the wife of the popular rector. To
count them all would be impossible.

The Rev. Clericus has been waiting half an hour
to speak to his wife, who is having a call from Mrs.
Longwind. Hearing the front door close he sup-
poses the visitor is gone.

The Rev. Clericus (calling from his study) :
" Well, is that old bore gone at last ? "

Mrs. Clericus (from the drawing-room, where Mrs.
Longwind still sits) : " Oh, yes, dear, she went an

hour ago ; but our dear Mrs. Longwind is here — I know you will want to come in and see her."

Nor can we visit every city, town, village, and hamlet, to add examples that plentifully exist : we must classify.

How do men dispose of such humorous literature as that given to us by Catharine Sedgwick, Eliza Leslie, Caroline M. Kirkland, Mrs. Whitney, Mrs. Stowe, Rose Terry Cooke, Mrs. Whicher of Widow Bedott papers, Mrs. Ellen H. Rollins in " New England By-gones," Mrs. Walker who originated that saying: " The total depravity of inanimate things," Mrs. McDonell, "Sherwood Bonner," whose skit in the Chestnut Street Radical Club of Boston will carry her name on for generations, Mary Wilkins, etc., etc., unless men only read their own wit and admire their own brilliancy. Junius Henry Brown thinks that man cannot change his long-held estimate of woman's mental calibre from which, as he made it up, he carefully eliminated all sense of the ludicrous. It is a wise man who writes, " Don't you know that men hate to meet women in the arena for any sort of contest but one—that of *hearts ?* "

In these progressive days when women are taking high rank in every profession and every business, when young girls are winning prizes for mathematics, oratory, essays, in fair competition with young men, when middle-aged women are managing yachts and riding bicycles, and the muscles of our college girls are being hardened by boating, golf, and tennis, it is simply absurd to cling to this moss-back fallacy of the past. Such critics remind me of a mole which, blind and living under ground, only comes out of his hole to nibble with sharp teeth at something growing *above* him.

The professional wit carefully reserves his good things for pay, in print, or for after-dinner display, but half the women of my acquaintance are saying and writing good things all the time, without the least effort or self-consciousness. At every age, from ninety to nine, I find an abundant fund of illustration : and even younger. Think of dear old Mrs. Wade. eighty-six years of age, more lively than many a maiden in her teens, fond of games, excelling in fancy work, admired by all. When a lonely old fellow actually proposed to her a few years ago, she relegated him to the position of a brother, and when he would not be sent away, and begged her to make the subject a matter of prayer, she said quickly, with a quizzical smile, " *No*, I'm not going to bother the Lord with questions I can answer myself." And she said she'd concluded to *wade* through the rest of her life.

Old ladies often continue to see the humorous side. One such old dame, living in New Hampshire, and nearing her centennial, was bidding farewell to her oldest son, who had come on from the far west to see her. " Kiss me again, mother," he said. " I may not have another." And she inquired, " Why, James, don't you feel as well as usual ?"

22

Another venerable woman, who could not remember some story she desired to quote, said: "Why, sometimes I seem to know nothing." It was during that period in politics when a certain party were known by that name, and her son said: "You'll have to join the Know-Nothings." "Well, I won't have to go far," she retorted, looking keenly at him.

At a large party given in honor of her arriving at her ninetieth birthday, she was heard to say: "I seem to be one among ten thousand, even if I am not altogether lovely."

"The woman clergyman is often witty, as is Anna Shaw." Once, when answering the question-box, at a meeting, the question was asked, "Who is responsible for the liquor business?" She answered tersely, "Men. Of course they have votes and the business can be voted up or down, according to the will of the voters." A minister in the audience said, "Sister Shaw, don't you think that is rather hard on the men? Don't you think the devil has something to do with the liquor traffic?" She looked thoughtful a moment, and then looking at the brother, said, "Well, yes, if the brother is willing to accept the company, men and the devil." A friend says:

Since I wrote you last I have recalled a sharp repartee made, in my hearing, by a little girl only five years of age. She was a member of the family that occupied part of the house in which I lived while studying at Andover. She was teased a good deal by a brother a little older than herself, on account of the color of her hair, which was an unmistakable red. The brother mentioned had a capillary covering of an indescribable hue, probably of the shade which the old lady defined as " half-way between a dander-grey russet and a fire-stone drab." He had ruthlessly tormented his little sister one day, when she suddenly turned on him and exclaimed, with flashing eyes : " Well, I can tell you one thing, Fred, I know what color my hair is, and that is more than you can say ! "

If the merit of a retort can be gauged by its success, this one ought to rank high, for it put an end to the persecution.

Susan B. Anthony represents the elderly spinster, witty to the last, as quick now as when, thirty years ago, Horace Greeley said to her : " The ballot and the bullet go together. You women say you want to vote. And you're ready to fight, too ? "

" Yes, Mr. Greeley, we are ready to fight — at the point of the *goose quill* — the way you always have ! "

The wit of young girls is apt to take the form of repartee, and to be highly spiced with pepper-sauce, as, at a church wedding, when an impecunious groom said impressively : " With all my worldly goods I thee endow," his cousin in the front pew whispered : " There goes his *valise*."

A young English attaché of the legation in Washington remarked to an American belle some years ago : " I am weally sorry to see that the Bering Sea affair is not likely to be amicably adjusted, for, of course, with our superior navy, we could just wipe you off the face of the earth." She replied with one word — "*Again?*"

Is not that as true wit, in condensed form, as the remark of Talleyrand, and a cruel one it was to the wretched sufferer on his deathbed, who said, "Oh, I suffer the torments of hell!" "*Déjà?*" (already?) asked the diplomat.

It was the younger daughter of Judge Chase, who, on passing General McClellan, who was leaning gracefully over the back of a chair at a reception: "Ah, General, behind your entrenchments, as usual."

Another girl, who had spent a winter in Washington society, with no end of admirers and attention, went for the summer to a seaside resort, where the flattering devotion continued.

Among the train was an addle-pated dude, who said to her one evening, in a patronizing way, in the intervals between his cane-suckings, "Weally, Miss Scott, you must have an awfully nice time, don't you know — so much attention. Why, sometimes I truly fear it will turn your head." "Indeed, Mr. Softy, I have more fear for my stomach."

Fashionable Doctor: "My dear young lady, you are drinking unfiltered water, which swarms with animal organisms. You should have it boiled; that will kill them."

His Patient: "Well, doctor, I think I'd sooner be an aquarium than a cemetery."

A well known society woman of the West end, unfamiliar with the niceties of the English language, spoke at one of those delightful teas which characterize this delightful season of the year, of a spinal staircase of great beauty which had been constructed in the house of a neighbor. There was a bright girl near by who heard this architectural — or anatomical — reference. She said, aside, and it was very mean of her to whisper:

" Perhaps the lady refers to her neighbor's back stairs."

It was at a state ball. The Englishman and the American girl were talking over some of those present, when the Englishman said: " That is Lord B—— who has just passed you. Have you met him?"

" Yes," was the answer, "and I thought he was extremely dull."

" You surprise me," said he, " he is one of the most brilliant lights of our service."

" Really?" she replied. " Then it is my turn to be surprised. His light flickered so when he talked with me that I set him down as one of your tallow diplomats."

And surely our married belles are not slow at retort.

At a supper party in London the other night the conversation turned on "talking shop." Some one declared that an actor or musician was never happy unless allowed to talk shop by the hour, and then it

was pointed out that doctors and barristers were
"just as bad." A witty lady present laughingly
added: "Yes, philosophers talk Schopenhauer, ladies
shopping, tipplers 'Schoppen,' musicians Chopin,
and actors shop."

Mrs. Lincoln's remark, as the vivacious Miss
Todd, to her lank, gawky admirer, is worth quoting:
Young Abe said, "Miss Todd, I want to dance
with you the *worst* way." And she added, "*he
surely did.*"

Mrs. Fred Grant is a witty woman, as is proved
by her remark to Frederick Douglass, who regretted
being dragged into a political excitement as a nom-
inee: "You'll have to figure as the dark horse, Mr.
Douglass."

Mrs. George Pendleton replied appropriately to
one of our English critics who complained: "You
have no antiquities; no curiosities in your country!"
"Antiquities will come in time, and as for our curiosities, we *import* them."

And that suggests the response of Miss Patterson,
who married a Bonaparte, and was asked at a dinner
in England why the Americans had such bad manners. She said she supposed it was because of
their direct English descent without any infusion
from the *Aborigines!*

It was a Washington woman who said: "Sumner
should never have married. His self-love was so
intense as to make it almost bigamy."

Rudyard Kipling's mother is described as the

wittiest woman in Northern India. She said of an extremely erudite but garrulous official, that he ought never to be allowed to talk, but should be consulted when required as a cyclopædia of information.

Married women do not lag behind when attacked. Rev. Dr. Trask of anti-tobacco fame said to his petite wife soon after their marriage: "I confess I am disappointed in your height." "No more than I am in your depth," she retorted.

Of wit in dramatic form let me say that Gilbert borrowed his "Palace of Truth" almost bodily from "The Tale of an Old Castle," by Madame de Genlis, and that those inimitable farces, "The Belles of the Kitchen" and "Fun in a Fog" were written by an Englishman especially for the Vokes family.

In our own country, Mrs. Monatt's "Fashion," a comedy in five acts, was played most successfully and for a long "run" at Wallack's in New York and in Philadelphia, and Mr. French, the publisher of plays, tells me it has been acted all over the Union, and has everywhere been a great favorite.

Mrs. Verplanck's "Sealed Instructions" also met with marked approval.

Miss Merington's plays written for Sothern are complained of by the masculine critics as being "*too* witty"! bristling with epigrams and over-radiant with brilliant repartee.

Lovers of mirth are now enjoying in New York Miss Martha Morton's comedy, "His Wife's Father," and Crane is complimented for the quality of *his* humor. Neil Burgess burlesques Widow Bedott, and is regarded as its author. The younger McCarthy does give to Madame Rejane genuine wit in her art. Miss Kate Vannah and Miss Bartlett are now collaborating a comedietta.

Women's wit never fails, even in the street cars:

Polite gentleman, rising, "Take *my* seat, Madame."

"Never mind, thank you, I get out here, too!"

Severe conductor, "Miss, this is the smoker's seat."

Young lady, "Must I smoke if I sit here?"

"You can't keep a good man down," said the proverb-loving boarder.

"Not," said the typewriter boarder, "not unless he has a seat in the car. Then you can't get him up."

The concise description of a ladies' lunch as "Giggle, gabble, gobble," was from a New York leader in society. It has been widely ascribed to Dr. Holmes, who assured me in an autograph letter that it did not belong to him.

Fully half the humorous poetry in our current magazines is from women. I know several who earn their pin-money sending their own off-hand jokes and those of their less enterprising sisters to comic papers for good pay.

In Dean Ramsay's "Reminiscences of Scottish Humor" he quotes Jimmy Fraser, an idiot, who said the cleverest thing of them all. I would gladly include a witty idiot girl in my collection, but cannot find an idiot *girl!*

Off-hand letters scribbled on shipboard fairly scintillate. Here is one bit from a very seasick girl:

" Life is intolerable and the whole world a huge mass of food. And alas for the busy, restless mind. I actually wished I had lost mine before starting, for the one thing you can *retain* is ideas. ' Ten minutes for refreshments,' ' hot fried oysters,' ' boiled eggs,' hotel gongs, etc., chase through my brain like mad. Still laboring under the delusion of ' must eat ' I take a cracker, one small, dry, hard, Boston cracker. Heller's tricks pale beside this one of mine, for I instantly threw up several dozen. I try a little brandy, but 'tis quickly converted into a ' brandy-sling.' "

Books of travel from the pens of women, are they deficient in humorous incident and vivid sense of fun?

Some man regards the absence of a funny column in a girl's paper as proof of no humor. It seems to me evidence of wit and sense — anything less humorous than those efforts I know not of.

After a careful consideration of masculine wit as shown to-day in the weakly efforts of professional humorists, the pathetic senilities of *Punch*, the tedious specimens of after-dinner fireworks, when nothing will go off, being damped by dullness and reiteration, the confessed inability of our noted story-tellers to invent or smuggle a new and really laughter-provoking anecdote, I deem it unwise to wish to live up to, or rather down to, this somnolent and twilight interregnum of masculine wit.

And in time this absurd, unmeaning fallacy will disappear, and the wit and humor of women will be generously and universally acknowledged.

If it is a " very serious thing to be a funny man," it is even more dangerous to be a witty woman. For remember :

> " Tho' you're bright and tho' you're pretty,
> They'll not *love* you if you're witty ! "